Praise for *The King of Con*

"*The King of Con* is for real and his story reveals how big money, big business, and the mob really work. Required reading."

—**Nicholas Pileggi**, author and screenwriter of *Goodfellas* and *Casino*

"Tom Giacomaro is a master manipulator and natural-born crime boss you'll love to hate and hate to love. His life story is a roller coaster ride of high finance, underworld intrigue, and dazzling riches that will leave you exhilarated, exhausted, and wanting more."

—**Nina Burleigh**, *New York Times* bestselling author of *The Fatal Gift of Beauty: The Trials of Amanda Knox* and national political correspondent for Newsweek

THE
KING
OF
CON

THE
KING
OF
CON

How a Smooth-Talking Jersey Boy Made and
Lost Billions, Baffled the FBI, Eluded the Mob,
and Lived to Tell the Crooked Tale

THOMAS GIACOMARO
and NATASHA STOYNOFF

BenBella Books, Inc.
Dallas, TX

BenBella Books, Inc.
10440 N. Central Expressway, Suite 800 | Dallas, TX 75231
www.benbellabooks.com | Send feedback to feedback@benbellabooks.com

Printed in the United States of America
10 9 8 7 6 5 4 3 2 1

Library of Congress Cataloging-in-Publication Data
Names: Giacomaro, Thomas, author. | Stoynoff, Natasha, author.
Title: The king of con : how a smooth-talking Jersey boy made and lost
   billions, baffled the FBI, eluded the Mob, and lived to tell the crooked
   tale / Thomas Giacomaro and Natasha Stoynoff.
Description: Dallas, TX : BenBella Books, Inc., [2018] | Includes
   bibliographical references and index.
Identifiers: LCCN 2018008469 (print) | LCCN 2018011275 (ebook) | ISBN
   9781944648039 (electronic) | ISBN 9781944648022 (trade paper : alk. paper)
Subjects: LCSH: Giacomaro, Thomas. | Swindlers and swindling—United
   States—Biography. | Criminals—United States—Biography.
Classification: LCC HV6692.G496 (ebook) | LCC HV6692.G496 A3 2018 (print) |
   DDC 364.16/3092 [B] —dc23
LC record available at https://lccn.loc.gov/2018008469

Editing by Brian Nicol
Copyediting by Scott Calamar
Proofreading by Chris Gage and Cape Cod Compositors, Inc.
Front cover design by Pete Garceau
Full cover design by Sarah Avinger
Text design and composition by Silver Feather Design
Printed by Lake Book Manufacturing

Distributed to the trade by Two Rivers Distribution, an Ingram brand
www.tworiversdistribution.com

Special discounts for bulk sales (minimum of 25 copies) are available.
Please contact Aida Herrera at aida@benbellabooks.com.

For my sweet Lauren

CONTENTS

PROLOGUE:
MAN OVERBOARD

Some motherfucker was trying to kill me.

My new Mercedes 560SEL shot off the highway and into the air like a rocket before nose-diving into the Passaic River—with me in it.

Ten minutes earlier, I'd been downing after-lunch $200 shots of Louis XIII cognac at a restaurant in Cedar Grove, New Jersey, when this broad I'd been seeing in nearby Passaic called me to come over for an afternoon quickie. This girl was nutty; she used to kiss the windows of my Mercedes and leave red lip prints all over the glass.

Within minutes of leaving the restaurant, I was speeding eighty miles per hour along the highway to get to her, and I was very, very drunk. That's when I noticed a white van on my tail.

It switched lanes and sped up next to me. I looked over quickly and saw the side-panel door swing open to reveal three goons, fumbling around like they was The Three Stooges. One was trying to hold the door open; the second was getting on his knees with a shotgun; and the third stood behind the second pointing a handgun at me. He began to shoot. Yeah, I sobered up damn fast.

I swerved and rammed my car—the heaviest, biggest, fastest tank-of-a-Mercedes you could buy at the time—into the van, knocking the Stooges off their feet while they sprayed my car with bullets.

The van fell behind me and chased me, zigzagging across the lanes, until they sped up to me again. I rammed the van on the side a second time, this time knocking it against the cement barricade.

Fuck! Who wanted me dead? Could it be any one of dozens of mob guys I'd done business with? Maybe it was the Nicky Scarfo guys in Philly. Or my partners in my $100,000-a-week cocaine racket who want to get rid of me and take my connections. Or it could be Little Al and the Lodi crew in Jersey, exacting revenge after I took the money and left them with companies about to crash. It could be a soldier from any of the other "families" in the area I associated with. I was mobbed up the ass with all of them without officially being a "made man" . . . and that made a guy like me the kind of guy they sometimes wanted dead. Never mind that I clipped them all for millions.

Spotting the exit ramp for Passaic, I made a sharp right onto a single lane, jug-handle curve directly over the river.

The van followed. I was doing seventy miles per hour on the curve when they crashed into me from behind, forcing me into a killer spin like an Indy race-car driver. The spin sent me through the guardrail and sailing into the air, over the black water.

The car's airbag inflated when I hit the guardrail and pinned me to the back of my seat as I plummeted into a free fall, hitting the Passaic River bumper first—it was like slamming into a concrete wall.

The airbag burst and my head smashed into the steering wheel. The car sank fast until it hit bottom with a muffled thud, like a submarine landing on the ocean floor. It was dark and quiet; I couldn't see nuthin'. But I could hear something—water rushing into the car.

My head throbbed and my hip was crushed. Within a minute the entire car was filled with freezing water, except for a small pocket of air at the top, in between the half-deflated airbag that had floated up and the car's roof. I stuck my head in the pocket, pressed my lips against the roof of the car, and sucked in air. The doors and windows wouldn't open.

I had only one thought in mind now. It wasn't about what mother-fucker was trying to kill me or that my Brioni suit and alligator shoes were ruined.

It was:

I gotta stay alive for Lauren. I can't let my baby girl grow up with a father who's been whacked. I gotta get the hell outta this car!

And then I remembered the gun. *Frankie's gun!* Hidden under the passenger seat was a stolen .357 Magnum with hollow-point bullets—on the street they called it a "cop killer." I took another deep breath and dove down and got it.

At the top again, I sucked in more air as I tapped the back passenger window with the gun's barrel to make sure I was pointing it at the glass and not myself. Then I squeezed my eyes shut and fired six times—*boom, boom, boom, boom, boom, boom!* I felt for the glass with my hand—gone. I took one more long, last breath and launched myself out the window, swimming upward toward the light.

A white light? Oh, shit. Was I dead?

I let go of the stolen gun as I rose upward. When I broke the surface and gasped for air, I heard applause and cheers—a crowd of people who'd seen me go over were lined up on the ramp I just flew offa, watching me from above. The white van was long gone.

Never mind the fucking ticker-tape parade. *"Motherfuckers. Help!"* I yelled.

Two construction workers had already climbed down from the highway to the riverbank. Now, they stripped off their jackets and dove in, pulling me to shore.

"An ambulance is on its way," one said, bunching up his coat under my head.

I tried to sit up and tell them my name.

"We know who you are, Tom," said the other, covering me with his dry jacket. "We've seen your picture in the papers. And we saw everything. The van that ran you off the road had Pennsylvania plates, and we got some of the license number."

I rested my head back down. I was broken up, bleeding, shaking, and about to pass out. But I was alive; I was not so easy to kill, assholes.

This was an attempted hit, no doubt. I was set up.

And no doubt, I deserved it. I was a stinking rich, arrogant, coke-addicted, narcissistic, money-hungry, alcoholic, power-driven, obsessive-compulsive, son-of-a-bitch liar, thief, con man, bully, extortionist, and sociopathic madman. I caused a lot of people a lot of problems in my lifetime.

But you try to kill a guy like me and miss?

Now *you* got the problem.

PART I

CHAPTER 1

SINS OF
THE FATHER

Dad calmly walked back to the car and dropped the
blood-streaked bat on the floor beside my feet.

A prison shrink once told me that by the time we're seven years old, we are who we are for the rest of our lives, and there's usually shit-all we can do about it. Our brains are hardwired forever, and it's too late to change anything.

Too late to go from bad guy to good, or from sinner to saint—as Father Stanley might have said. Unlike the shrink, Father Stanley thought you could change your fate in the time span of one confession.

"You've reached *the age of reason*, Tommy," he pronounced, solemnly, as I knelt in the jail-cell confines of the dreary confessional to make my very first confession, soon after my seventh birthday.

"From this day onward, you are morally responsible and accountable for all your actions. You have free will to *choose* your behavior."

Well, I gotta be candid with you. If Father Stanley was delivering a message from his god, my parents and I never got the memo.

Because by 1960, the year I reached this age of so-called reason, my father had been beating the crap outta me for years and I was already an accomplished thief. So apparently the Giacomaros of North Haledon, New Jersey, didn't do so good with this morally responsible accountability thing. Or *ting*. That's how the guys I run with say it.

By my first communion I was already a crime boss.

My father, Joseph, went out bowling and card playing every Friday night. He'd return home stinking of booze and strange perfume, carrying a thick wad of bills he'd won gambling. Dad was an accountant; he was smart with numbers and knew how to get money outta people from right under their noses.

And so did I.

I'd be wide-awake when he staggered in at 4 AM—even as a kid, I slept only three to four hours a night, a habit that wore down my mother's sanity—and listened closely as his footsteps echoed down the hall, into the den, then downstairs to the basement where he'd pass out asleep. He always slept in the basement on Friday nights so my mother wouldn't wake up and know what time he got home.

I'd lie motionless under my blankets until I heard his floor-rumbling, boozy snoring through the floorboards directly below me.

And that's when I'd rob the motherfucker.

Armed with a mini flashlight, I'd slip out of bed, move silently down the hall, and tiptoe into the den. I'd quietly slide a chair across the floor until it nudged against the bookcase—that's where he stashed his wallet, on the top shelf. If I stood on the chair and stretched my arm as high as it could go and fished around, sooner or later my gloved fingers would bump into the thick leather lump. Yeah, I wore gloves when I slept—still do, but I'll get to that later.

Hitting up dad's wallet was like winning a lottery. It's what we in the money-stealing business called "easy money"—the sweetest kind. It was always a sure bet. I'd peel four or five twenties from the bulging billfold and return it to the shelf. Back in my room, I'd hide the money in a hole I cut in my mattress.

Early Saturday morning I'd knock on Eddy LaSalle's door to come out and spend the ill-gotten loot with me. Eddy's dad had some important job as a business executive in Hoboken. In looks and personality, Eddy and I were exact opposites. I was dark, wiry, frenetic, and never shut up; Eddy was tall, shy, blond, and stocky. But we understood each other, Eddy and me. We both had trouble at home and there was shit-all either one of us could do about it.

But on Saturday mornings with my dad's twenties burning a hole in my pocket, we hadn't a care in the world. Back then Bazooka chewing gum cost a penny a piece, and I was a kid with a hundred bucks to blow. I was a fucking millionaire.

First we'd go to the Rendezvous, a nearby shopping emporium that sold girlie magazines and comic books, and stock up on *Superman*. Two doors down was Jay's Luncheonette, where we'd hoist ourselves onto the counter stools and order deluxe cheeseburgers, French fries, and all the Coke we could stomach.

I loved the feeling of importance and power that the money gave me. Contrary to Father Stanley's little morality lesson, I had no remorse about stealing from my father's wallet. In fact, I was pretty confident that it was my *moral responsibility* to do so.

I ate fast, wolfing down the food like I was starving, and I was. But it wasn't a physical hunger. I was feeding emptiness, stoking a burning anger, and numbing a pain inside of me with the stolen money and fast food. Every bite I took was a conscious *fuck you* to my father.

"This'll show him," I'd say, as we sat stuffing our faces. Eddy would shove ketchup-drenched fries in his mouth and nod. He knew exactly what I meant.

I was five years old when I first saw my father's fierce Sicilian temper. We were driving home from a relative's house on a beautiful spring afternoon. My mother, Yolanda ("Lonnie"), was in the passenger seat and I was sitting in back reading a comic book. Even my father seemed in a rare good mood—that is, until the driver next to us swerved in front and cut him off. That driver obviously didn't know my father was the last person in the world you want to fuck with, and until that day, neither did I.

Joseph Thomas Giacomaro had been a technical sergeant in the US Marine Corps and had seen combat in both World War II and Korea. At a lean 5'8", he was neither tall nor beefy, but that didn't matter when you were a trained expert in hand-to-hand combat.

He returned from Korea after being discharged in 1954 with a trunk load of combat memorabilia: his banged-up canteen; a utility belt with a leather holster for a sidearm; two standard-issue field blankets; his camo-green Marine Corps jacket (which he wore once a week when he mowed the lawn); and his prize possession, a menacing, black-handle bayonet with a ten-inch blade. He kept the bayonet locked up in a closet and once, just once, he demonstrated how it was used.

My father in his US Marine Corps uniform

My mother and I were in the kitchen, and she was showing me how to make tomato sauce. From an early age, she taught me how to cook and sew.

"You never know when it's going to come in handy," she used to say, as I stood on a chair and stirred the bubbling sauce. That's when my father came into the kitchen with his bayonet and drew the blade out of its fiberglass scabbard. Suddenly, cooking wasn't so interesting to me anymore.

"Did you use that to hit people?" I asked, hopping down from the chair.

"*Hit people?*" he scoffed. "You don't hit someone with a bayonet— you *jab* them, you *poke* them," he said, gripping the weapon tightly in his hand. He lunged across the linoleum and thrust his arm out in front of him. My mother and I both jumped back.

"You jab your enemy in the guts and then twist the blade to cut him up inside. One less enemy to worry about," Dad said to himself, smiling.

Like I said, Dad wasn't big, but he could fight. And anyone who knew him will tell you he had a certain lunacy in his corner—when he got worked up, he was a fucking madman.

On the road that day, Dad blared his horn at the other driver and screamed out the car window: "Pull over, you motherfucker!" A couple of minutes later, we caught up to the car at a red light and two huge, very angry-looking black guys climbed out and started walking toward our car.

Before they had a chance to say or do anything, my father had grabbed the Louisville Slugger he kept under the back seat and was on top of them.

"Joe, *nooooo!!!*" my mother screamed.

My father didn't swing the bat, he lunged and *poked* and *jabbed* the two men all over their bodies—in their stomachs, their chests, their faces, and then the back of their heads after they crumpled to the ground, begging him to stop.

"Fuckin' nigger mother*fuckers*," he hissed, as he kept on jabbing them as hard as he could. The fact that they were black made their beating twice as brutal as it might have been; my father was a racist son of a bitch.

I watched through the car window, trembling, as my mother sobbed. When Dad first jumped out of the car, I was worried he'd get hurt in the unevenly matched fight. Back then, he was still a hero to me. I proudly wore his Marine Corps jacket and belt when Eddy and I played army in the woods.

But it was those towering black guys who didn't stand a chance. When my father was done with them—it was over in a couple of minutes—they lay in the street, curled up and still, as a frightened and confused crowd began to gather. Dad calmly walked back to the car and dropped the blood-streaked bat on the floor beside my feet.

"Two less enemies," he muttered.

He got behind the wheel and sped away. The only sound in the car the rest of the way home was my mother's whimpering. I have no idea if those two men lived or died.

A few months later Dad started beating the shit out of me, too.

For reasons I didn't know or understand, he'd snap—he'd fly into a sudden rage and chase me all over the house until he cornered me, usually in the dining room.

"You're no fucking good!" he'd shout, as he hit me hard with his open hand. I'd yell for my mother to help, but what could she do? How do you stop a maniac?

"Not the head, Joe, don't hit him in the head! Not the face!" was all she could offer. She was afraid I'd get brain damage, or that everyone in church would see my bruises. Back then, it was normal to take a swipe at your kid, and it wasn't anyone else's business. But even for that era, she knew what he did to me was too much.

I'd crumple to the floor just like those guys in the street, and then he'd spit out the words to me that he'd repeat for the next forty years:

"You will never, *ever,* amount to anything," he'd say, looking down at me. He looked like a monster. "*You. Are. Nothing!*"

When it was over, I'd run across the backyard to hide in the woods behind our house and sit on a rock and cry. I'd stay there for hours, embarrassed to go to school or play with Eddy because everyone would see the purple blotches spreading across my arms—defense wounds.

Please, god . . . make my father stop hitting me. Please help me, god.

From my rock, I'd hear him go after her. My mother was so bony, thin, and frail; her screams would travel through our open windows, rise up in the woods to reach me, then fall silent.

The next morning she'd wear a scarf to try and hide the welted handprints around her throat.

"Please, don't call Uncle," I'd beg her. My mother's truck-driving brother, Anthony Foglia, was a Teamster and built like a brick shithouse. He was the only one I knew who had the balls and strength to kill my father if he wanted to. But despite the beatings my father gave us, I couldn't stand the idea of him getting hurt. So whenever I could, I'd get in between his hands and my mother's throat, even though that bit of heroics always cost me a second pounding.

I assume it was my father's abuse that drove Mom to drink, just like it drove me to steal. She'd start on her wine at 5 PM—"the bewitching hour," my father called it—in anticipation of his arrival home from work at 6 PM. As soon as he walked through the door, he'd pour himself the first of many vodka martinis or straight-up scotches of the night. But he'd hit me whether he was sober or drunk; that didn't make a difference.

My beatings continued—two or three times a week—until I was sixteen. My mother wasn't so lucky. Her sentence went another forty years, until my father died.

And that's why, Father Stanley, I chose to steal my father's money when I was seven. That's why it was reasonable for me to take revenge on him with my small act of petty larceny without feeling the least bit guilty.

That's when getting back at my father *started*.

I'm not sure it ever ended.

CHAPTER 2

THE MAKING OF A CRIMINAL MIND

The less I reacted, the harder he hit; but nothing he did could make me even flinch. And I refused to stay down.

I was born on January 30, 1953, in Paterson, New Jersey, and grew up in the leafy, upper-class suburb of North Haledon. My parents were also born in Jersey and so was one grandparent, while the other three stepped off the boat from Sicily.

When I was a baby, my mother used to tie my hands to the high chair while she fed me so I wouldn't make a mess—in handcuffs at six months! As soon as I could walk, she tied me to the backyard clothesline with a ten-foot rope so I wouldn't escape the confines of our yard.

I was so hyperactive that I barely slept, and I got worse depending on the lunar calendar.

"You're possessed!" my mother used to say, "and it's worse during a full moon."

I couldn't figure out if I was born bad, like my father insisted, or if I became that way. Did he hit me *because* I was bad, or did I act out *because* he hit me? This I would try to figure out as I sat on the rock in the woods. More than a few shrinks tried to pick my brain to untangle the mess in there, too. I do know that around the time my father began beating me, I started getting into trouble.

With my father, before the hitting started

In kindergarten at St. Paul's elementary school, I refused to nap like the other kids or stand and put my hand on my heart to pledge allegiance to the flag—not because I didn't love my country, but because I couldn't stand being told what to do. I also couldn't sit or stand still, never mind *sleep* in the middle of the day. No one talked about attention deficit disorder or attention deficit hyperactivity disorder back then so instead of getting help from a school counselor or being pumped full of Ritalin, as they do today, I was simply labeled A Bad Kid.

Sister Ann patrolled the rows of desks like a gestapo officer. She was in her eighties and wore a heavy black habit and a starched-white cornette that projected from her head like Satan's horns. During her rounds, she often found good reason to stop at my desk and yank my hair or jab my head with her ruler—her version of the bayonet. It wasn't the pain that bothered me—I got it way worse at home. It was the humiliation I felt in front of my classmates when I'd put my head down on my desk and sob. A bunch of those kids bullied me for years.

Crybaby!

When one ferocious ruler attack left a gash across my ear, my father saw it and recognized it wasn't his own work. He marched into the rectory, dragging me with him, to confront Father Stanley—it was one of the few, perhaps only, times he ever stood up for me. Apparently it was okay for him to beat his kid until he was black and blue, but *goddammit* there was no way in hell anyone else could lay a hand on me.

"You and your *people*," he said to the priest, "keep your fucking hands off my fucking kid." My father was not a religious man and he harbored no reverence for nuns and priests.

———

My parents moved me to a public school with no ruler-wielding nuns—Memorial School in North Haledon—but I got in trouble there, too. Pranks like putting tacks on kids' seats or shooting spitballs made me a regular in the principal's office.

"What did you do this time, Thomas?" the principal would ask.

"I didn't do it!"

"*What* didn't you do?"

"I dunno. Whatever it was, it wasn't me!"

I was excellent at convincing him there'd been a misunderstanding, or that I was the innocent victim of some other kid's scheme of the day. As I convinced him, I convinced myself, too. *Yeah, yeah, that's what happened. It's the truth!* Or maybe the principal was a soft touch because he'd seen the bruises peeking out from under my shirtsleeves. Whatever the reason, he felt sorry for me and I played to his sympathy.

"The teacher picks on me," I'd say, eyes downcast.

"Okay, Tommy. You can stay in the office for the rest of the day. Go sit in the corner."

Only I couldn't sit still there either. So I ran errands and organized files for the secretaries, who hugged me and fed me cookies. I learned an important lesson by being sent to the principal's office:

that my bad behavior would be richly rewarded. Hanging out with the secretaries was a vacation next to the rigid structure at home, where my parents—both undiagnosed obsessive-compulsives—ran our house like a military boot camp.

After my father was honorably discharged from the Marines, he began working full-time as an accountant for a highfalutin firm in Clifton. He was so smart, number savvy, and precise that he could make any ledger line up like the blades of grass along the edge of our driveway. He'd lie down on the front lawn in the evenings and clip each individual blade of grass by hand to make sure their heights were uniform. His own father was like that, too. Grandpa Sal owned a barbershop in Paterson and he'd trim each hair on people's heads until it was just so—one strand at a time. (My mother's father had a barbershop, too. Later on, I learned that one of them was a front for a numbers racket.)

At night, my father was in high demand to balance the books for local mob-owned restaurants and meat and produce markets. They knew he'd keep his mouth shut about the money they pulled in off the books, and with the extra cash he could buy his Cadillacs and Oldsmobiles. He used to hand-wash his four-door, white 1958 Oldsmobile, a real mob car, in the driveway, and I was not allowed to touch it or play in it.

My mother was an old-fashioned Italian mom, devoutly Catholic, and a germaphobe who kept every stick of furniture in our home hermetically sealed in industrial-strength plastic, as though humans didn't live in our house. If she could have boiled the living room couch in rubbing alcohol to sterilize it, she would have. She painstakingly dusted her Hammond M3 organ in the living room every day using a special yellow cloth, then waxed it with canned butcher's wax.

I don't know how they found each other. Together, my parents made the world's most anal-retentive couple, and I was their dysfunctional protégé and whipping boy.

My parents on their wedding day

My mother ordered me to wash my hands every hour with Lava soap—the kind used by coal miners, oil-rig workers, and auto mechanics. It burned and ripped the skin off my hands so badly that at night she'd slather them with Vaseline and give me cotton gloves to wear as I slept. Those gloves summed up my life: I lived in a home I couldn't touch, with people who didn't touch me (except in the wrong ways). Even at night when I acted the stealthy cat burglar, ripping off my father's money, I left no fingerprints behind.

I slept beneath Dad's Marine-issued blankets—they were woolen and itchy but warm as hell. He taught me how to fold them and make my bed like a proper Marine.

"Hospital bed corners, like we do in the corps!" he'd say at inspection time every morning, and toss a coin onto the bed to make sure it bounced.

Each room in the house had to be organized to my parents' exact specifications—the canned goods in the kitchen were lined up by height with labels facing forward. Ever see the movie *Sleeping with the Enemy*? That was my father. The socks in my drawers were lined up by color and the rows couldn't touch each other. Even my toy soldiers had to be put away in proper formation, standing at attention and at the ready.

It was a sickness: my parents desperately needed order; there was no room in their lives for chaos. My misbehaving, that was a mess. Affection or hugging, that was messy. Even at five years old, I could see that other families weren't like mine. I watched *Leave It to Beaver* and *My Three Sons* on our black-and-white TV and saw how they talked nice at dinner, and how June and Ward asked Wally and Beaver about their day. Sometimes, I'd pretend to be like those TV families. I'd hold my mother's hand mirror up to my face and kiss my reflection.

I love you, Tommy, I'd say to myself.

There was something else that happened when I was age six or seven that wasn't quite right. It was a potential mess that had to be hidden away, and even though I have a photographic memory about everything else in my life, this I remember in a blur of images.

For six months or so, my mother went away. I didn't know why, but I remember my father signing papers and my mother leaving in an ambulance. I remember him taking me to visit her on Sundays in a big gray building, surrounded by people wearing white coats. She'd beg to come home but my father would shake his head. During those months, Dad took me to his sister's house, Aunt Millie's, instead of school. I played with my cousin, Anthony Bianco. We were the same age, but he was a nerdy, smart bookworm with thick glasses. Aunt Millie would take us to the Jersey Shore and we'd run up and down the beach all day long. Then one day, Uncle Anthony went and signed papers and my mother came home.

If it wasn't for Charlie and Midge next door, I'd have turned out crazier than I did. Or I'd be dead. The Gerhardts were our neighbors from the day we moved into the house in North Haledon. They didn't have kids of their own. Charlie owned a sporting goods store in Paterson, and Midge worked for New Jersey Bell Telephone. They were my parents' best friends and to me, they provided my first "safe house." If I knew they were home, I'd run to them instead of the rock after my father's beatings. I'd get into their house through the back door, which they left unlocked for me, and stand in the middle of their kitchen, silent.

"*Tommy* . . ." Midge would say, pulling me into a hug. She knew.

Charlie would come over to me and put his hand on my shoulder, shake his head, and mumble something under his breath.

After hamburgers and fries with Eddy on Saturdays, I'd go to the Gerhardts' for hours and play with their kitchen gadgets and make a mess in the sink. Charlie let me drive his red 1957 Chevy up and down his driveway with the radio blasting. He was a kind, soft-spoken, easy-going man. He brought me baseball gloves and footballs from his store and signed me up for Little League when I was nine years old and took me to all the practices. He tried to make things better between my father and me, but it never worked.

On the night of my first Little League game, Charlie convinced my father to attend with him to surprise me. I'm sure it took a few vodka martinis. When I got to bat, I scanned the bleachers and saw Charlie's smiling, encouraging face . . . and my father's scowl next to him.

Holy shit.

I kicked the dirt and got into position. This was my chance to make my father proud, to show him I could be *something*, that I wasn't nothing. But the first pitch was so fast and far inside, it hit my left shoulder and knocked me off my feet. And just like in kindergarten, I burst into tears. The coach led me back to the bench to put ice on my shoulder, and I caught sight of my father's face on the way: pure disgust. Nothing Tommy had struck out and I stayed benched for the rest of the game. Charlie tried to console me in the car as we drove home, but my father wouldn't even look me in the eye.

I never played baseball—or any sport—ever again. And after that day on the field I never cried again, either—not for another forty years.

———

At home, I found small pockets of happiness. Sunday was a special day regardless of what violence had taken place in our home during the week. I seldom got hit on Sundays. My mother cooked roast beef or leg of lamb, and my father let me watch the New York Giants with him if I kept quiet and out of his way. We also played chess; my father learned it in the Marine Corps barracks and was so desperate for an opponent that he taught me how to play. I took to it immediately, maneuvering the men on the chessboard, knowing instinctively how to see the best moves several plays ahead and win the game, which infuriated my father.

When I was alone, I imagined escaping my world. I was obsessed with *The Wizard of Oz* and wished that I, too, could go to a fantasyland far away.

Every year after the Labor Day weekend, I'd start counting down the days to Christmas. I'd take out my Frank Sinatra, Perry Como, and Dean Martin Christmas tapes, which I'd recorded off the transistor radio, and play them while pretending to do homework. Schoolwork bored me, but Christmas music made me feel happy—it sounded hopeful. And even though I still got beaten at Christmas, my mother would decorate her dining room mahogany furniture with cotton so it looked like snow—so at least I got beaten with a festive background. Starting in early September, I played the crackling tapes over and over:

Jingle bells, jingle bells, jingle all the way . . .

My father would bang on my bedroom door.

"It's *September*, dammit! Stop playing those goddamn Christmas carols!" Whatever attention I lacked from my parents in some areas, they overcompensated in others. (*Overcompensated*—a useful word I learned later in prison therapy.) I was the best-dressed kid in school—wearing green-and-blue silk Nicky Newark guinea chinos, leather shoes, and Italian knit shirts when other kids wore junky dungarees and turtlenecks. And up until I was ten, my mother insisted on tying my shoes for me. After school, she'd be waiting to drive me home at 3 PM.

"Overpossessive" was another term I heard later in therapy. My mother literally—and I do mean literally—wiped my ass for me right up until my tenth birthday. I'd call her from the bathroom after I was done pooping.

"Ma, I'm done!" A few seconds later she'd be running up the stairs with a warm, wet towel in her hand to finish the job.

"Bend over," she'd say.

Meticulous. Germaphobe. Obsessive. And more than a little anal-retentive, that was my mom. She even flushed for me. Why did I let her do this? I knew it was warped, but it was as close to physical affection and love that I got. Freud woulda had a field day with that one, a fucking wet dream.

I went to my first psychiatrist around the age of eight. My parents were worried because my acting out in school was getting worse and my marks were plummeting. They really had no idea what could possibly be troubling me. Neither, it seems, did the headshrinker.

In the backyard playing with the sheath of my dad's bayonet

My mother waited in the Cadillac as I sat in his mildewy office twice a month for four months, answering the same questions each visit.

"How are you feeling, Tommy?"

"I'm all right."

"How are things at home?"

I stared at the heavy, dusty drapes on the window. No wonder my mother wouldn't come in.

"Like I said, my father beats me."

After which he'd talk to my parents, and they'd explain I got spanked for misbehaving, and all three would unanimously agree that I was A Bad Kid. My father now had official confirmation from a professional of the diagnosis he'd reached on his own years before!

The doctor gave me a multiple-choice IQ test to determine if I was dumb as well as bad. But as it turned out, I was very, very *not* dumb. The first time I took the test I scored 159; he looked at the results and said, "This can't be right." I took the test again and scored even higher—189—which landed me somewhere between "very superior" and "genius." The doctor looked baffled but didn't ask me to take it a third time. I don't know if he told my parents about the scores, but if he did, they said nothing to me.

Needless to say, my first shrink wasn't any help, and by the time I reached age ten, my stealing had gotten worse—or *better*, depending on your point of view. Already the little businessman, I decided to expand beyond the regular looting of my dad's wallet and diversify. Every good thief knows the importance of a diversified portfolio.

Behind our house and beyond the woods, a row of split-level homes was under construction on a vacant strip of land, and the unguarded site was like catnip to my stirring criminal sensibilities. I knew there had to be something there I could steal and sell, but this wasn't a solo job; I needed backup. I recruited my first crew—my best pal, Eddy, Mikey "The Bike" Tossellini (whom I met in catechism class), and Danny Gravano (whose father, we were told, was a cement truck driver).

I drew up the plans for our first job—we'd break into the unfin-
ished homes and steal cases of lightbulbs, nails, plumbing supplies,
and toilet bowls, and resell them to hardware stores in town at a
ridiculously discounted price they couldn't refuse. Even earning pen-
nies on the dollar—like ten bucks for a $100 toilet—I made a small
fortune. And the thrill of pulling off my organized crime gave me a
total adrenaline rush.

Like with Dad's wallet, I didn't feel a trace of guilt or remorse
over it. But since my mother made me go to confession every Saturday, I did tell Father Stanley about it. He wanted me to be accountable, after all, so I gave him a full accounting. I'd been an altar boy
since I was seven and went to church with my mother on Sundays.
But I had doubts about this god she worshipped. After five years of
praying to him to stop my father from beating my mother and me,
the beatings had gotten worse. I didn't feel this god looking after me
at all. The year I turned ten was also the year President John Kennedy was assassinated. The entire country was sobbing in the streets,
and it made no sense: If this god was all-powerful, all-loving, and
all-knowing, why would he let such a tragedy happen? Fuck mysterious
ways. Maybe I wasn't important enough to watch over, but President
Kennedy was.

My mother, on the other hand, was certain someone or something was protecting me. She started believing this after I got into
a bike accident at age six that should have killed me. I went flying
down the driveway and flipped over the handlebars, slamming my
head into the cement sidewalk so hard I got a major concussion and
my mangled teeth were pushed up into my nose. I was rushed to the
hospital and into intensive care . . . but the next day when I woke up,
"It was a miracle," my mother would say, looking heavenward, when
she retold the story over the years.

"The doctors and nurses were in shock to see that he'd completely
healed! You're special, Tommy," she told me after that. "You have a
gift that saves you from trouble."

Maybe so, but Father Stanley wasn't buying it. He told me I was a sinner, so I lined up with a hundred other kids at the confessional. Inside, I'd start with the smaller sins and work my way up.

"I was disobedient in school," I'd say, peering into the latticed grid. "I talked back to my mother. And me and the other altar boys drank wine from the chalice . . ."

I had inherited my parents' genetic propensity for booze. Eddy, Danny, and I used to get into my father's bar in the basement and mix gin, vodka, and scotch into Coca-Cola bottles and get drunk in the woods. We also siphoned off homemade wine from the barrels in the Gravanos's garage. Getting drunk was another good way to escape my abusive world, I found.

"And, oh yeah, Father"—I'd save it for last—"I broke into a bunch of empty houses and stole everything that wasn't nailed down."

He yawned.

"Say twenty-five Hail Marys," he'd say, "twenty-five Acts of Contrition, and twenty-five Our Fathers. *Ego te absolvo*, I absolve you from your sins. In the name of the Father, the Son, and the Holy Spirit. Amen."

I was in and out in less than a minute; he had a big line to get through before lunch. By twelve, when puberty struck, I refused to go to church anymore. If there was a god, he clearly didn't give two shits about me.

Eddy and I had graduated from plastic toy guns and comic books to BB guns and *Playboy*. And something else had changed inside of me that I couldn't articulate, but I knew instinctually: I was losing the ability to feel fear or pain.

My father had been beating me up and telling me I was no good for more than half my life, and now I felt something inside of me cross over. A decision had been made; a wall had gone up. If no one could stop my father from hitting me, then I'd stop him from *hurting* me. How? I would refuse to feel the pain.

The next time Technical Sergeant Joseph Giacomaro lunged toward me in the dining room for hand-to-hand combat, I didn't put my hands up to block his blows.

"Go ahead," I said, "beat me as much as you want." My voice was so cold and far away, I barely recognized it.

My father hit me, again and again, until I fell to the floor. I got up.

"Is that it?" I said, smiling at him. "Give me some more."

So he did—he kept pounding on me until my mother screamed so loud, I'm sure they heard her down at the Rendezvous. Blood and spit flew from my mouth. The less I reacted, the harder he hit; but nothing he did could make me even flinch. And I refused to stay down.

Even when he threw me against the wall and I slid to the floor, I got up and laughed in his face.

"Is that all you got?"

My mother begged me to be quiet and begged my father to stop—but neither of us did.

He was out of his mind. And I felt nothing.

CHAPTER 3

HIGH SCHOOL CAPO

We were more than a fraternity; we were a mini-mob.

Sometime after my sixteenth birthday, I snapped.

My dad came at me with his hand raised and his face twisted, and I fought back. I didn't hit *him*, no. My Sicilian blood prevented me from decking my own father; it was too disrespectful. And a small part of me still clung to my childhood image of him as my hero—I wasn't ready to completely kill that. Besides, the son of a bitch was two inches taller than me and a trained killer.

But what I lacked in height and training, I made up for with *anger*. I had learned rage from him, but I was smarter than he was. I knew where to attack to cut him the deepest without laying a finger on him: his perfectly ordered world. I was going to wreck his house.

He had me cornered in the dining room again. As he geared up to swing, I picked up a chair and hurled it across the room, aiming for my mother's beloved Hammond M3 organ and hitting it.

"C'mon Dad, let's go!" I yelled. He stared at the organ in horror, then at me, shocked. His arm was frozen in the air.

"You want to hit me all the time? You know how many times you've hit me, you motherfucker? Fucking hit *this*."

I moved to the organ, picked up the bench, and smashed it against the carefully polished cherrywood—gouging the top panel and music stand and breaking a bench leg. My mother rushed into the room and screamed.

"You ruined the bench!"

"Yeah, fuck you, Ma. You love your furniture more than you love your son. I took beatings all my life. Now your organ is taking one, what do you think of that?" I reached for another dining room chair. "How about I start breaking everything in the fucking house?"

Their faces were as white as a New Jersey blizzard in February. I looked at my father: "You beat me one more time, and I'll destroy this place. You wanna see crazy? *I'll show you who's fucking crazy.*"

My father put his arm down and my parents backed away. It was the last time he ever raised his hand to me.

I taught my parents a lesson that day, oh yeah; now *I* was the one not to fuck with. The following week the furniture repairman fixed the leg on the organ bench, but the deeply etched grooves and scratches on the wood would remain forever—an everyday reminder to us of the time I staged my coup and seized power in the house.

My high school yearbook photo, just before I took over the school

I took that new attitude with me to Manchester Regional High, and in my junior year became boss there, too.

In the late sixties and early seventies, high school fraternities in Jersey were basically gangs who tortured and beat up each other. We had Kappa Gamma Lambda (KGL), Omega Gamma Delta (OGD), and Alpha Beta Sigma (ABS)—they were all mostly jocks—and Sigma Kappa Delta (SKD), who were street thugs.

Hell nights were brutal. SKD called their pledges "dogs" and KGL called theirs "moose." They stripped the guys in the woods (where no one could hear them scream) and gave them seventy whacks with a wooden paddle until they were bruised from ass to thighs. Assuming the pledges survived that, they then had their balls smothered in chili sauce and deep heat until the skin fell off. Lastly, the frat would pelt the pledges' heads with eggs until their skulls pounded. This went on for eight to twelve weeks.

"Fuck that," I said to Eddy and Danny and my new buddy, Billy Stone. I wanted the power of being in a gang, but on my terms.

"We're going to start our own fraternity," I announced. "And we're going to get big. And it's going to be the most powerful one of all."

That's how I talked now, in blustering hyperbole. I had the idea for ten seconds and was already plotting expansions and takeovers. I dubbed us Gamma Sigma Delta and ordered sweatshirts and sweaters in navy and gold to wear under our leather jackets.

I began with a crew of twelve—like a bunch of badass apostles and their false messiah. I was the president, treasurer, boss, and brains of the outfit. We didn't stay twelve for long because I had a talent for luring, organizing, and convincing others to join and do what I wanted. I moved people around like pawns on a chessboard, like when I played with my father—thinking a few steps ahead of the game with the grand plan to win, be the biggest, be the most powerful.

Our first stop to recruit new frat members was the toughest high school in South Jersey—Paterson Tech. That's where the biggest, meanest black guys went, and no fraternity had dared recruit there before. To me, they were fresh meat, potential marks, and an untapped market. Eddy and I hopped into my secondhand, light-blue metallic 1965 Chevy Impala and crashed their after-school dance the following Friday. We intended to leave that crepe-papered gym a few hours later with either broken noses, new frat brothers, or their women . . . or all the above.

I arrived with Eddy, my official bodyguard, at my side. At seventeen he was now 6'2" and a lean, mean basketball star at Eastern Christian High School. Like me, he also had a screw loose in his brain and a rage from his own father beating him. Eddy could turn into a lunatic in one second if provoked, ideal bodyguard material. As soon as we got on the dance floor, a circle of big black guys surrounded us.

"Who are you?" the biggest one asked me.

"We're Gamma Sigma Delta, that's who we are," I said. "And we want to bring you into our fraternity. I'll give you your own chapter. You'll make a lot of money. And all the girls will want you. And *you*," I said to the biggest one, "you're going to be president of your chapter."

I was no dummy and neither were they. They wanted power, too, and they knew it came in numbers. I also knew these guys sold drugs, and they were at that moment tabulating in their minds how many new customers they'd inherit by joining a fraternity.

I needed them and they needed something from me. And that, in a nutshell, is the art of the deal. I sweetened the pot by describing the girls, the money, and the cool sweaters, and in one hour I'd added forty of the toughest guys within a fifty-mile radius to our gang.

The following Friday we crashed a dance at Paterson Catholic, where I had an even bigger deal in mind.

Kappa Gamma Lambda had been around since the fifties and had the most jocks—it was new compared to the older frats OGD (established in the early 1900s) and SKD (established in the 1920s).

I knew KGL guys would be at the dance, so when we got there, I zeroed in on one of their members, Stevie Moretti, and gave him my pitch. Stevie's job was to bring in new members, but what I suggested was heretical.

"I want a merger," I told him. "You need us delinquents for your fights with those SKD street thugs." Stevie nodded, and said he'd take me to his leader.

A few weeks later I was standing in front of KGL's grand president, Dennis Greenwood, in his parents' basement in Hawthorne. That's where frats often held meetings—in their mommy and daddy's finished basements, complete with wet bar, dartboard, and an original edition of Twister, circa 1966.

Dennis was a blond, WASPy-looking kid headed for prep school, no doubt, and the whole damn football team surrounded him that night. Next to them, Billy, Danny, Eddy, and I looked like a bunch of long-haired hoodlums in leather jackets, bandanas, and knives hidden in our boots.

"How many guys you got?" Dennis asked. We had fifty-three.

"We got a hundred guys," I lied. The falsehood slid off my tongue effortlessly, like butter sizzling across a hot skillet. It came so naturally, I didn't see it as lying at all: I was telling the truth as it *could* and *would* be. Alternative facts, you might call it. I could get another fifty guys no problem so in my mind it was already done.

"We want to merge with you," I continued, "but we're not doing no regular hell night or taking seventy shots on the ass and getting messed up. You want us? My top three guys here and me will do three shots each to show our loyalty and that's it. We'll give the KGL oath to the rest of our guys."

Dennis eyed the knives in our boots and agreed to my terms. Right there in the basement, they whacked our asses with wooden paddles they'd made in woodshop class. They were two inches thick, twenty-four inches long, twelve inches wide, and the shape of a pizza paddleboard. You had to use oak or maple so the paddle wouldn't snap when you hit a guy hard.

That night, we traded in our navy and gold colors for green and white—we were officially a chapter of KGL with me retaining my titles of president and treasurer.

Over the next several weeks, I continued my plans for expansion. I made the rounds of high schools in the nefarious regions of town with my crew—crashing dances and luring in the toughest fighters with promises of money, girls, power, and no hell night humiliation. It was good training for the mergers and acquisitions I'd do later as a salesman.

We drove from school to school in my Chevy, but I never paid for gas. I'd back my car into the driveway of someone's highfalutin mansion late at night and send Danny out to stick a hose into their gas tank and drain it. We kept a hose in my trunk, buried under stinking sports equipment and shit-stained underwear—another one of my early, brilliant ideas. I got Stevie to put *real* skid marks on a bunch of ratty underwear, and we laid them across the junk in the trunk in case a cop stopped us and took a look. The entire trunk smelled like dirty ass. One glimpse and sniff of the shit-stained skivvies and the search was over.

In two months, I added one hundred more members to KGL and had big plans for how I'd play my new pawns.

One of my after-school jobs was working the cash register at the local A&P—then called The Great Atlantic & Pacific Tea Company. Once I saw that the assistant manager on night duty was either drunk or asleep in his office, I organized my chess pieces.

During my shift, a bunch of guys would come in and load up shopping carts with steaks, chops, ribs—hundreds of dollars of meat, expensive produce, and imported tinned specialty items.

Ka-ching! I'd punch in a few items and let them by with the rest for free.

Meanwhile, I organized a whole other operation in back. Four
of my guys would pull up at the delivery door in their hippie van
and we'd load it up with boxes of meat out of the freezer and storage fridge. The next day we sold it to local markets, and what we
didn't sell, we'd cook and eat at our frat house and wash it down with
Rheingold Beer.

We found a run-down house in Paterson and rented it for $150
a month, furnishing it with used sofas, mattresses, and a stolen juke-
box. It was a top-secret man cave—no girls allowed, not even for
fooling around. That's what cars were for. Stevie and I picked up girls
and made out with them in my Chevy until the cops banged on the
steamed-up windows. One girl I had my eye on was the gorgeous
captain of the cheerleading squad, Angela DeAngelis, who was older
than me and didn't give me the time of day until after we'd both
graduated. We smoked hash, had sex, and she dragged me to radical
political meetings. She urged me to rob banks with her—"not for the
money," you understand, but "as an antisocial statement." After I lost
touch with her for a year or so, I saw her face in the newspaper: she'd
become a founding member of the Symbionese Liberation Army,
the American terrorist group that kidnapped Patty Hearst in 1974.
In May of that year, she was killed at the SLA's safe house during a
shootout with police that was broadcast live on television.

With my A&P operation, the money was rolling in. After the
first month the inventory was short $43,000 and the shocked man-
ager thought it must be a mathematical error. The second month
we were short $67,000. In month three, the general manager of all
the New Jersey Great Atlantic & Pacific Tea Companies arrived to
investigate. They didn't have surveillance cameras back then, so he did
it the old-fashioned way—by watching us. Specifically, he watched
me. From the parking lot he saw me pretend to press the cash register keys while my buddies walked out with bags of filet mignon and
caviar. He rushed in and grabbed my arm.

"Take off your apron and get the fuck out."

I was fired, but so what. I had another scheme in mind. My next job was at Larkey's, an expensive menswear shop in Paterson. Billy Stone and I worked as "pickup" guys—bagging the altered suits in the basement and running them up to the waiting customers on the main floor. It didn't take too much of a pitch to enlist a handful of salesmen, black guys, to work with us. They had access to the merchandise on the main floor and in the stockroom. I instructed them to fill plastic garbage bags with Botany 500 suits and leave them by the dumpster for me to pick up later, promising them half the money we made selling the $500 suits for $200 to an outlet store.

This went on for six weeks, and in that time we stole forty-five to sixty suits, about sixty pairs of slacks, and shoes, making about $50,000. Until the general manager for all of Larkey's, Guy Zoppi, hired a private investigator and planted him undercover on the sales floor—a move this chess master didn't foresee. I recruited the spy, and a few weeks later a bunch of cops and detectives burst in and raided the place. The black kids got handcuffed, and I got sat down in a room alone for interrogation.

"You're the kid who's masterminding this whole thing," one of the detectives said.

"We're going to arrest you," said a cop.

"I'm calling your parents," said Mr. Zoppi.

This was not good. My father would take out his humiliation and anger on my mother. In that moment, I discovered a new talent to go along with my lying—crying on cue.

"You can't do that," I sobbed. "My mother's *sick*. She's going through 'the change.' If you tell her I've been fired or arrested, she'll kill herself!"

My performance was worthy of an Academy Award for Best Melodramatic Bullshitter because it worked, and it earned me my high school nickname, "The Worm," since I could slither out of any tight spot. The other guys were arrested, but they let me and Billy go without calling our parents.

Later that night, I drove to the phone booth in front of the North Haledon Fire Department and called Mr. Zoppi at home.

"What the fuck are you calling me for?" he asked.

"Please, Mr. Zoppi, I'm sorry!" I cried again. I was on a roll. "Those black guys at the store put pressure on me to steal. They scared me! I'm just a little guy. Um . . . can I have my job back?" I had balls the size of watermelons, but Mr. Zoppi busted them.

"Kid, you ain't ever, ever, ever coming back."

Click.

But again, I wasn't without a scheme for long. Everywhere I looked I saw dollar signs and easy marks. My palms got itchy when I sensed a potential big score.

When the drama department at school put tickets on sale for the annual play, I bought one and a made hundreds of counterfeits at a print shop and double sold every seat. The night of the performance was pandemonium. I managed the school store for a few weeks until the inventory came up $12,000 short the first month. The worm wiggled out of that one, too, and I talked my way out of being expelled.

Stealing car parts was another mastermind of mine. We'd hit three outdoor car lots in three different suburbs and take the radios and tires off the Super Beetle Volkswagen bugs and Triumph TR6s.

The car lots didn't have any fences or security cameras back then— it was a different world when people just trusted strangers not to steal their stuff. We'd go to the lots after midnight and pop the side windows with a screwdriver, reach in and open the door (no car alarms back then, either), pop the latch for the trunk, and get the spare tire. To get the AM-FM radios, Eddy stuck his hand under the dashboard and unscrewed the bolts. We were fast, at a speed of one minute per car, and we'd hit twenty cars per night. At $50 per car, we'd make $1,000 in a few hours. When the lots installed security cameras three months later, we adapted and got ski masks. I was unstoppable.

We started selling drugs to other students. I bought them in Newark from a guy from the Dominican Republic who sat around playing cards in front of a coffee shop. We made the exchange in the bathroom, then transported the drugs behind the emblem on my steering wheel. We could fit about $1,000 worth of drugs in that little pocket—pot, LSD, and orange sunshine—before taking them to my basement, where we sorted them out into little plastic bags.

Soon, I expanded our business distribution network and started selling to the guys who owned the "roach coach" lunch trucks parked outside the manufacturing plants in the area. "You wanna provolone sandwich?" they would ask their customers. "You want any pot with that?" Those blue-collar guys needed a little escape from their shitty, humdrum lives.

As treasurer, I kept the money we made in a metal cash box on the floor of my bedroom closet. We were more than a fraternity; we were a mini-mob. And I was its High School Capo.

With drugs came rock 'n' roll, and the world was changing. Apollo landed on the moon in the summer of 1969 and Woodstock happened.

I drove up with Danny and another friend, Stan Parrot, on the Saturday night of Woodstock weekend, but a few miles from the stage, traffic came to a standstill. We pulled over and started walking in the rain and through the mud with thousands of others kids, getting high along the way. A mile from the concert, we could see the lights bouncing off the stage and hear the Who singing, *Sometimes I wonder what I'm gonna do . . . ain't no cure . . . summertime blues . . .*

After Jefferson Airplane finished the night with "White Rabbit," we slept in the car, soaking and stinking, and left in the morning inspired.

In junior year, Danny and I started our own band, the Sound Effect. Out of the petty cash in the metal cash box, I bought myself a Farfisa electronic organ and a Leslie 147RV speaker and got Danny a rhythm guitar. We practiced Hendrix, Cream, Vanilla Fudge, and the Who in Danny's muddy backyard barn and performed at high schools and birthday parties. The kids came to hear music and to get stoned or fucked up, and we provided all three—a diversified portfolio, remember?

But with drugs come drug wars. And with drug wars comes violence. I wasn't worried. I was building more than a crew; I was building a fucking militia.

CHAPTER 4

BLOOD ON
THE STREETS

We were armed with chains, bats, zip guns, and our newest,
most dazzling piece of weaponry that I designed myself—
homemade Molotov cocktails . . .

By senior year, KGL was a massive army.

We had nearly five hundred members and it was all my doing—I was a born leader. It was time for a hostile takeover.

Eddy and I had a new sit-down with Dennis, the grand president, and told him how it was gonna be from now on.

"*I'm* the new grand president," I informed Dennis, matter-of-factly. Eddy stood next to me, silent and huge. Dennis was quiet; there was nothing he could say or do about it. I'd turned his fraternity of jocks into a gang of thieves, and his original members were so afraid of me, they followed my orders. Now that I was to be the real capo of all the KGL chapters, they'd have even more to fear.

Every morning I swung my Chevy into the prime spot in the school parking lot—there was no name on it but everyone knew it was mine, including the teachers. I got a new bodyguard—Corky Quant, my most massive and menacing recruit to date. Corky was 6'6" and 280 pounds, and everywhere I went, Corky was sure to go.

When I had to bust up ABS's Monday night frat meeting to challenge them to a showdown, Corky was by my side.

The tension between ABS and KGL had been building for months—especially after I found out they tried to steal our drug clientele. I stoked their anger by spreading talk around school that they were pussies and scared to fight us. I knew what I was doing; I knew how these games I was playing were going to end—with a knockdown, bloody war. It's what I wanted.

In retaliation, the wusses took it out on Stan Parrot, my Woodstock buddy. Stan was a jock and played football with them. (One of their players, by the way, was Bruce Huther, later a linebacker for the Dallas Cowboys, the Cleveland Browns, and the Chicago Bears.) After practice in the spring of 1971, they cornered Stan alone in the locker room and smashed his face with a shot put, busting his nose and teeth.

They messed with Stan, so I declared war. I arranged for three hundred of our guys to wait on the hill by Manchester High with baseball bats, chains, knives, and zip guns—a cross between a slingshot and a crossbow that shot nails. Meanwhile, Stevie and Corky came with me to bang on the basement door of the ABS meeting a few blocks away.

"You busted up Stan," I said to a roomful of football players, "so now you gotta meet us down the street at the school. You think you're so tough? We'll be waiting for you. You better show up, you punk motherfuckers."

Thirty minutes later they came up the hill, and like a scene out of *Braveheart*, my guys appeared from behind the crest and charged, taking them by surprise. When those *scooch a menz* jocks saw my armed militia running toward them, they turned around and fled. Like I said—*pussies*. Fucking meows. The cops showed up and made everyone disperse, which was too bad because I was looking forward to breaking some heads.

Our biggest gang war was with SKD—we called them "Skids." They wore black and gold. Our two gangs were bitter rivals, like a teenage version of the Bloods and the Crips. And when I heard that they, too, were trying to hone in on our drug clients, I went berserk.

Danny and I and twenty of our guys crashed a dance at St. Teresa's, where we knew some Skids would be, near the end of our senior year. Outside in the parking lot, I had 150 of my soldiers waiting. My plan: to lure the Skids out and beat the shit out of them, like we tried to do with ABS before they ran away like little girls.

Inside, though, there were hundreds of them and they swarmed us.

"Giacomaro, what the fuck are you doing here? We're gonna tear your head off," said one SKD guy, "and stick it up your ass."

"Oh, yeah? Well I'm gonna kick your fucking dicks in!"

But we were outnumbered times ten. Even the band onstage could see that and struck up Black Sabbath's "When Death Calls."

In other words, we were dead.

We made it to the front doors and they followed, but outside we were greeted by dozens of squad cars surrounding my waiting army and shining their high beams on the sea of green, white, black, and gold sweaters pouring out of the school. Once again, the cops had thwarted my fight. But not for long.

"Meet us by the warehouses next Saturday at midnight," I said to the SKD president, as we were being shuffled away. He nodded.

I was a volcano ready to erupt.

The police had been keeping an eye on me and knew I was the instigator of the thefts and fights in the area. Sergeant Healy of the Paterson Police Department lived on our street and paid a visit to my father.

"Your son is a bad kid," he told my father. As if Dad didn't know already. My father was humiliated, and Charlie next door felt a sense of impending doom around me.

It'd been years since I'd used Charlie and Midge's kitchen as my safe house. After I stood up to my father and got my car, I was rarely home and didn't need them anymore. What a cocky, ungrateful son of a bitch I was.

That week before the big warehouse showdown, Charlie tried to talk to me. He knocked on our back door when he saw that I was home.

"You're going down the wrong path, Tommy," he said, sitting at our kitchen table, full of concern.

"You're hanging around bad kids, you're stealing . . ." I saw something in Charlie's eyes I'd never seen before—disappointment. And just like always, love. He was trying to warn me, trying to set me on a better road. But I was such an arrogant kid, I wouldn't listen. All I knew was that he was telling me what to do, like my father.

"Mind your own business," I told Charlie, and I got up and left the room—and Charlie's life forever. I refused to talk to him after that day. He tried to approach me many times over the next year when he saw me coming or going, but I ignored him and left him standing in the driveway, hurt.

That moment when Charlie tried to help me could have been a turning point in my life, but I dissed it. Another turning point arrived that same week by certified mail.

"Tommy, did you apply to *Princeton*?" my mother asked, excited, as she handed me an envelope from that day's mail. Inside were the results of my SATs—I had a near perfect score—and a letter from the College Entrance Examination Board:

Mr. Giacomaro,

We question the validity of your SAT scores because of your lack of academic performance at Manchester Regional High School. Please come to Princeton and take the test again under our watch . . .

Because I was getting Cs, Ds, and Fs at school, they didn't believe I could get such high marks on my academic tests. So just like I retook my IQ test with the shrink, I drove to Princeton and retook the SATs. The second time, I got a near-perfect score again.

My parents didn't understand what any of that meant, but I did: I was very, very smart, just like those childhood IQ tests showed. With these scores, I could go to Princeton or any Ivy League school of my choosing. I could get a scholarship. I could change my destiny.

Instead, I chose to fight down at the warehouse, sealing a different kind of fate for myself. I was too angry not to. And so was Eddy, especially after what happened next in his life.

On a sweltering hot and humid afternoon, he showed up at our front door, out of breath and terrified.

"What the fuck's wrong?" I asked.

He motioned for me to follow him, and he led me back to his family's garage, running. Eddy's father, James, lay on the cement floor with a rope around his neck, dead. Eddy had arrived home from school and found him hanging from the septic pipe, and he'd cut him down using gardening shears. Mr. LaSalle's face was blue and his body was rigid. Because of the heat, swarms of flies were already circling his puffy, decomposing corpse.

Eddy didn't cry and I felt nothing. We were both in shock and barely said a word to each other about it then, or ever. My parents took me to the funeral, and my mother told me on the way home that Eddy's dad was a kleptomaniac and had been caught stealing something at the grocery store and was going to be arrested, so he hung himself.

The details of Mr. LaSalle's death would remain a mystery to many neighbors and friends. I had a big mouth—I could be a real *chiacchierone*—but in honor of my friend I never told anyone what happened in the garage that day. It might be the only secret I ever kept in my life. (Until now, that is.)

In that tragic moment, I suspected that Eddy's fate was now sealed, too. I could have gone to an Ivy League college and Eddy could have been a pro basketball player.

Instead, we both needed to fight and believed we had nothing to lose.

———————

The following Saturday night Eddy, I, and hundreds of our crew gathered in the warehouse district in Paterson. The barren area was made up of old dye houses and storage facilities that would ten years later be a broken-down, looted ghost town. We'd be its ghosts.

We were armed with chains, bats, zip guns, and our newest, most dazzling piece of weaponry that I designed myself—homemade Molotov cocktails made from empty Rheingold beer bottles from the frat house. We filled them with gasoline and lead BB pellets and stuffed rags in the bottlenecks. Before the Skids arrived, I choreographed the ambush, sending some of our guys to hide on the cobblestoned side streets.

"You got my orders?" I asked. They nodded.

When our enemies arrived, we started pushing and shoving, then I gave the signal to the hidden group and unleashed hell.

The flaming cocktails flew from the alley through the air like missiles, smashing onto the road and exploding with hot BB pellets shooting out like machine guns. The boys who were hit grabbed their burning clothing and looked up to the sky.

That's when we attacked full force and charged. We beat the shit out of SKD that night until we heard the police and ambulance sirens on their way and took off into the dark alleyways.

That summer night my vision became a reality: KGL was now the biggest, most powerful high school fraternity in all of Jersey. As I ran, I took one last look behind me.

My fallen enemies were on the ground, bleeding and burning. I wasn't sure if they were dead or alive.

I left them there like that, just as my father taught me.

CHAPTER 5

HIGHWAY ROBBERY

We called it "legal corruption" and everybody got a piece of the pie.

R otting garbage, burning flesh, and a steaming pile of shit—
that's what it smelled like.

The New Jersey Meadowlands dump on Route 20 in East Rutherford burned day and night, seven days a week. If you lived or worked nearby, you got that stink in your clothes, in your hair, and shoved up your nose so deep you never got rid of it.

When I was a kid, people used to say the Mafia dumped dead bodies there after a late-night hit. By morning, whatever happened in the night was shrouded in the thick, early fog.

My first legit job out of high school in the summer of 1971 was at Maislin Transport, a trucking company with an office fifty yards from the dump. The Maislin brothers owned thousands of acres in the area, including the dump site, on which a new, clean, shiny Giants Stadium would be built five years later.

Maislin was the largest trucking company in the country at a time when trucking routes could be worth millions, before Ronald Reagan deregulated the industry in 1980. Back then a company like Maislin had the power to "run lanes"—they were awarded exclusive contracts by the government to haul specific merchandise. The international runs were the most coveted routes, and booze was the most valuable, desired merchandise to transport. The drink of choice at that time was Seagram's Seven Crown and Canadian Club whisky. This cargo arrived in New York and New Jersey from Montreal by one carrier only—Maislin Transport.

Ever since the Maislin brothers began their business in 1945, they continued the time-honored tradition of Al Capone in the twenties—the prosperous partnership of booze, cops, transport, and organized crime. You had to pay the government and the Mafia to get the liquor contract, then pay again to keep it.

In 1971, Maislin had ties with New York's Genovese crime family and the most corrupt labor union of all time, the International Brotherhood of Teamsters—specifically, Teamsters Local 560 out of Union City, New Jersey.

My uncle Anthony was a proud member of Local 560, and it was his idea to get me a job at Maislin after I (barely) graduated from high school. He knew an important guy who knew an even bigger guy. His idea was for me to start at entry level and work my way up to truck driver and Teamster, like him. My father was livid—he wanted me to go to college and be an accountant, like him. Plus, he knew the trucking industry was mobbed up the ass.

"Don't get involved with these people!" my father yelled at both of us. "These are bad people!"

"Mind your fucking business," my uncle shot back. No one else talked to my father like that and got away with it. At 6'2", Uncle Anthony towered over my father. He had a red mole over his eyebrow and a broad, ruddy face like a real old-time *ginzo*, an old Sicilian.

"Tommy can't go to college," my uncle said. "He's a dummy. Well, actually, he's really *smart*, but he won't do good full-time at school; he can go at night. Right now, he needs to grow up and get a job."

The following week Uncle Anthony took me to the Tick Tock Diner in Clifton to get approved by Maislin "friend" Anthony

Provenzano—aka "Tony Pro." Tony was VP of Local 560 and, I didn't know it at the time, a *caporegime* in the Genovese crime family. He'd just gotten out of jail after doing time for embezzlement and extortion. Tony Pro was powerful because of his strong ties with Teamsters Union leader and Mafia associate Jimmy Hoffa.

Both names meant nothing to me; I was clueless about organized crime except for the kind I organized myself. What I was also clueless about then, and found out later, was that my own family was "connected."

My father's mother, Josephine Laplaca, was related to Pete Laplaca—the capo of the Gatto crew in the Genovese crime family. Which further explained why my father flew into a rage at the thought of me getting involved with these "bad people": they were his own flesh and blood; they were *his* people. Which meant they were mine, too. My family pedigree, along with Tony Pro's vouching, is what got me the job at Maislin. I was one of their own; I could be trusted.

Before I started the job, my uncle pulled me aside to warn me.

"These are mob guys, Tommy. Be polite. You gotta be careful. Keep your mouth shut. Be respectful. Don't give them none of your attitude. And one more thing," he added, "whatever you're doing in the basement stops right now, you hear me?"

I nodded. With high school over, I was losing a lot of my drug customers anyway, so I put that on hold. It was kid stuff compared to the dangerous world I was entering.

The trucking industry in New Jersey was the most mobbed-up business in the country, followed by garbage. And my new boss, Alex Maislin, a Canadian Jew from Montreal, had his hands in both. Short, bald, and chubby, Alex was a conceited, flamboyant, powerhouse of a character who wore Yves St. Laurent suits and swaggered around the office with a pearl-handled, .45-caliber chrome gun in his belt, resting against his big belly. At lunch he got bombed on vodka, then spent the afternoon chasing the secretaries in miniskirts around his desk. When he talked to you, whether you were a cop, a mobster, a union boss, an employee, or some nice-looking tomato—he talked rough, with balls as big as the one that dropped in Times Square. Alex Maislin would be my first role model for the guy I later became.

"You're gonna be my gopher," Mr. Maislin told me at our first meeting in his office. "And you're gonna go for this and go for that. And I'm gonna to start you off at $145 per week."

That was double the usual salary for a job like that. I looked over at his gigantic bodyguard, Rocco, hovering in the corner, his thick arms crossed. Antonino "Argentina" Rocca was a former Hall of Fame wrestler who sang opera around the office, but never talked. He was like a mountain—big and immovable; he was Alex Maislin's version of Corky Quant.

"All right, Mr. Maislin," I said, in my polite voice. I could do polite.

"No, no, noooo. Tommy. Call me Mr. Alex."

For the job I wore a tie and stuffed my shoulder-length hair under a Yankees cap. In my light-blue Super Beetle Volkswagen (I traded in my Chevy), I picked up lunches for the staff and dropped off Mr. Alex's dry cleaning and picked up sports tickets; whatever Mr. Alex asked me to do, I did. I picked up groceries to stock his fridge in his mansion in Fort Lee, and drove his wife to the beauty parlor. When she interrogated me about Mr. Alex's nineteen-year-old girlfriend at the office, I lied for him.

"He don't have no girlfriend, Mrs. Maislin," I'd say. "He's a good man."

I was already learning *omertà*—the Mafia's code of silence. Uncle Anthony said to keep my mouth shut, so I did—especially about what I saw down at the loading docks late at night. Sometimes when I was walking through the terminal, I'd see a black Cadillac speeding past the security post and drive to the back. Two guys would drag a screaming guy out from the trunk and beat the shit out of him. In the middle of the Meadowlands, surrounded by acres of eight-foot wetland cattails, you could scream your lungs out and no one'd hear you. Just like the torturing of the frat dogs in the woods. It was the perfect place to whack someone. And, conveniently, the dump was right there to get rid of a body.

Mr. Alex loved me for my discretion and because I was fast, smart, immaculate, and never late. He told me to come in at 8 AM so I was there before 7 AM—setting up the ledgers, organizing his office, and laying out his booze. Every other day I took his 1972 Fleetwood Brougham black-on-black Cadillac with XXX license plates to the car wash and did the detailing myself—wiping the mats and the inside of the windows. Mr. Alex hugged me and kissed my cheek hello every morning and goodbye every night.

"You're doin' good, kid," he'd say, slipping me a fifty-dollar tip. He kept three-inch-thick wads of C-notes and fifties in his pockets, held together with rubber bands.

My favorite task was to drive Mr. Alex and Rocco to Frankie & Johnnie's Steakhouse in Manhattan, where they'd meet Frank Sinatra for dinner. I'd wait in the car playing "Nice 'N' Easy," with a smile, knowing Sinatra was just inside with my boss.

Sitting out there one night, I decided that I wasn't gonna steal from Mr. Alex. I could have easily pinched the joint good; I had the keys to everything—the offices, the warehouses. I could have called up my old crew to bring their vans to the loading docks and fill them up—TVs, stereos, washing machines, musical equipment, lawn mowers, and furniture. My hands got itchy just thinking about it.

But the money Mr. Alex gave me got so good so fast, I didn't need to. There was *big* money to be made at Maislin if I played my cards right. And Mr. Alex would shoot me with his .45 if I ever stole from him.

One afternoon in a drunken rage, he went after one of the dockworkers when he thought the guy had ogled Mr. Alex's teenaged *goomah*.

"I'm gonna kill that sonofabitch!" he said, storming through the terminal with his gun to find the guy.

"Mr. Alex!" I ran after him with Rocco. "Calm down! You don't need to shoot this guy. *Fugghetaboutit.*"

It was a phrase I first heard at Maislin, which was immortalized in the movie *Donnie Brasco* twenty-five years later. All the Maislin guys were saying it, and I was learning to speak their language. *Hey, youse guys got da ting wit da ting wit da ting?*

I even started getting my hair cut by the barber to the mob, Marty, who had a shop in Paterson. They all loved him because he was quiet and they'd sit in his chair and spill their guts and he never ratted. Every two weeks I was Marty's first appointment of the day at 6:30 AM for a trim. No more hippie hair for me; he slicked it back like a real mob guy.

Mr. Alex calmed down about the dockworker and didn't remember a thing the next day. The guy lived. Mr. Alex was so impressed with how I handled him that he offered to pay my tuition for night classes at Bergen Community College and William Paterson University, where I had just signed up to study business administration. He had big plans for me, he said.

Four weeks into the job on a hot and sticky August afternoon, I was summoned to his office. He was in his usual vodka-induced stupor with his loaded .45 dangling over his belt.

"Tommy, we got ten loads of Canadian Club coming in tonight from Montreal and the security guard called in sick. You're gonna do security tonight."

"What do you mean," I asked. "All night?"

I'd overheard the dockworkers talking about overnight guards in the transport business calling in sick when they thought there'd be a hijacking. Liquor was a big target because, unlike TVs and stereos, the bottles didn't have serial numbers.

This is how a hijacking went down: A car pulls up to the security post around 3 AM, at the same time the trucks carrying the booze arrive. The hijackers jump out with guns, order the driver out, take IDs from the driver and security guard, and say, "If you say anything, we know where you live." Sometimes, they shoot the truck driver and the security guard. Sometimes, they died. The empty trailers were found a few days later, abandoned somewhere.

"Sit in the guard shack," Mr. Alex continued, pouring a new drink, "and when the trucks come in, write down the trailer numbers and the times. It's easy! I'll pay you time and a half, and here's an extra $100 bonus."

I felt myself go pale. I looked over at Rocco—arms crossed and stone-faced.

"Hey, Mr. Rocco," I whispered, "don't you never talk?"

"What's that, Tommy?" Mr. Alex asked.

"Oh, nothing, nothing." *Motherfucking guardhouse duty. I don't need this shit.*

"Tommy, you look a little nervous," Mr. Alex slurred. "If you run into any trouble there's a phone in there, call the cops," he said. "Or . . ."

He took out his .45 and handed it to me. "Take my gun. Just start shooting."

It was so heavy I fumbled and nearly dropped it.

I looked over at Rocco again. Now the wrestler in the corner looked nervous, too.

The guardhouse was a tiny shack fifty feet from the highway. It had a rotary phone on the wall and an air conditioner in the window, which I didn't turn on. I wanted to make sure I'd hear the hijackers barreling down Route 20 when they arrived. I carefully placed the gun on the counter and opened the windows. Flies from the rotting-garbage-burning-flesh-steaming-shit dump rushed in. *Motherfucker!*

By midnight the fog began to roll in. I grabbed the phone and called my new girlfriend, Debbie Carini, a pretty blonde I'd met at the Jersey Shore on Memorial Day weekend. She walked past me in a blue string bikini and I reached out, grabbed a string, and pulled her toward me. Yeah, I was smooth with the broads all right.

"Hey, baby," I said on the phone. "I'm scared out of my fucking mind over here."

Deb and me, high school sweethearts

I called her every thirty minutes as the flies buzzed around me like vultures circling a soon-to-be-dead body. By 3 AM, the fog was so thick, coming in through the window, I could barely see the phone or the gun in front of me. But I could see a pair of headlights heading my way and it wasn't a delivery truck.

Screw this! I thought. I grabbed the gun and ran blindly out of the shack to the truck terminal and crawled under a trailer. The fearless capo of Manchester High who vanquished his enemies months earlier with chains and firebombs was hiding like a sissy. Not my finest moment. But this wasn't high school anymore; these guys were the real thing.

From the ground, I saw the wheels of a car idle in front of the guard shack, then I heard a *boom-boom-boom*. A few minutes later, the car was gone. I ran back to the guardhouse and called the police. When the cops showed up, I explained about the place being hijacked.

"Yeah, right kid," they said, chuckling and getting back into their squad car, "not *this* place."

The booze trucks arrived after that and everything was fine. And as the sun came up it finally dawned on me: *other* trucking companies got hijacked, but not Maislin—and for good reason.

The next day, I told Mr. Alex everything.

"Mr. Alex, please don't make me do that fucking job no more. I almost had a nervous breakdown."

"Jesus Christ, Tommy, take it easy," he said, reaching into his pockets. "Here, take more money. You'll feel better."

He handed me two hundred-dollar bills. I smiled and looked over at Rocco, who grimaced in the corner. I just invented yet another way to get money—whining. Mr. Alex told me I'd passed an important test doing guard duty, proving my loyalty to him.

"I need loyalty, Tommy. I demand it," he said, announcing I would now be promoted from gopher to runner. My new duties beginning the next day were to deliver briefcases "to certain very important people," he explained.

One of my first regular runs was to the offices of the New Jersey Sports Authority at the new World Trade Center. In the fall of 1971 the iconic center was still under construction, but the lower half of one building was in use and already busy. The first time I stood in front of it on the street, I looked up in awe. The roof disappeared into the clouds.

Once a week I was sent to meet a man from the Sports Authority in the lobby and hand him a briefcase. I wasn't told what was inside, but I knew damn well it wasn't briefs. Bribe money? Several months later I went to that same lobby to fetch a big fat check from that same guy. Maislin had hit the jackpot and sold their East Rutherford property, including that stinking dump, to the Sports Authority as the site for the new Giants Stadium. The deal would make all seven of the already-wealthy Maislin brothers even more stinking rich.

Soon, another World Trade Center stop was added to my routine—the US Customs office. They were in charge of clearing the shipments that came in from Canada so, of course, the kindly customs agents received a weekly briefcase for their hard work and loyalty from their friends at Maislin Transport.

I drove my trusted Beetle to deliver money

By October, I was making out-of-town deliveries. I'd roll down the windows and play cassettes of Sinatra singing "Summer Wind" full blast in my Bug as I drove to Albany, Philly, Baltimore, and Cherry Hill to take top-secret briefcases to different Teamsters Union presidents. I was like Henry Hill in *Goodfellas* when he was a runner for the bosses.

Each time I left the office, Mr. Alex handed me a fifty- or one-hundred-dollar tip. Or he'd say, "Go put some gas in the car, Tommy, and keep the change."

Why were the union presidents getting paid? Because it was their guys who drove the Maislin trucks and if they were ever to strike, your trucks stopped moving and your business was dead. An interruption in service could kill your business, so we had to keep the union bosses happy.

The only day I didn't do deliveries was on Friday—that was State Police Day at Maislin. That's when more than a dozen New York and New Jersey police captains, sergeants, and lieutenants came to have lunch with Mr. Alex. They had to be kept happy, too. On Friday mornings I'd go to the docks with a dolly and bring back cases of Seagram's and Canadian Club to have ready in the office. After lunch, as they were leaving, Mr. Alex handed each one a few bottles and a briefcase.

"A little gift," Mr. Alex would say.

It's what kept our trucks from being pulled over by cops or hijackers, I finally understood. No one was gonna stop a Maislin truck if so many powerful people were making money off us.

I was learning the importance of bribe money, but we didn't call it that. We called it "legal corruption" and everybody got a piece of the pie—including me.

I was making more money than I ever imagined, about $4,000 a month. For an eighteen-year-old kid, that was fucking ridiculous. Every other night I took Debbie to the Steak and Brew on 43rd Street in Manhattan, and we'd order the most expensive steaks on the menu and Blue Nun wine; we were some hotshots. After dessert, in the parking lot, we smoked the best pot that money could buy.

My father was going mental watching all this unfold.

"Where are you getting all this money?" he demanded. "What are you doing for it?"

He thought I was doing something illegal with the "bad people."

The irony, if he only knew, was that it was the first time in my life since I was seven years old that I *wasn't* stealing from someone, including him.

I was simply benefitting from other people's corruption.

CHAPTER 6

WHITEY AND JIMMY

"Welcome to the brotherhood. You're gonna go far."

My previous top-secret deliveries were warm-ups for what came next.

In November of 1971, Mr. Alex began sending me on what he reverently called "the confidential runs." It was an assignment for only the most trusted and loyal of employees, he told me.

Mr. Alex was looking to expand his liquor delivery to include a Montreal-to-Boston route, and there was only one way to get that. He had to pay a kickback to the guy who was already leaning on the local distributors there—that guy was Boston crime boss James "Whitey" Bulger.

At that point the Irish Bulger, 42, wasn't a crime boss yet. He'd done time at Alcatraz and was a top lieutenant to mobster Howie Winter, the leader of the Winter Hill Gang—the top Irish Mob syndicate on the East Coast. Seven years later he'd be boss of that gang and kill his way onto the FBI's "Ten Most Wanted List" for his role in nineteen murders. He was a cunning, charismatic, "hands-on" killer—the kind of guy who'd shoot your testicles off and enjoy watching you slowly die as blood poured out from where your balls used to be.

In 1971, all I knew was that Whitey was the guy we had to pay off if we wanted our trucks to make a stop in Boston. If we even wanted to *pass through* Boston without paying Whitey, he'd steal our loads.

I arrived at the office in early November to find Mr. Blumenblatt, Mr. Alex's VP, waiting for me. Mr. Alex was the boss, but Mr. Blumenblatt was the brains. He wore old fedoras from the forties and underneath them his mind worked overtime. Mr. Blumenblatt did everything for Mr. Alex, including sucking his ass. If Mr. Alex stopped short, Mr. Blumenblatt's face slammed into his butt.

When I arrived that morning, Mr. Blumenblatt handed me the usual briefcase—a black, beat-up Samsonite with a combination lock. These were leftover, used suitcases the salesmen at Maislin had worn out and tossed. This time, Mr. Blumenblatt also gave me a piece of paper with an address scribbled on it, a wad of petty cash, and a plane ticket on Allegheny Airlines.

"You're flying to Boston this morning," he said. "The briefcase goes to Mr. Bulger. We gotta take care of him."

Just like Hoffa, the name meant nothing to me. Mr. Blumenblatt proceeded to give me specific hand-off instructions.

"Tommy, when you give it to Mr. Bulger . . . hand it to him low."

"Low?"

"Yeah. Under the table like, so nobody sees."

A few hours later I was landing in Boston with a briefcase full of $125,000 in cash on my lap. That was the beauty of the seventies—no security opening your bags, no X-ray machines to worry about.

———————

I took a cab to Triple O's Lounge in South Boston, where Mr. Bulger was waiting for me at the back. The place looked dark and sticky, and it smelled of spilled beer and stale cigarette smoke.

I didn't need anyone to tell me which one he was. First of all, the joint was empty because it was strictly used for the gangsters and their crew. Second, Whitey's whole demeanor had *boss* written all over him. After I was frisked at the door, I was escorted past the pool table and dance floor to Mr. Bulger, who stood up to shake my hand. He had a guy sitting with him. Guys like him always had a guy sitting with them.

The first thing I noticed were his wrists—they were as thick as tree trunks. They were the kind of wrists that were connected to the kind of hands that killed people.

"Ha ya doin', kid?" he said, in an elongated Boston accent, and smiled.

"I do just fine, Mr. Bulger."

I handed the briefcase to him low, as instructed, and he put it under the table.

"You did good. Thank you. You hungry? *Djeet?*" (Translation: Did you eat?)

On the table was every antipasto and pasta on the menu.

"No thank you, Mr. Bulger. I'm good."

The entire exchange lasted less than five minutes and then I was out the door, on my way back to the airport.

That was my routine with Whitey every four to six weeks. We didn't say much more than that, and I never sat down when he asked *Djeet?*

On a snowy day in February 1972, I was given a new confidential run. Mr. Alex told me the assignment himself; it was that important.

"We have a VP coming in from Detroit," he said. "You're going to the airport to pick him up; he's coming in on the Blue Goose. His name is Jimmy Hoffa."

I still had no idea who he was. ("Tommy, you're green apples," Mr. Alex used to say, when I didn't know these guys. "You ain't ripe yet.")

Six weeks earlier, Teamsters Union leader Hoffa, 59, was sprung from a Pennsylvania prison after serving less than five years of a thirteen-year sentence for attempted bribery and fraud. Richard Nixon himself pardoned Hoffa—after the union leader allegedly bribed him. Also part of Hoffa's sweet deal with his pardon was a one-time lump sum of $1.7 million for a pension—a first of its kind in Teamsters' history.

A few weeks before I was sent to pick up Hoffa, Nixon announced his candidacy for reelection. The International Brotherhood of Teamsters would endorse Nixon for a second term as president later that year, of course.

Mr. Alex tossed me the keys to his Cadillac.

"Take my car. At the airport, hold up a piece of paper that says 'Hoffa.' I told him you're a scrawny kid wearing a baseball cap and he'll come to you. Go pick up this motherfucker and bring him back here. And Tommy . . . for god's sake, drive slow."

I wasn't sure if he was worried about Mr. Hoffa or his car.

At the arrivals gate I held up my scribbled sign and two men approached me. One had dark slicked-back hair and the face of a bulldog. The other guy was one of those guys who was always with the important guy.

"Are you the driver?" the bulldog-faced one asked. I nodded.

"I'm Jimmy Hoffa." He stuck out his hand. "How you doin'?"

"I do good, Mr. Hoffa, real good."

"No, no. You call me Jimmy."

"All right, Mr. Hoffa. Here, let me carry your bags."

"No," said Hoffa, "we carry our own bags. Just take us to the car."

I had parked illegally outside the front doors, but I knew the cops circling the airport would recognize Mr. Alex's XXX plates and protect the car. The drive back to the office was quiet, uneventful, and slow—at Mr. Alex's orders. When Hoffa's meeting with Mr. Alex was over a few hours later and I took him back to the airport, he was talkative.

"In prison they built a special cell just for me," he told me, "with accommodations to my liking."

"Is that right, Mr. Hoffa?"

Talk in the back seat shifted to the Kennedys. In the fifties, Bobby Kennedy worked for years investigating labor racketeering and tried to nail Hoffa then, but he couldn't. After John Kennedy was elected in 1960, Bobby continued his crusade as attorney general and put together a "Get Hoffa" squad of prosecutors and investigators in the Justice Department to get him behind bars, which they finally did. John Kennedy was assassinated four months before Hoffa was sentenced, and Bobby Kennedy was assassinated while Hoffa was in prison.

"Slimy pricks set me up," he was saying to the other guy.

At Newark Airport, I hopped out of the car and opened the door for him. Before he left, he shook my hand again.

"Tommy, how long you been in trucking?"

"Just a few months, Mr. Hoffa. I graduated high school last year."

"Ah, a real working man, I see. Well let me tell you something. They love you at Maislin, kid. You're smart and fast; I can see that and so can Alex Maislin. We talked about you. You're going to have a big career in the trucking business, lemme tell you. Welcome to the brotherhood. You're gonna go far."

"That's beautiful, Mr. Hoffa."

And just like that, standing in front of the Blue Goose entrance-way at Newark Airport, the powerful and corrupt union leader predicted my future and solidified a new fate for me.

When I got back to the office, Mr. Alex and Mr. Blumenblatt were giddy drunk on whisky, and Mr. Alex hugged me.

"Hoffa loved you!" said Mr. Alex. "Did he tell you we're going to send you to the Academy of Advanced Traffic? It's a private school, very expensive. His idea. We're going to take you under our wing and you're going to learn everything there is to know about trucking. We're going to groom you to be an executive here."

"Oh, that's beautiful, Mr. Alex!"

Hoffa liked me so much that we added him to my out-of-town confidential runs every four to six weeks, just like Whitey.

Why was Hoffa getting a briefcase full of cash if we were already paying various union presidents? Because Hoffa was more powerful than the president of the United States.

Every two weeks, I was either flying to see Whitey or Hoffa. I never knew who or when. I'd find out when I arrived at work that day and Mr. Blumenblatt or Mr. Alex handed me a plane ticket.

I'd meet Hoffa in Detroit at a restaurant called Machus Red Fox in Bloomfield Hills. It smelled like an old-fashioned gin mill. He always sat in the back, like Whitey, with his back to the wall, and he had a guy with him.

Like with Whitey, I'd hand the case to Hoffa low, and our entire exchange would only last a few minutes and I'd be on my way back to the airport.

"You're doing great, Tommy," he'd say each time, then added, "You're going to be a big success. *Djeet?*"

Sometimes Hoffa would say, "Do the right thing, Tommy." That meant: Take care of yourself, take care of me, take care of Mr. Alex, keep your mouth shut, and most of all—don't fuck up.

When winter weather was bad, the handoff happened at the Detroit airport without Hoffa—he'd send his bodyguard, a short guy with a big gun, to meet me at my gate. We'd walk to a coffee shop and do the handoff there. A few minutes later, I'd be back on a plane to Jersey.

Delivering money to Whitey and Hoffa, I never had a real concept of the danger I was putting myself in. I look back now and know I could have been robbed or beat up or worse. To me, it was just part of my job. I didn't know enough to be scared or overly in awe of these guys. I still didn't have a full understanding of what the world of organized crime was until a month after my first meeting with Hoffa, when *The Godfather* was released in movie theaters.

Debbie and I went to see it and I couldn't take my eyes off the screen. The Cadillacs, the suitcases filled with money, the guys beaten up by the docks, the guns, the corrupt union bosses. I'd seen it all, but in real life.

"Holy shit," I whispered, under my breath. I went to see the film three more times, alone. I was thrilled by the danger, riveted by the power, and mesmerized by the money. Being a small part of something so big, so feared, and so notorious made me feel strong. I couldn't wait to get my own black Cadillac.

Mr. Alex was true to his word about grooming me. During the spring and summer of 1972, he put me in different departments at the office for weeks at a time to learn about over-shortages and damages, customer service pickup, dispatch, sales coordination, receivables, payables, accounting, and mergers and acquisitions.

In the sales department, Mr. Blumenblatt watched me charm potential clients on the phone while aggressively pitching them, and he reported back to Mr. Alex.

"I hear you're a natural-born salesman, Tommy," said Mr. Alex. "I have good news. I'm going to groom you to take over the New Jersey division."

I told this to my mother when I got home from work that day, and for the first time in my life she said, "I'm so proud of you, Tommy. The way you've changed." She made sure to say it in front of my father just to *scootch* him. He didn't say anything.

That weekend, I went next door to see Charlie. I'd ignored him all year but now I was feeling so good about how I was doing, I wanted to tell him. And maybe, I wanted to brag and rub it in his face a little—no, *a lot*. I was making money, and I was in school and wasn't stealing and I had a big future in trucking—Mr. Alex and Mr. Hoffa said so! I wasn't on the bad path he predicted for me.

When I approached Charlie on his driveway, this time he was the one who walked away from me. *Motherfucker*, I thought. I was hurt, and that made me angry. *I'll show him.*

But I never did.

A few months later, Charlie died of a sudden heart attack. I refused to go to his funeral and I would feel a lot of regret about that later—but not just yet.

My mind was elsewhere. It was with the dangerous, enticing world I'd seen on the movie screen. In that moment, I felt like Michael Corleone in *The Godfather* when he realizes that this world is in his blood.

I belonged to a new crew, a new kind of family, and that was my world now. I was a teenager associated with some of the most powerful Mafia associates in the country. My mother was proud of me for turning my life around and being a good boy, but I knew the truth about that.

By the end of 1972 Nixon had been reelected in a landslide victory months after the Watergate break-in, and he was all over the news. It would be a while before we'd hear about slush funds and Deep Throat and bribes, but when I looked at his face and into his eyes on our old black-and-white, I saw the crook that he was.

I knew one when I saw one, because I looked at one in the mirror every morning. Even though I'd been good all year at Maislin, the thieving con artist in me was like a dormant monster, waiting to take over.

It would again, soon enough. Not just yet, but soon.

Like the stench of the dump, it was in me for good.

CHAPTER 7

GOLDEN TONGUE

*Paul Lucy had his own pet name for me that soon got around: Golden
Tongue. "Because you can talk anyone into anything," he said, proudly.*

A great salesman is a great seducer, a Rudolph Valentino on
the sales floor.

He plays to your fantasies and promises you everything
you think you need and want. He gets you excited and makes you feel
special. He never takes no for an answer. And then, like every other
son of a bitch, he fucks you—literally or figuratively or both.

After two years at Maislin, I was hungry to move up and be that
great seducer.

I had the raw goods—Mr. Alex had educated, groomed, and
trained me—and I had the endorsement of trucking god Jimmy
Hoffa. So when the next executive position opened up and Mr. Alex
gave it to one of his spoiled, Harvard-reared nephews instead of me, I
told him I was leaving. Fuck that. I wasn't gonna wait around and get
muscled out by Maislin offspring every time a job opened up.

The following Sunday, Uncle Anthony came over to reprimand
me. He and Tony Pro had put their reputations on the line for me, he
reminded me, and Alex Maislin had trusted me with top-secret tasks.
I was an ungrateful, stupid kid. Before he left, he gave me another
one of his warnings:

"Whatever you saw and did at Maislin," he said, "you better keep your fucking mouth shut about it. *Capisce?*"

I nodded. In other words, don't be a rat.

I always knew I was a natural at sales, even before Mr. Alex and Mr. Blumenblatt told me so. As a kid, I convinced hardware stores to buy plumbing supplies from me! I pulled my frat recruits into my moneymaking schemes, and wormed my way outta trouble with teachers, cops, and bosses—all that was being a salesman. I was selling a story, a product, a vision . . . *me.*

In the fall of 1973, Debbie and I got married around the time Nixon insisted, "I am not a crook!" Standing in front of the priest at St. Anthony's Church and promising to love and cherish one woman until the day I died was quite the sales pitch on my part. I was twenty years old and didn't even shave yet. I tried to get out of it the night before.

"You are not going to shame our family!" my father yelled, pounding his fist on the kitchen table and sending dishes flying (which made matters worse because now we had a mess, too). "You're gonna marry this girl and get the fuck out of the house!"

I did want to get the fuck out of the house. And Debbie was a beautiful girl. But I didn't know a thing about loving someone.

At the wedding, my father's mother, Josephine LaPlaca—the one related to the Genovese capo—sat in the front pew wearing a sphere-like, netted picture hat circa 1945 that dwarfed her 5'2" frame and blocked everyone's view. Uncle Anthony refused to come, he was still angry at me for leaving Maislin. My parents sat in the front pew, too, nervous as hell that I wouldn't go through with it. When I said the words "I do," I nearly retched at the altar. Part of that could have been because I was footing the bill for the whole damn sacramental occasion.

Not that I had to worry about money. I'd already talked my way into a new job in the dispatch department at North American Van Lines on Route 46 in Little Falls. It was a gigantic corporation owned by PepsiCo in Purchase, New York, with a corporate structure that had boundless potential for someone like me. They gave me my own office, my own secretary, and started me at $250 per week. With my first paycheck, I got Debbie a white Camaro and put a down payment on a one-bedroom apartment for us in Wayne.

I was only in dispatch a few months before Sam Spector, the sales manager and East Coast VP, noticed I was a "natural" and bumped me up into sales. My salary doubled to $500 per week, and they handed me the keys to my very first company car—a brand-new silver Ford LTD with a blue interior. To me, you could always measure a man's success by the company car he drove. Problem was, they'd never had someone as young as me in that division. It was now early 1974 and I'd just turned twenty-one—too young to be insured to drive the company car.

"So?" said Sam, with a Yiddish lilt. "We'll make an exception for the boy." Sam was a balding 6'2" Jew from Manhattan. His ill-fitting, plaid sport coats were stained with the drippings from oily lunch coleslaw.

What was about to happen, you gotta understand, was unprecedented. I was an aggressive, energetic new kid plopped into a corporate world of old, tired men. The executives were all in their fifties and sixties and got there by paying their dues and slowly moving up the ladder. No companies at that time had a salesman my age, making that kind of salary and driving a company car.

But Sam and the new national VP, Paul Lucy—a quick-witted Harvard guy who wore wide-lapelled leisure suits—had a hunch. At forty, Paul was their youngest exec and had been transferred from Pepsi to recruit youthful energy into the fuddy-duddy place. I was the first of a new breed of brash, young salesmen, poised to turn the old regime on its head.

I put away my baseball cap and sports jackets and went to Bamberger's department store to outfit myself with new suits. I saw how the other salesmen at NAVL dressed—like shit. I would dress like the powerful VP I intended to become.

Early seventies by the Jersey shore

As soon as we got the paperwork done, they put me on the road. My job was to convince big-name appliance manufacturers to give us contracts to transport their goods. The only training I'd had was a few weeks in the Maislin sales department, but I wasn't worried; I knew how to maneuver people.

Let loose in the Tri-state area, I was like a swaggering gunslinger in the Wild West, shooting at everyone. I cold-called major companies and sweet-talked secretaries to set up meetings for me with their bosses. I hopped in my Ford and showed up at their offices unannounced.

"I'm Tom Giacomaro from North American Van Lines. How ya doin'? You ship this stuff everywhere? Where do ya ship to? Let's go to lunch, you want to go to lunch?"

If I could get them to lunch, I'd pour wine and tell them how much money they'd save and make with NAVL because we were faster, smarter, and better than the other guys. Another glass of wine and they'd take out wallet photos of their snot-nosed kids and I *ooohed* and *ahhhed* and blew sunshine up their ass. I told them their middle-aged wives were beautiful and that their kids would go to Princeton. I exaggerated, but so what. I was perfecting the persona of a funny, earnest salesman who blew into your office like a tornado and wined and dined you until your *no* turned into a *yes*.

I sold them on the American Dream and it worked. I started bringing in two to three new accounts each week.

"So? Tommy? Such deals you make this veek!" Sam would say, stopping by my office. "Such good deals!" My desk was fastidious— Inbox on left, Outbox on right, with files lined up like my rows of socks. Outside, I Windexed the glass and mirrors of my Ford LTD and shook out the floor mats every day—twice a day in warm weather, to get the sticky bugs off.

Sam and Paul were so impressed with my work ethic and success that they started sending me out farther, to territories and big companies where their other salesmen had failed. The first was General Electric's major appliance division in Columbia, Maryland. In the appliance world, GE was like the gorgeous tomato every guy wanted to fuck, but couldn't get to first base with.

"We've tried to open dis account for ten long years," Sam said, before I set off in my pristine car. "Let's see vat you can do, Tommy my boy."

"Don't worry, Sam. I intend to get my hands on their washing machines."

I got to Maryland and I checked into the local Holiday Inn with my very first credit card, a corporate American Express, then called up the GE office, *schmoozed* (as Sam would say) the secretary, and got the big boss, Paul Bluestein, on the phone.

"How ya' doin'?" This is Tom Giacomaro from North American Van Lines and I happen to be in the area and I'd like to stop in and . . ."

"You *just happen* to be in the Columbia, Maryland, area?"

"Well. You want me to tell you the truth? I didn't even know where Columbia, Maryland, was until today. But everybody says they can't open this account so I came down especially to see you."

"Is that so? And what do you think is going to happen?"

I ratcheted up the Jersey accent. The farther from Jersey I drove, the more these guys loved the accent.

"You're gonna gimme all yer freight, dat's what."

He laughed. And that's when I knew I had him. Always make 'em laugh.

"You talk funny."

"So listen, Paul—can I call you Paul? I'm ten minutes away and ..."

Ten minutes later, he was giving me a tour of his huge warehouse packed with appliances stacked to the ceiling. Dollar signs danced in my head. I had a vision of *our* guys loading those boxes into *our* trucks. A rival company was scheduled to take a humungous order to Little Rock, Arkansas, but I did some calculations in my head and whipped out a pen and notepad from my briefcase—the same black Samsonite one I used to use at Maislin to deliver money to Hoffa and Bulger.

"Listen, Paul. I got the power of the pen. Do you know what that means? It means I have the power to make you an offer you can't refuse. What do you pay that other company? I'll cut that rate by twenty percent."

"Is that so. And how fast can you do that?" he asked.

"Effective tomorrow."

His eyes widened.

"Kid, if you're that good and you can get twenty trailers here by Friday morning to take this load," he waved his arm across the expanse of the warehouse, "you got the account!"

"Twenty?"

"Yeah. And I need them here by seven AM. And I need you here, too, to have your picture taken with me for the company newsletter."

It was Wednesday afternoon; I only had a day and a half to make it happen. Our biggest orders at NAVL usually involved one or two trucks—three at max. What he was asking was impossible. If you were anyone but me.

"Paul," I stuck out my hand, "you got yourself a deal."

I drove to the nearest pay phone and called up our dispatcher to get twenty trucks in Maryland, pronto.

"Are you crazy?" the guy yelled. "We need those trucks for a bunch of other accounts we already got moving in New York tomorrow!"

Fuck your incompetence, I thought. *You will never do anything great with your life.* But what I said was, "Get Sam on the phone."

A minute later, Sam was talking through a mouthful of deli.

"Tommy, my boy. Vat's dis I hear? It can't be done!"

I took a deep breath. "Sam, respectfully, fuck those other accounts. Postpone them. Buy new trucks. I don't care what you do, just do it. I just landed us a multimillion-dollar deal with General Electric that's so huge it will make you and Paul rock stars."

A day and a half later the twenty trucks and I arrived at 6 AM, an hour before deadline. I watched the workers load the trucks, just as I had envisioned, and shook Mr. Bluestein's hand for the photographer. I was on such a high that, on the drive back to the office that day, I stopped at Black & Decker in Towson, Maryland, and nabbed that account, too. I was the fucking rock star.

Paul and Sam were elated. After my big score they put together a "hot sheet" of the dream accounts throughout the entire country they wanted me to go for; I was to be their new "account buster" and they would fly me wherever I needed to go, first class.

At the top of the list was Lee Hayes, the transportation manager at Maytag, in Newton, Iowa.

"He won't talk to nobody," Sam warned me, as I left for the airport.

"I'll get him," I said, cocky as hell.

I flew down, checked into the hotel, and called up Mr. Hayes.

"This is Tom Giacomaro," I said to his secretary. "I'm a top VP at North American. What's your name, honey? Uh-huh? That's a *bee-oot-iful* name. I need to speak to Lee. Please tell him I'm on the phone, baby."

You could get away with talking to women like that in the early seventies. Mr. Hayes got on and I tried a new tactic.

"Let me ask you a question," I started off. "Why've you been roughing up all our Midwest salesmen all these years? What's wrong wit youse, don't you like us?"

Hayes was an old-regime guy, born and raised in the Midwest. I'm sure my Jersey accent sounded like a foreign language to him.

"What? Why do you talk funny? Are you *I*-talian?"

"Whattaya talkin' about, I talk funny? I'm from Jersey. I'm with North American and my boss says I got to come out there because you're nasty and ornery to everybody."

He laughed. I had him.

"Hey listen, can I call you Lee?"

"I prefer you call me 'Mr. Hayes.'" Right. Old-school guy.

"All right, Mr. Hayes. I'm hoping to swing by and take you out for lunch. It just so happens I'm going to be in your neighborhood anyway and . . ."

"In the neighborhood of Newton, Iowa? *Nothing's* in the neighborhood of Newton, Iowa. Unless you're standing in the middle of a cornfield."

"Ah, well, ya got me there. In fact, I just so happen to be down the street from you right now this very minute."

Two weeks later I wrapped up that account, and Maytag became one of the largest customers North America Van Lines ever had.

———————

And that's how it went for the next two years.

Sam and Paul flew me all over the country, and I went after the biggest companies that transported huge, bulky appliances like washing machines, refrigerators, and stereos because the more space the merchandise took up, the more trucks they needed and the more money we made. I opened up Whirlpool in Benton Harbor, Michigan, and Westinghouse in Columbus, Ohio. I wined and dined the Black & Decker execs in Towson, Maryland, and the Roper Stove guys in Baltimore. I entertained the bosses at Toshiba in Irvine, California. In the industry, I became known as "The Appliance King," but Paul Lucy had his own pet name for me that soon got around: *Golden Tongue.*

"Because you can talk anyone into anything," he said, proudly.

I couldn't wait to get to work each morning. The office opened at 8 AM and I'd arrive at 6 AM to write reports and structure my itinerary. With every new account, the money came rolling in via monthly bonuses and commissions. I upgraded my wardrobe yet again, with a dozen Pierre Cardin and Yves St. Laurent three-piece suits, including my favorite—a lime-green number pinstriped with gold that cost $500. I remember staring at my reflection in the mirror at Macy's as the tailor pinned the suit for alterations, thinking: *The more expensive the suit, the more powerful the man.*

With my new money, clothes, and prestige came the inevitable—the women. I was a big shot and my nickname was Golden Tongue, after all. That made me a chick magnet for the broads in the office, hotties wearing miniskirts, crushed-velvet bell-bottoms, and platform shoes. I was twenty-three; I couldn't resist any of them.

As I worked my way to the top, the leaders around me were falling.

In August 1974, Debbie and I sat riveted to the TV with her parents and watched Walter Cronkite on the CBS Evening News announce President Nixon's resignation days after a "smoking gun" tape was released, tying him directly to the Watergate scandal. "I have never been a quitter," he said in his resignation speech later that night, but he didn't admit to any wrongdoing. Deny, deny, deny. I knew that trick since forever.

Less than a year later, in July 1975, I got an urgent call from Uncle Anthony saying to get to his house right away.

"Sit down, Tommy," he said, in the kitchen. (With Italian families, all important things happened in the kitchen.) "Jimmy Hoffa is missing."

"Are you kidding me?"

"No. So you gotta be prepared in case the FBI comes and talks to you."

In other words, don't be a rat.

Hoffa had gone missing with the same bodyguard I'd seen him with, and our friend, Tony Pro, was one of the last to see both of them alive and was a suspect.

"You need to tell the FBI the truth about everything they ask youse," Uncle Anthony continued, putting his giant trucker hands on my shoulders and squeezing hard. "*Tell them you don't know nuthin'.*"

A few days later, one of the switchboard girls at the office rang me from the lobby to say, in a whisper, that two FBI guys were standing in front of her and wanted to see me. *Fuck!* I met them in the lobby—two fat, sloppy-looking guys in their sixties—and took them to a conference room, closing the door.

"We've got some questions about working at Maislin Transport," one began. He had a pad and pen to take notes. "What do you know about Jimmy Hoffa?"

"I don't know nuthin'."

"We know you used to pick him up at the airport," said the other one. "Did he ever say he was afraid for his life?"

"No."

"Why did you go meet him in Detroit?"

Shit. "I used to take paperwork to him."

"Did you ever see this paperwork?"

"No."

"What did he talk about when you saw him?"

"Nuthin'."

I could do this. I'd been interrogated my entire life by my father, principals, bosses, cops.

"Did anyone ever follow you when you were with him?"

"No."

"Did he say anything to you about anybody?"

"No."

They pressed harder, asking how many times he'd come to Maislin and how many times I'd met him in Detroit and who else did I see him with and what did they look like?

I shrugged. "They looked like those guys who are always with those guys."

"You have an uncle who works for the Teamsters. Has he said anything to you?"

"No."

"Do you know the name Tony Provenzano? Tony Pro?"

Shit. "Yeah. He's my uncle's friend; he helped me get the job."

"How many times did you meet with him?"

"Just once, at the Tick Tock Diner. He wanted to make sure I was a good, straight kid."

I emphasized the words "good" and "straight." After an hour of questioning they left, saying they'd be in touch. They could see I didn't know anything about Hoffa's disappearance. But I wondered what *they* knew. I would learn in years to come that it wasn't just mob guys who ordered contract hits on guys and tossed them into the river or the dump; the government did it, too, when they wanted to get rid of a mob guy without the hassle of prosecuting him. For the rest of the day, I couldn't get the Meadowlands dump out of my mind, or the stench of burning flesh and garbage from my memory.

Golden Tongue kept busting accounts, and the following year, in mid-1976 during the nation's triumphant bicentennial, I went to Fort Lauderdale to receive the National Salesman of the Year Award at NAVL's yearly convention. Out of hundreds of salesmen from all over the country, I'd opened the most new accounts and brought in the most revenue.

For the occasion I wore a white suit and vest, an orange shirt and orange tie, and platform shoes. I was ahead of my time; *Saturday Night Fever* wouldn't come out for another year at least. I looked like a cross between a Times Square pimp and a Creamsicle. With my award came a doubling of my salary, up to $50,000. But a new VP title was what I was after, like at Maislin, and again I wasn't going to get it—this time because of my age. At twenty-three years old, they told me I was too young and it just wasn't done; it was too fast. Besides, all their VP positions were filled so I'd have to wait until someone either was fired, quit, or died—the latter being most likely.

Paul Lucy could see I wasn't the patient type. By early 1977 he floated the idea of taking me over to mergers and acquisitions at PepsiCo in Purchase, New York. He was a visionary, like me, and wanted to diversify Pepsi into the restaurant world to acquire chains like Kentucky Fried Chicken, Taco Bell, Pizza Hut, and Wilson Sporting Goods (all of which he later did), "And you're just the young man to do it," he said.

But by then I had a situation at home, something I didn't even consider: Debbie was pregnant. I was already a cheating, piece-of-shit husband; there was no way I could be a decent father. Look at the example I had.

"I want to get rid of it," I told Debbie's doctor, as we sat in his office. "I'm not ready. I don't know how to love a baby." I wasn't sure I knew how to love at all. People were either useful or not useful to me.

Debbie was horrified, but her doctor—a silver-haired Greek guy—talked to me calmly and dissuaded me out of an abortion.

"You will love this baby," he assured me. "You will see."

I didn't believe him, but I decided to let Debbie do what she wanted. I was never home anyway so she might as well have it and keep herself occupied. I wouldn't be involved. I had a career trajectory to plan out; I was going to be the King of Trucking.

The summer of 1977, before the baby's birth, was a summer of death.

The serial killer "Son of Sam" was stalking and murdering women in New York with a .44 pistol, and a power failure threw Manhattan into a blackout for two days of terror and looting during a brutal heat wave. The summer ended with the sudden death of Elvis, the King of Rock and Roll.

It was on that funereal note that Debbie went into labor in September. Despite my protests about being a father months earlier, something happened to me after the first contraction. I needed to be in the delivery room; I didn't know why. Fathers weren't even doing that sort of thing then. I insisted, and put on a gown and mask and watched the entire labor without blinking. I saw all the blood, shit, piss, and gunk, and then my first child, my daughter Lauren, pushed her way out of Debbie's body. I cut the cord and the nurses cleaned her up, wrapped her in a blanket, and placed her in my arms.

I inspected her face. She had my eyes, and my grandmother's nose, and my mother's chin, and I couldn't breathe or speak.

I'm sorry, I apologized to her in advance, in my mind. *I'm sorry that I'm going to be a terrible father.*

First Christmas with Lauren

I didn't plan or foresee the next moment, it just happened. I lifted her tiny body and kissed her soft, warm forehead. *I'll keep you safe*, I promised.

For the next few hours, I was thunderstruck and didn't take my eyes off her. I followed the nurses when they took her to be finger-printed and tagged, to make sure no one swapped or stole her. She was mine; this child was *mine*. Then I followed her back to the hospital room. As Debbie slept, I stared at Lauren all night.

––––––––––

When I put my focus back on work a few days later, I went into overdrive.

A competing company, Allied Van Lines, flew me out to Grand Rapids, Michigan, to offer me a position as their VP of Sales at a salary of $65,000. It was the position Mr. Alex and Sam Spector said was impossible, but I didn't believe in impossible.

"What kind of car do I get?" I asked.

"Whatever you want."

I took the job, and picked a red Lincoln Town Car with a white interior and white roof. With the moving allowance they gave me, I put a down payment on a ranch-style home with two fireplaces in Grand Rapids. Each new job came with new cars, new clothes, and a new house—better than I had before. I was living the American Dream and getting addicted to the adrenaline rush of such rapid success.

Four months after I started at Allied, I got an even better offer from another trucking company, Deliverance.

"We'll give you $95,000 and a brand-new Cadillac," said a top guy at the company. "And," he added, "as senior VP you get a *carte blanche* expense account."

A Cadillac—just like my father and Mr. Alex and the mob guys in *The Godfather* have. Now *this* was success. I took the job and told Debbie to get packing again, we were going back to Jersey.

In six years I'd gone from a gopher in a baseball cap to senior VP with a limitless expense account and my own Cadillac.

Who was better than me? No one!

Unless you were my father; in his eyes I was nothing, no matter what I accomplished. By the spring of 1978, Debbie and Lauren had flown back to New Jersey ahead of me while I sorted things out with

Allied and finished packing up the house. To help out, my parents drove out to Grand Rapids to fetch our French poodle, Tara, and drive her back to Jersey. My house, as always, was impeccable for their visit. And not only did I intend to impress my father with the house and details of my new job, I had a surprise waiting for him in the driveway: a 1978 burgundy Oldsmobile with spiked, gold-rimmed Vogue tires. It was just like his favorite car that he had when I was a kid. I went out to greet them as they pulled up and showed my father the car.

"Look, Dad . . ."

"I don't give a fuck," he cut me off. "You're a piece of shit. You're nothing."

In a fraction of a second, the high I was feeling about my accomplishments plummeted, like a plane in a death spiral. Apparently what happened was that before they'd left Jersey, Debbie told them about my cheating. So now my father had something new to beat me up about.

After they left with the dog a few days later, someone affiliated with Deliverance arrived in town to seal our new deal and celebrate. He took me out to my first strip club and convinced two big-titted dancers to come back to my place with us. I was still death spiraling; I wasn't in the mood.

"You gotta try this," he urged, taking out a vial of white powder and pouring a line of it on the glass coffee table. Cocaine. I didn't even know what it was.

"It'll make you feel great," he promised. "It's the new drug of choice!"

"Nah, I smoke pot," I told him, and took out a joint.

I didn't do so good with hard drugs. When I tried Orange Sunshine in Danny Gravano's barn as a teen once, I tripped out on the mud floor surrounded by chickens and goats and hallucinated farm animals for weeks afterward. A guy with a frenetic brain like mine shouldn't do cocaine.

He handed me a rolled-up hundred-dollar bill. I knew I shouldn't. But I could hear the echo of my father's voice—*you're nothing; you'll never be anything*—in my head and I wanted it gone, I needed to kill it.

I leaned over the glass and snorted. The drug raced through my body and brain like a runaway train. *Oh, shiiiiiit.* It was better than stealing money or getting senior VP or Cadillacs or sex with big-titted strippers. My heart raced and I could feel my pupils dilate so wide I thought my eyes would pop out of their sockets.

From that moment onward, I was no longer the future King of Trucking; I was King of the World, headed for trouble.

CHAPTER 8

AN UNMADE MAN

I was on fire. *I blared my favorite disco tune, "Crank It Up,"*
on the radio as I drove around with my police shield.
My heart was pounding-pounding-pounding.

I wore three pairs of white Jockey underwear on top of each other—
we used to call them "Superman" underwear—under my pinstriped Pierre Cardin suit. They smoothed the bunched-up Ziploc
sandwich bags I had stuck against my sweaty *cogliones*, my balls.

I had big balls, all right—stone fucking balls.

It was my first time smuggling cocaine and I wasn't nervous. I
shaved the tops of my thighs so that I could duct-tape the bottom
of my underwear to my legs to keep the coke from sliding down as I
walked and boarded the flight at Newark.

It was 1979 and they didn't stick you in body X-ray machines or
sic drug-sniffing dogs on you then. Those were the good old days.
I was a top executive at Deliverance, with their official logo on my
Hartmann briefcase, on my way to a meeting at our Indianapolis
headquarters. Who's gonna suspect I got drugs in my crotch?

After landing I met my new coke buddy at his apartment.

"Get this fucking shit offa me!" I said, dropping my pants to my
knees in his kitchen and pulling at the duct tape. We ripped off my

skin and I got the glue off using paper towels soaked in liquid Carbona. For a day, my balls would stink like gasoline mixed with turpentine. As soon as my balls were covered again, he handed me a manila envelope with $18,000 in cash. Easy money, my favorite kind.

When he gave me my first hit of coke that night in Grand Rapids a few months earlier, it was the beginning of the unraveling of the new-and-improved Tom Giacomaro—the one who shot to success in the trucking world using wit, charm, smarts and finally made his mother proud. The unraveling had begun, and in the end it would reveal the Tom my father always knew I was: the fuckup. The nothing.

I woke up the next morning after that first coke hit, called in sick at Allied, and spent the next three days getting fucked and fucked up with the strippers. My next few months in Michigan were more of the same. Coke, I discovered, wasn't like my previous shitty Orange Sunshine trip. It was fantastic—it made me into Super Tom with a perpetual hard-on in my Superman underwear. And it made the girls wanna fuck all night.

Grand Rapids was the asshole of the world, but the strip clubs were filled with rosy-cheeked college girls rebelling against their Republican, Amway-cult families. They weren't whores, exactly. I took them out to dinner and gave them drugs, but I didn't pay for the sex—not with money, anyway. They loved the coke as much as I did.

When I finally returned to Jersey in 1979 to join Debbie and Lauren, I arrived an official cokehead.

The first two things I did was buy my first Rolex—an eighteen-carat-gold one with a diamond-studded face, paying $12,000 cash for it. Then I went to get my new Cadillac—a black, 1979, two-door Coupe de Ville with a burgundy interior, white-and-gold gangster Vogue tires, and chrome wheels—a real *guinea* car—over at Brogan Cadillac. Hard to believe that eight years earlier I was stealing car radios and tires. Before I left the dealership that day, I treated myself to a second car—a black Sedan de Ville with a red interior. The salesman, Freddy Minatola, said I was his new favorite customer. Little did we know he would soon be one of mine.

Debbie, Lauren, and I settled down in a Cape Cod house in Hawthorne that I bought for $87,500, then spent $100,000 to renovate. I sent Debbie, with Lauren, to her mother's for two months while I slept in a cot in the living room to "oversee" the renovations. In other words, I took broads there and partied all night. The coke, the coke . . . how can I explain what the coke did to me and my life?

Before I left Michigan, I was made VP and became my coke buddy's new East Coast connection.

"You need to find someone with access to large quantities of coke," he said, excited. "You have no idea how much money we could make with this stuff!"

I had some idea, since I saw firsthand how easy it was to get hooked on it. But I hadn't sold drugs since my pot-dealing days in high school, and my connections were rusty. There was only one person I could think of to call—my old KGL brother Stevie Moretti.

After I defected to Maislin, Stevie continued selling pot to my connections for a while and was now studying at some hoity-toity school in upstate New York. He'd gone straight, like me—until I called. (*"Just when I thought I was out,"* Michael Corleone says, *"they pull me back in."*)

Sure enough, Stevie knew a guy who knew a guy. Within a few days, we were back in the drug-dealing business together in my mother's basement.

I started off buying six ounces, once a week. I was our main buyer and Stevie bought his stash from me at a discount. Within a few weeks I upped the amount to eight ounces, then ten. Two months into it, I was buying and selling kilos. That's when I bought my second Cadillac from Freddy—an Eldorado Biarritz with a beige interior.

Our drug dealer brought the coke to my office on Route 46 in Clifton—a mile from my old office at North American Van Lines—in a plain brown paper bag. He was a degenerate kinda drug dealer, nothing fancy. But his Peruvian coke was pure and gorgeous. So good, that by month four I was buying seven kilos at a time. That's when I went to see Freddy again for my third Cadillac, a black Seville with a beige interior.

The coke dealer's wife always gets a fur coat—with Debbie

Stevie stored the drugs for us in a rented safe house in West Paterson, but my mother's basement is where we performed the smashing, cutting, weighing, and packaging ritual.

While my father was at work, we cleared the papers off his table where he did his accounting and tax work and lay down a cheap, plastic tablecloth—the kind old-fashioned Italians used on Thanksgiving and Christmas to protect the nice one underneath. Then we placed the coke in the middle of the table and covered it with a towel, so it wouldn't fly all over the place when we smashed it. It looked like a big brick of hard cheese. Using an eighteen-inch-long machete I'd smash it until it crumbled, then pour it into a spaghetti strainer and grind it against the wire mesh with my fingers until it was the consistency of baby powder.

In a ceramic bowl, we cut it fifty-fifty with a powdered vitamin we got at the health food store—inositol hexanicotinate (IHN), a form of niacin. It looked like coke and was tasteless. When we were done, it was a big sand dune of white dust.

I poured it on a triple-beam scale using flour scoopers for weighing, then divvied it into separate Ziploc baggies, one ounce per bag. We rolled up and burped each baggie to get the air out, then double-bagged them.

The entire production took four hours, and by the end, we were high as kites. In prison more than two decades later, I found out why. As we handled the coke with our bare fingers, we absorbed it into our bloodstream through our pores. Who knew?

The final task after we removed our equipment was to scrub my father's desk clean. The son of a bitch would have noticed one speck.

———

As we got our drug cartel off the ground, Stevie and I started another side business, buying a dumpy little travel agency in Paterson. The owner, Joan Reiser, was married to the chief of detectives for Passaic County, Oatsie Reiser. It was a connection we knew would come in handy in our new line of work. Oatsie was good friends with all the New Jersey politicians and cops, and if there was one thing I learned from Mr. Alex, it was to be nice to cops—*really* nice. Oh, yeah.

We kept Joan on as manager and kept the name, Reiser Travel Agency, so that everyone could see we had the law on our side. We used the front part of the office for the travel agency and hired pretty girls in tube tops and jumpsuits to answer the phones. The back part we used for Deliverance and our drug business.

Buying the travel agency was just a way to get closer to the cops and buy them. I'd seen Mr. Alex do it with his briefcases full of cash and "gifts" of booze, and now it was my turn. I wanted one of those gold-and-blue police shields to put by my car's back windshield so cops wouldn't pull me over and so I could park wherever I wanted.

"Ya gotta make a 'donation' to the Jersey State PBA—the Policemen's Benevolent Association," Stevie said.

The next time I saw Oatsie at his club, I did. The Reiser Social Club was kind of like John Gotti's Ravenite Social Club in Little Italy, but a guy cave for the noteworthy Democrats in the area—firemen, detectives, state police, senators, and congressmen. Stevie and I went on Sunday mornings to get chummy with the cops and politicians so they'd keep their mouths shut about our cocaine business. We donated generously to the club, to their political election campaigns, and to the Benevolent Association. Sometimes, we donated directly to Oatsie, if you know what I mean.

"For the Benevolent Association," I'd say, handing him an envelope with a $25,000 check.

I got my police shield immediately. As long as we "donated" on a regular basis, we never got into any trouble. And so, we expanded our business.

While my Indiana buddy sold coke to buyers there, Stevie and I developed our own client networks in Jersey. Stevie reconnected with our old "roach coach" vendors parked at the local factories, and I gathered a group of friends to sell to: Freddy Minatola, who sold me my Cadillacs, became a regular customer. So did a few of my childhood buddies. I also sold to the waiters and restaurant owners in North Jersey, who sold to their patrons. In the mid- to late seventies, cocaine was the big high and everybody wanted it, everybody was doing it. Walk into any bar or club and people were doing lines in the bathroom.

By month eight of our cocaine business, I was grossing $200,000 a week and I was *on fire*. I blared my favorite disco tune, "Crank It Up," on the radio as I drove around with my police shield. My heart was *pounding-pounding-pounding* and my days ran at fast-forward speed.

We recruited a team of "runners"—friends, freight salesman from conventions, guys we partied with—who became our airport mules. We were transporting so much coke out of town that Stevie and I taped the pouches of drugs under their armpits as well as in their underwear. We sent our mules to Detroit, St. Louis, Chicago, Cleveland, Pittsburgh, and Des Moines. It was helpful to own a travel company so we could get airline tickets on the cheap.

By month ten, Stevie and I had a dozen safe houses all over North Jersey. We stored drugs in walls and ceilings of townhouses and in boxes of refrigerated iceberg lettuce in restaurants. Coke absorbs scents, so packing lettuce around it keeps it smelling clean.

The more coke we bought, the more coke I snorted, the more my pulse raced, and my life crumbled.

At first, I used it mainly as a party drug. It was the death rattle of disco and Stevie and I did lines and then went to Studio 54. I'd slip the doormen and bouncers hundred-dollar bills and we'd walk past the long lines waiting behind velvet ropes. I wore silk shirts unbuttoned to my navel, with my 18K gold chain and cross against my chest. And a Rolex, always a Rolex—by then I'd bought five more.

Within the year, by the end of 1980, I was carrying around a vial of powder in my pocket and dipping into it every hour with a little gold spoon I bought at a head shop. My respiratory and nervous system rode a continuous roller coaster—up and down, up and down, *pounding-pounding-pounding*—with one ride leading seamlessly into the next.

John Lennon died and I barely noticed. I was doing coke all morning, then started drinking at 3 PM to bring myself down enough to have business dinners with my Deliverance clients—vodka became my poison, just like Dad. I took clients to a hotel in West Orange where Connie Francis and Liza Minelli performed, and they came by our table to say hello. I wanted to tell Liza that *The Wizard of Oz* saved my sanity when I was a kid but I was too fucked up to say the words. I think I said something like: "Toto . . . home . . . man behind curtain . . ." and that was pretty much it.

At my Deliverance dinners I'd invite Ira from Toys "R" Us, Tom from Samsung, Joe from Emerson Quiet Cool, and their various wives, girlfriends, or mistresses. I'd call out to the waiter:

Bring us eight bottles of Château Lafite Rothschild!

And Dom Pérignon!

And Louis XIII cognac!

Money was no object on my limitless expense account, especially after I'd excused myself a few times to go to the bathroom and do more coke.

When my business dinners were over, Stevie and I did more coke before hitting the nightclubs and strip joints to pick up broads to bang. At 6 AM, as the sun rose, I'd finally get home. This went on almost every night.

After I made it up the circular stairway at home, I'd stop by Lauren's bedroom door and peek in. Sometimes I went in and watched her sleep. She was there; she was safe. She was the only good, pure thing about me.

The only way I could get to sleep was with quaaludes. They made me crash for two days, and my Indianapolis buddy had to cover for me with the big bosses there. He didn't care what shape I was in as long as I kept our top accounts going (I did) and kept the coke coming (I did).

He didn't care, and Debbie didn't realize how bad it was getting. But I did.

I was starting to get paranoid, thinking everyone was watching me or following me or looking at me funny. I was jittery; I couldn't breathe. I could hear my heart pounding against my ribs the skinnier I got.

One afternoon I drove my Cadillac northward to Seven Lakes Drive in the Hudson Valley, winding up to Bear Mountain, where my father had taken me as a kid once and we'd had a good day. *I'll be able to breathe there*, I thought. I drove up as high as the road would take me, parked, and sat on a rock overlooking the valley. The day before, Debbie had told me she was pregnant again.

"What am I doing to myself?" I asked out loud, to no one.

———————

Tom Jr. was born in June 1981 and again, I was in the delivery room. When he came out, I held him in my arms and kissed his forehead, speechless once more. I knew I'd never be home for him either, but I wanted kids—lots of them. I wanted the big family I never had as a lonely, only child, and I wanted them to have each other. I felt protective over them and, yes, I did *love* them. I just had no idea *how* to love them or how to be a family man.

I knew how to make money. By the fall of 1982 I was raking in $300,000 a week in cocaine sales alone. My salary at Deliverance, now $150,000 a year—I got a raise after bringing in Zenith and RCA—was pocket change in comparison. Debbie and I moved to a big house in Wyckoff—I paid cash. She bought furs and wore Jackie O sunglasses.

I had so much cash I didn't know what to do with it. I started storing it in shoeboxes in the basement. I'd put $10,000 in each box, duct-tape them shut, and stack them. At one point I had eighty boxes in the basement, that's $800,000.

I wasn't even thirty yet, but I was worth millions. And that made me the cockiest, most arrogant fuck you'd ever meet. Which is how I walked into Gaspar's Nightclub one night with Stevie, tossing hundred-dollar bills at the staff. Gaspar's was the hottest place in Jersey and I knew the owners well. It was hopping with broads and a haven for selling drugs. I had my own table and made drug deals downstairs in the basement.

That night, in the fall of 1982, I walked in with my cocky attitude and noticed a hot blonde and two mob guys at the table next to us drinking and doing coke on the sly using snuff bullets. I'd seen them around and they'd seen me.

Frankie Camiscioli ("Frankie Cam") and Joe Albino were two associates of the Genovese crime family who ran numbers and sports. Their boss was Genovese capo Lou "Streaky" Gatto, who'd taken over a few years earlier. The Gatto crew controlled illegal gambling, loan-sharking, and bookmaking rackets in the area and was known for their violent methods and shrewd business deals. The blonde was Kim DePaola, whose mother, Dotty, was married to the head of the Assassination Squad, "Murder Incorporated" for the Gambino crime family.

Frankie Cam

With one glance I could see that Frankie—loud and stocky like a pit bull—was The Muscle and Joe, a quieter, James Caan lookalike, was The Brains. Kim was The Broad. I introduced myself.

"We're in the numbers and sports business," Frankie said to me, over the synthesizer beat of Soft Cell's "Tainted Love."

"Yeah? Well I'm in the trucking business," I said, eyeing Kim.

"Yeah? Well, it just so happens that we'd like to expand into the trucking business," said Joe.

"Oh yeah? You got that kind of money to expand into trucking?"

"Oh, yeaaaah," said Frankie. "We got tons of money."

The next day I met them at Joe's house in Clifton to talk business. I already had cops in my pocket, I was thinking. Add a few mob guys and I'd be protected across the board. Joe had put out a spread—cold cuts, rolls, this and that.

"We want to go fifty-fifty with you in a trucking company," Joe began.

"Oh yeah? Well, I don't see what you have to offer me," I said. "I'm already the biggest and the best in trucking because I have all the important accounts. What do I need you for?"

"We're organized crime," Frankie said, proudly.

"That don't impress me much," I said. "No one's more organized than me."

"We got control over at the Teamsters; the union guys work for us." Joe continued, "We're with the Genovese crime family."

"Oh, yeah?" I cut him off. "Well, I got my own Teamsters contacts. And I gotta be honest wit youse guys, I'm with the *Giacomaro* crime family."

That shut them up for a minute. Frankie looked confused; Joe looked hesitant. And in that moment, I decided that these two dumb goons could be useful to me. They were mob, but they'd be easy to control. And starting up a new trucking company was a good idea. Deliverance couldn't handle the amount of business I brought in; there was always a surplus and my contacts went elsewhere to pick up the slack.

"You guys know I move cocaine, right?"

"Yeah. You can't tell anybody you do that," Frankie said. "We're not allowed to do coke; our boss won't let us."

"Fine."

"Okay."

We stood up and shook hands.

"Next week, we'll take you to meet our boss. You're wit us now."

Fuck. I didn't want to meet Streaky. He'd wanna get his claws into me and my legit business and make me a "made man" and tell me what to do and fuck everything up. No way. I wanted their protection and connections, but I wanted to do things my way, as always.

"Lemme explain something to you so youse understand," I said, still gripping Joe's hand. "I ain't *wit* you guys at all. You're wit *me*."

But there was no getting around it. The next week we set up our new corporation, Lone Star, and looked for warehouses. And I went for my first Mafia sit-down with Lou "Streaky" Gatto.

We met at Vesuvius in Newark. Streaky sat at the head of the table, flanked by his sons, Joseph and Lou Jr., and his son-in-law, Al "Little Al" Grecco. Streaky was a skinny little guy who barely spoke, but his ego was big enough to suffocate the entire restaurant. Little Al did all the talking and as he spoke, Streaky systematically placed hundred-dollar bills, one at a time, in between his knuckles, made a fist, and held each up in the air. One by one, waiters came up to him like moths to a flame, kissed his hand, and took a bill.

"Thank you, Don Luigi," they said, worshipfully.

Fucking son of a bitch, what a freak show. Meanwhile, Frankie and Joe were sitting at either side of me shoving sausages, peppers, and *pasta fagioli* in my face. I had my usual coke-vodka-quaalude hang-over so all I wanted to do was vomit.

"I don't want to eat this fucking shit, Frankie," I whispered. "I'm gonna throw the fuck up!"

"Just eat the fucking food," Frankie whispered. "You'll offend Mr. Gatto."

While waiters kissed Streaky's fist and I struggled to hold back my retching, Little Al began his pitch to me. As a salesman, I wanted to give him some advice: this was not the best time to suggest a merger. But I was too nauseous to even try.

"Tommy, we want you to consider being with us all the time," he said.

"Explain to me what that means," I asked.

Little Al raised his hands and made a gesture that looked like praying, then he pulled his hands apart.

"We wanna open up the books for youse," he said.

Goddamn it. Can't the guy be clear and just say it?

"You want me to become a made guy, is that what you're saying?"

"Yeah," said Little Al. "We got big plans for you."

Their plans, I knew, included me giving them a percentage of my own money every week—which is what Joe and Frankie did—and them using Lone Star to launder money. It meant they'd own me.

I'd had enough and wanted to get out of there. I suddenly had less than zero patience for this. And dammit, I needed a hit.

"You must be kidding," I said to Little Al. "What could you possibly offer me that I don't already have?"

Frankie kicked me under the table. Streaky looked like he wanted to leap across the *pasta fagioli* and stab me in the eye with his fork. I didn't care; this salesman wasn't for sale. But I was still a salesman, so I repeated my question to Little Al, but nice.

"What I mean to say is I'll consider what you said. Thank you very much for lunch and I'll let you know. In the meantime, Mr. Gatto, we're going to make you richer than you can imagine."

His ears perked up at that. They had plans for me? Arrogant assholes. I had my own plans.

I planned to use the mob for everything they had, but never be one of them. I planned to infiltrate the world of organized crime all the way to the top, but never be made.

The only crime boss I planned to answer to was myself.

CHAPTER 9

MOBBED UP

My ego loved the power, fear, and respect
I got being associated with mobsters.

We had ways of making them pay.

If someone was late paying the cocaine money they owed us, we started off nice. We charged them a *vig*—weekly interest on their debt amount. It's a loan-shark industry term.

Then if the guy missed a few weeks on his vig, we were done with nice. We slapped him around a little. We had guys with names like Billy No Neck, Ralphy Balls, or Tony Scratch do the slapping around. Every week there was always some guy somewhere getting slapped around.

If that didn't convince them to pay up, we sent two gorillas to their house at 3 AM to drag them out of bed, beat them up, and throw them in the trunk. That's usually when people start to beg, when they go in the trunk. Sooner or later, everybody begs. They beg for more time; they beg you to believe them; they beg you for their lives.

We didn't wanna hear it. We knew the guy probably spent the money he owed us on expensive, flashy shit—a new car, a Rolex, a fur coat for his *goomah*. Remember Johnny Roastbeef in *Goodfellas* showing up with his pink Coupe de Ville? Like that. Stupid, stupid, stupid. A little time-out in the trunk (Me: "Don't get your fingerprints on the lid, I just had it waxed!") usually convinced a guy to give us the expensive shit they bought with our money so we could sell it to pay down their debt.

Then there was the dumpster method. Some of the waiters who owed us coke money ended up in their own restaurant dumpsters. I always thought that was a little poetic. We had about twenty-five Colombian and Dominican guys at the high-class restaurants in the area buying coke from us to resell. I kept the books on who bought what and who owed what, so I knew. When too many of them were late, the total in arrears could be millions of dollars. Now that wasn't fair to us, was it?

For the waiters, we offered the convenient dumpster method. It was a no-brainer—the dumpsters were right there! We still gave them a choice, though, like Monty Hall in *Let's Make a Deal* asking what door you wanted.

"Do you wanna get put in the dumpster, or do you want us to throw you off a fucking bridge?"

I remember when a waiter at Archers was two months late. I told Frankie to subcontract two guys to rough him up when he came out of work at 2 AM. They grabbed him and duct-taped his hands and feet and smacked him around, then threw him in the dumpster with all the stinky vegetables and rotting fish. The dumpster was especially disgusting in the summer. They stuffed the guy's mouth with lettuce so he couldn't scream but could still breathe—lettuce is porous don't forget. He was moaning in the dumpster all night until a busboy found him the next morning.

As far as I know, no one ever died from being dumpstered. And our victims never called the cops on us afterward. What are they going to say to the cops, "I owed them $200,000 for a cocaine debt"?

My all-time favorite way to make someone give us money was the fish tank.

At the office we had a five-foot-long saltwater fish tank filled with a dozen triggerfish and a moray eel. The triggerfish were like piranhas, with strong jaws and sharp, pointy teeth for crushing sea-shells. The moray eel had two sets of jaws like a raptor, to capture and restrain large prey and swallow them whole. Underneath the big fish tank I kept a small goldfish bowl. Several times a day I'd scoop up a bunch of goldfish, pour them into the big tank, and watch the triggerfish swarm them in a feeding frenzy.

"Come to the office to talk," Frankie would say to a delinquent client.

Once there, I'd explain to the guy about the teeth and jaws of the triggerfish and eel, and demonstrate how they savagely devoured flesh by pouring in a scoop of little, defenseless goldfish and watch-ing the triggerfish and eel rip them apart. That's when Frankie would grab the guy, drag him to the fish tank, and stick his arm in, up to the elbow. Frankie was a former Golden Gloves boxer, I had learned, so he could drag anyone across a room.

I liked the way the tank water turned bloody, but Joe didn't have a stomach for it. He didn't have the same killer instinct as Frankie and me.

"If you don't have our money tomorrow," Frankie would say, after he took their arm out, "we're gonna chop your hand off and feed it to the fish for dinner."

All the above methods usually worked and we got our money, but once in a while, nothing worked. That's when a guy would disap-pear. It happened to a waiter named Fat Mike who was late with his payments and driving around town in a new Cadillac. It only took one call to Freddy Minatola to get the details of his new purchase. Freddy, by the way, was buying and selling coke for us at the car deal-ership. Everyone at Brogan was high as a kite.

We gave Fat Mike the fish tank treatment, but that didn't work. Then he was beat up in front of his four children in a restaurant park-ing lot, and still he didn't pay. After that, he disappeared. Just gone. The Genovese Lodi crew was known to be dangerous killers and I'll leave it at that.

Marty the Barber, whom I was still seeing every two weeks for haircuts, always knew the updates on who was alive and who was whacked.

"Hey, Marty, what happened to so-and-so?" I'd ask, as he clipped around my ears.

"Dead."

"And what about . . . ?"

"Also dead."

He was a man of few words, but they were essential ones.

It was a whole new regime working with Joe and Frankie, but the violence didn't bother me. Maybe it was because I'd been training for it my whole life—from childhood beatings to high school gangs to bodies being dumped behind Maislin.

So I embraced the mob ways, and that changed everything. I was linked to a mob family now and everyone knew it. Most of the drug clients I'd had for years paid me faster and gave me more respect because I was "with the Lodi crew." I got more freight for Deliverance because word went around that I was connected. My ego loved the power, fear, and respect I got being associated with mobsters.

I started smoking cigars—Arturo Fuente and Maduro—to look the part. I went to Frankie's connect in the diamond district on Canal Street and bought a duplicate of his checkerboard diamond ring. I was reinventing myself from salesman to drug dealer to mob guy, and my association with Joe and Frankie put me in the major league. As Frankie once said, *I was wit dem, now.*

I was a family man, all right, just not the regular kind. I barely spent any time at home with Debbie and the kids and still, Lauren loved me like crazy. Our time together was on Saturday mornings when I'd lie sprawled on the couch trying to recover from a night of coke, booze, and strippers. Lauren would snuggle next to me, as close as she could get, and watch cartoons. I made her little sandwiches for lunch and the kid loved me; she really did love me. I didn't deserve it.

Lauren around age seven

A few months into Lone Star, in May 1983, my son Nick was born and again I was in the delivery room and held him and kissed him on the forehead. But soon after he popped out, I was out with Frankie, Kim, and Joe at the hottest clubs—Regine's or New York New York—where we'd see Sammy the Bull or John Gotti across the room and they'd give me a nod. *I was wit dem.*

When the big mob guys weren't there, we'd do coke out in the open at the table, not bothering to hide it. The staff didn't dare tell us to stop.

"Hey, Frankie, hand me da ting that goes wit da ting to use da ting," I'd say, when I wanted him to pass me more coke.

"Tommy! Listen," Frankie would say loudly, grabbing me by the shoulders. "I can't see dis fucking ting. I drank too much. My eyes are *diluted*. I can't see, and I gotta *circumcise* my watch!"

Like I said before, Frankie wasn't the brains in this outfit.

―――――――

My office in Clifton was now a full-service business—we juggled drugs, travel, and trucking. Customers for Reiser Travel, Joan's very legit domain, used the front door to reach the front office, and trucking people or drug deliveries came through the side door for the back office. Even though they'd been forbidden by Streaky, Joe and Frankie began buying coke from me "on the arm" or "on the cuff" and selling it.

Joe was smart, as I guessed, and a quick learner. So I taught him about trucking and we worked hard and built Lone Star together. He taught me more about kickbacks.

"Why do you waste your time taking these trucking people to dinner and strip clubs?" he asked. "Give them cash! Watch how fast they give you their business!"

Frankie did fuck-all in our office and spent his days running numbers at another office and hanging out with Kim, taking her to fancy restaurants or shopping, spending the money Joe and I worked hard to bring in.

"Stick with me, baby," he used to tell Kim, "and you'll be fartin' in silk." Not a bad line, I thought. I stole it to use on my trucking clients.

Once in a while I passed by the office Frankie used for illegal betting. It changed locations every few months, but it was always over the George Washington Bridge in New York where betting was only a misdemeanor instead of in Jersey, where it was a felony. The office was always a one-bedroom apartment with a table, metal folding chairs, and a handful of people answering push-button phones with tape recorders attached.

Frankie and Joe were glad to have the Hudson River between them because they'd get on each other's nerves. They were both running numbers in Jersey on their own when the local mob guys who ran the area paired them together, ordering them to consolidate and share their contacts. I was in their betting office the day Frankie found out Joe held back on some of his contacts. Frankie picked up Joe and threw him across the room into a bunch of chairs.

Frankie had one of the worst tempers I'd ever seen. It was worse than mine and it rivaled my father's. Once when we were driving on the highway, I complained that a dump truck behind us was riding my ass. Frankie pulled a .38 from his briefcase, opened the sunroof, stood up, and fired at the truck—blowing the front to pieces.

"Is there something wrong with your brain?" I yelled at Frankie. "You crazy fuck! And besides, you wasted six bullets on a stupid dump truck!"

That was Frankie's biggest flaw; you can't fix stupid.

Joe and Frankie had to haul me out of bed on days after my all-night coke sessions. But even though I sank deeper and deeper into my coke addiction that year, Lone Star grew like crazy. We started doing $1 million per month in accounts, then $2 million. It was easy because I just took the overflow from my national accounts at Deliverance that they couldn't handle and diverted them to us. Deliverance wasn't losing anything, and my clients were happy to keep all their accounts with me. It was perfect!

Except the execs at Deliverance didn't see it that way.

When they discovered I was behind this new trucking company that had burst onto the scene and become their rival, they were fuming. I was called to Indiana for a sit-down with the top brass, including my coke colleague Jeff Goldman. In the boardroom, they accused me of being disloyal. I told them they didn't have the grand vision or ability to handle the magnitude of business that a Silver Tongue like me could bring in.

"We just bought one hundred new trailers," said the Deliverance chairman. "How is that not enough for you?"

"I need two hundred more. And for your information, I just bought a hundred trailers myself—with cash." I took out my pad and pen. "At $18,000 per truck, that makes . . . yeah, I paid $1.8 million. From my own pocket."

The chairman and the other board members looked both stunned and in awe. I could hear my coke buddy in my mind, begging me telepathically: *Please don't tell them about the coke!* The top execs were so insulted, they gave me an ultimatum—it was them or Lone Star.

I'd built Deliverance from a mediocre company to one that made more than one hundred million a year in general freight, but now I was done. I quit right there in the boardroom. If there was one thing I couldn't stand, it was a businessman who thought small. Deliverance would be one of the last purely legit jobs I ever had.

The bigger Lone Star grew, the more Streaky wanted me to get made. He never asked me directly—they never did that. They didn't want to look stupid if you turned them down, like when I insulted Streaky and Little Al at our first meeting at Vesuvius. But they kept strongly suggesting it. I didn't understand why Streaky was so surprised at my refusals until I heard Frankie and Joe mentioning a name in my father's family—"LaPlaca." I asked them about it, and that's when I discovered that I already *was* connected, since the day I was born.

I asked around and found out more. My family relative, Peter LaPlaca, was nicknamed "Lodi Pete." He started out as a driver for an underboss and rose up the ranks to capo, where he remained for several years until Streaky took over. It all made sense now. Streaky knew my lineage even before I did, and so did Alex Maislin. It's why they wanted me officially in the fold. I was "family."

Streaky loved me because I was what the mob called a "big earner." I wasn't sharing my money with him, but every week Frankie met up with Streaky and Little Al at Sorrento Bakery to give them an envelope of $10,000 cash—Streaky's cut from Frankie and Joe's Lone Star earnings. After a while I started adding to the envelope, thinking it would keep Streaky happy enough to get him off my back about getting made. But it didn't help much; the pressure was still on.

In the early to mid-eighties, the Mafia was peaking and diversifying, and while they'd always looked to recruit guys who could earn a lot of money or had no problem killing people, they were now on the prowl for guys who had legit businesses to be used for money laundering purposes. No wonder Streaky wanted me so bad: I pretty much fit all three categories they needed.

"Don't get made," Joe warned. "Once they get their hooks in you, you gotta pay them for life; they'll lean on you forever."

Even though Joe paid Streaky money every week, he wasn't made. He didn't want to be and they never asked him. He wasn't the type. Frankie was a brute, and I was a tough motherfucker and big business earner. Joe was smart, but he was a bit *finocchio*—kinda gay, though no one said it. That wouldn't do with the Lodi crew. But they took his money anyway.

Joe's dad ran numbers and sports with another mob family, the Luccheses, and as I infiltrated my way into the Genovese crime family, I plotted to make contacts there, too. I knew that as long as I stayed unmade, I might be able to float from one organized crime family to another if I needed, or have them all at once—that was my plan. Frankie had a meeting set up with Michael Perna, a soldier in the Lucchese New Jersey faction, and he wanted to take me and show me off, like, *Here's my new trucking guy. We're in the trucking business now, assholes!* Michael's brother, Ralph, was the current capo.

We met Michael and his crew at Casa Dante, a restaurant in Jersey City. They were no different than the other mob guys I'd met—they looked, talked, and acted just like the Genovese guys—cookie cutters, all of them. Frankie set up the meeting to offer Michael a chunk of our sports-numbers action. Our business got so huge we were worried we wouldn't be able to cover the bets. Frankie's idea was for the Lucchese crew to run some of it and give us a commission. They shook hands on it. It was a good deal among rival families that usually had no business doing business together, but sometimes it was allowed. You do them a favor and they owe you one. It gave you power to have another family in debt to you.

Back in Lodi, the old man was getting restless.

At our next sit-down at Vesuvius, talk drifted to the following week when they were gonna "open the books" for a few guys at someone's house. Frankie was gonna go get made and once again, Little Al pressed me to go, in his vague way.

"We got dat ting happening next week," Little Al said, "and youse gotta show up. You know, we're doing da *ting*."

"Yeah, the thing, okay, yeah, okay," I said.

Streaky heard me waffle from across the table and couldn't shut up about it any longer. His craggy, coughing voice drowned us all out.

"Ding-dong. Ding-dong," Streaky yelled out, looking over at me. "*Ding-dong*. All you do is take the dings. But we don't get no dongs."

He sounded like a crazy person. What was the old man saying?

"He's saying you're like a pendulum," Little Al translated. "You know how a pendulum goes?"

"No, Al. I don't."

Streaky rallied again from his seat.

"You won't make a decision!" he yelled. "You're wishy-washy, like a linguine when it's been boiled too long. There's no substance to you!"

"What did he call me?" I asked Frankie, who was sitting next to me.

"A linguini," Frankie said, trying not to laugh. "He wants you to make up your mind and come next week."

"You're mushy!" Streaky yelled. "You gotta toughen up!" Then he went on a rant about certain crewmembers who didn't know how to whack someone right.

"You don't pull out a gun and say, 'Stick 'em up!' like you was in the movies! When you take a gun out, you kill the motherfucker. Don't take your gun out unless you're prepared to kill a guy!"

Everyone nodded.

"Frankie, do me a favor and tell him I'm not mushy."

Frankie kicked me. I kicked him back.

"Shut the fuck up," said Frankie. "Or we'll both get whacked!"

A few days later Frankie took the oath of *omertà*. He did what was required before being inducted—every potential made man has to carry out a contract killing ("making your bones") or at least be part of one before getting made. He did it, and that's all I'm going to say about that. While he was getting made, I was out getting high and drunk and didn't show up.

The next day the shit hit the fan. The old man was insulted again by me and sent Little Al to find out why I was a no-show. I wormed out of it, then Little Al brought up another problem: Streaky found out we'd been dealing coke, and we had to go back to Vesuvius for a sit-down about it.

"I know you're doing that fucking white shit," Streaky said at our meeting the next day. His grating voice was like little stones scratching against glass. "If you don't stop, there's gonna be a problem. By the way, where's my money this week?"

Having a problem was never good. It could mean you were about to be beat up or whacked; who knew? Streaky only gave you one warning, if you were lucky enough to get that. He was a killer. But in our case, he was more interested in the money than the cocaine *sitch*. That was Streaky's mantra: pay me, pay me, pay me. He wanted us to keep giving him a cut from the coke, trucking, sports, and numbers, but not be so obvious about our drug dealing.

Meanwhile, I was planning a con to get money out of Streaky and Little Al.

I'd been buying coke off the cuff from Frankie V, a limo company owner in Hackensack. I used his limos when I went out with broads and got coked up. He was a good guy to know because he had all the local politicians in his pocket.

I'd run up a coke tab of $100,000 with him and I didn't want to pay it. I had the money, of course—I had $1 million in cash at home in my duct-taped shoeboxes. But I didn't like Frankie V and I just didn't want to pay him.

I decided in a stroke of brilliance that Streaky and Little Al were going to get rid of the debt for me. They wanted me so bad they'd do just about anything. So now I was going to fuck all three of them at once—Frankie V, Little Al, and Streaky.

I set up a meeting the following week with Little Al at La Couronne in Hawthorne. At the table, I put on my worried face and told him I'd been thinking about what Streaky had said, and I wanted to get out of the drug racket.

"Good, good. I'm glad," he says.

But there was one problem, I told him.

"There's this guy busting my balls for the hundred grand I owe him and I ain't got it. I put all my money into Lone Star. Al, ya gotta help me. I wanna make Streaky happy and stop with the drugs."

Little Al smiled. I knew what he was thinking. I was asking a favor, and then I'd owe one. *Now I'm gonna get my claws into Tommy. I'm going to bring him in for Streaky, and it'll look good on me.*

"Don't worry about it," said Al. "Set up a meeting with the guy to come here and I'll pay him. I got you."

It was just like playing chess, and I was getting all my men into place.

A few days later, Little Al and I arrived early to the meeting and brought Frankie Cam as our muscle. When Frankie V arrived and saw Little Al, he looked quietly petrified.

"What's going on?" he asked, sitting down.

"Listen," Little Al began. "As you might know, Tommy's wit us now. He's a legit guy in trucking and we're involved with him in the trucking business."

Frankie V nodded and Little Al paused when the owner came to the table with menus, filled our water glasses, then quickly left when Al waved him away.

"Now, Tommy come to us and he says you're busting his balls for this fucking money he owes you for the dope," Al continued.

"He owes me a hundred grand."

A couple came into the restaurant and the owner sat them as far away from us as possible. Little Al got up.

"Let's go to the bathroom."

We all got up and followed Al into the men's room. Inside, Al took out a wad of cash from his coat pocket and handed it to Frankie V.

"Here, take this. It's twenty grand. The debt's cleared now."

"Fucking Tommy owes me a hundred grand!" Frankie V said.

Frankie shifted his position by the sink, putting his hand on his gun. I leaned against a stall door and watched it all unfold like a scene in a movie.

"You're not understanding me, Frank," said Al, his voice getting tense. "The debt's cleared up now."

"But . . ."

No more words came outta Frankie V's mouth because someone stuck his head in the toilet and held it there, under water, for almost too long.

"Take the fucking money and get the fuck out of here!" Little Al's voice echoed against the tiles. "Or there's gonna be a *problem*. Do you understand? Get the fuck out—*now!* He don't owe you no more motherfucking money, you got it, motherfucker? *He's wit us now.* Now get the fuck out of here!"

Frankie V was let loose and ran out of the bathroom, dripping toilet water in his path. Honestly, it was bee-oo-tiful.

My next move on the chessboard was to fuck Frankie Cam, because that's what mob guys do. I wanted him out of Lone Star, and I was gonna use Little Al for that maneuver, too.

Joe and I were sick of Frankie never working but getting one-third of the Lone Star money while he played hooky all day with Kim. The next time he and Kim left in Kim's car to go have fun while we worked, I took action. Through the window I could see Frankie's disgusting, beat-up, silver Seville in the parking lot. Shitty, unkempt cars—now that offended me.

"Hey, Joe. Watch what I'm gonna do to Frankie's car."

We were at our warehouse that day and in the lot we had a forklift. Joe watched from the window as I climbed into the fork-lift, stabbed Frankie's car with the blades and picked it up, then tossed it in the nearby dumpster—crushing it until it looked like a tin can.

"Jesus Christ, Tommy, Frankie's gonna kill you!" said Joe, after I returned and went to my desk. "He's gonna kill *both* of us!"

I took out $50,000 in cash from my desk drawer and put it on the table.

"Go buy him a brand-new fucking Seville," I told Joe. "Fuck him and fuck that car. When he comes back, tell him he's out and to get the fuck out of our office."

Now, I already knew that the only way to get rid of a mob guy was to replace him with a *bigger* mob guy, and that's where Little Al came in. Joe and I met up with Al at a posh country club for dinner, and I played to Al's greed and need to impress Streaky. Before the meal was over, he'd agreed to take Frankie's place as our business partner and force him to take a buyout. He didn't like Frankie's attitude, either, and he was salivating at the prospect of getting his hands onto Lone Star.

To seal our deal, Al took me to the men's room and pulled out two wads of cash from his pockets, $50,000 each.

"Fifty for you," said Little Al, "and give the other fifty to Frankie and tell him we bought him out and he's thrown the fuck out."

After that, it was World War III in our Lodi faction of the Gatto crew.

Frankie went berserk when we told him he was out. He yelled and broke shit and punched walls. Later, he sent a warning through Joe that he wanted to kill me for what I'd done, orchestrating his removal.

"Tell him to bring it on," I told Joe. Later on, I'd feel bad about turning on Frankie. He was devastated, and in the long run, would end up proving more loyal to me than any of them. But that's what mob guys do—we turn on each other. It's greed. Get the other guy out of the way and get more money. That's what Little Al was thinking.

After we turned on Frankie, he turned on us. He took the money we gave him and started his own trucking company, Camway, and tried to steal our clients.

"Tell him if he doesn't stop," Little Al said, "there's gonna be a *problem*."

Again with the problem. And more followed. Right after Little Al came on board, Joe arrived in the office with a list of fifteen names to add to our payroll at Little Al's orders.

"They're 'no-show' jobs," Joe explained. "We'll receive an envelope every week full of cash and then we'll give these guys paychecks. We're washing the money."

I didn't mind being a money launderer so much, but I *did* mind being leaned on and told what to do; it was the thing I hated the most. Now it was my turn to wanna kill Little Al and Joe. Everybody wanted to kill everybody, it seemed, so someone was bound to die; one night, I thought that someone was me.

I was seeing a cocktail waitress at the time, Suzanne—jet-black hair, bit tits, tiny waist. It was Halloween night of 1983 and I'd just finished banging her brains out at one of our safe houses in Little Falls when the doorbell rang. I was so fucked up from drugs and booze I answered without thinking. The street was filled with trick-or-treaters ringing doorbells so I assumed it to be kids looking for candy.

Two guys dressed as hockey players, wearing masks and carrying sticks and guns, busted in and knocked me backward to the floor. They dragged me to the bedroom where Suzanne was still naked and threw me onto the bed with her.

"Where's the cash?" asked one, putting a gun to my head. "Where's the coke?"

I pointed to my Hartmann briefcases on the counter—one was filled with $100,000 of coke and the other was filled with $250,000 in cash. They took the briefcases and Suzanne's $80,000 diamond ring, on the table next to them. They didn't bother with my Rolex sitting next to the ring.

Motherfuckers; it was an inside job. How else would someone know where I was and that I had the cash and coke with me, and to keep their hands off my Rolex? With a gun at my head, one of them stuck a knee into my ribs and forced me to watch as they put their hands all over Suzanne's still-naked body. She cried, but there was nothing I could do.

They had ways of making me pay.

I left town soon after and went south to Cherry Hill, New Jersey, to start anew with the mob guys there. I never paid Little Al the $20,000 for my coke debt or the $50,000 he gave me as our deal starter. But I had a feeling he got his money.

Don't listen to what anybody tells you; there ain't no honor among thieves.

CHAPTER 10

SLEEPING WITH THE FISHES

It was dark and quiet; I couldn't see anything. All I could hear was my heart thumping against my ribs and the sound of water rushing into the car.

With his slicked-back silver pompadour and French-cuffed shirts, Nicodemo "Little Nicky" Scarfo reminded me of Sinatra. But that's where the comparison ended. Scarfo was a little guy, maybe 5'5", and had a high-pitched voice at odds with his brutality. Everyone knew that underneath his finely stitched suits beat the heart of a ruthless, tyrannical killer.

Which is why anyone who was mobbed up in the Philly–South Jersey vicinity at the time wanted to be linked with Scarfo, the boss of the Philadelphia crime family. If someone fucked you over, Scarfo could order them whacked at the snap of his manicured fingertips.

Was my new business associate, Vito Zitani, mobbed up?

All I can tell you is this: If you were doing certain types of business in Philly and South Jersey in the eighties, you were most likely mobbed up—or beholden to them somehow.

When I first met Scarfo in the spring of '84—an introduction by a mutual associate—there was no doubt in my coke-addled mind that if I was to double-cross Zitani, I'd have Scarfo to answer to.

During his reign in the eighties, Scarfo would order the murders of nearly three dozen people. Around the time of our meeting that spring, he would have been plotting the murder of Salvatore Testa, his protégé and top hit man (who was gunned down that September). Testa was the son of Scarfo's predecessor, Phil "Chicken Man" Testa, Scarfo's mentor and close friend.

That is, if a mob guy can have real "friends"—which they can't, not like normal people do. Mob guys are always looking to steal from, con, or whack each other—it's their nature. They hug you, they kiss you, they make you godfather to their babies, and then they kill you. That's just how it was.

Nicky Scarfo and I hugged and kissed when we met at the Saloon, a well-known mob hangout in South Philly. Not only was the meeting meant to intimidate me but also, I suspect, to show me off as Zitani's new golden boy and Big Earner. If Zitani was beholden to the mob or Scarfo in any way, meeting me was a way to assure Scarfo that Zitani would be able to make whatever payments he'd be required to make.

Vito Zitani was a businessman in South Jersey and owner of the trucking company Cargo Transportation Lines (CTL) in Cherry Hill, New Jersey, a stone's throw across the Delaware River from Philly. If he was mobbed up, that probably meant he was paying Little Nicky for his connections and protection, and maybe even for help to get a prestigious government contract.

A few months earlier Zitani had run into money problems. He'd tried to expand his business, made a few wrong decisions, and his company went down the shitter. He was desperate for help.

That's when yours truly, Golden Tongue, came swooping in to the rescue.

After getting out of Jersey, I needed to find a new home for my client base and trucking accounts. I heard about Zitani's trucking troubles through the mob grapevine, and the timing was as impeccable as Little Nicky's shirts.

At our first meeting, when I told him my longtime clients included heavyweights like GE and Samsung, Zitani got excited. When I added that I'd recently snagged a combined contract with Coleco and Toys "R" Us to exclusively distribute the hottest toy of the year, Cabbage Patch Kids dolls, he stood up and hugged me. I was hired on the spot as his VP of sales with a starting salary of $300,000, and we put my Golden Tongue in action.

The plan was for me to commute to Cherry Hill three days a week and work with Zitani in the office there and work in an office close to home the other two days. Zitani bought me a stretch limo equipped with a state-of-the-art Motorola car phone as big as a bread box—and hired me a driver, Miguel, a chubby Mexican kid. On the drives back and forth I'd hear from Lauren, now seven, who giggled at the idea of calling me in a car. "Are you coming home, Daddy?" she usually asked.

Like before, everything I touched turned to gold.

I wined, dined, coked up, and kickbacked the client base I already had and added new ones, including a multimillion-dollar company that made top brands of laundry detergent and soaps. I showed Zitani the trade tricks I'd learned, like how to get a cash flow fast. Most companies stuck an invoice in the mail and received payment forty-five days later. I devised a way to get paid immediately by typing out invoices and faxing them to the banks every night. In the morning, the money would be deposited in our account. This gave us millions of dollars earlier to put back in the company.

Within my first six months working with Zitani, I was booking $20 to $30 million a year in business. We started off renting five to ten trailers, and within three years we would own three hundred.

Is there any wonder why Vito Zitani loved me?

He promoted me that first year, doubling my salary and giving me half the business on a handshake. The following year my salary would double again and reach the $1 million mark.

When it came to style, I became Zitani's protégé. His class was a whole new level for me. He took me to Barton & Donaldson to buy custom-made, hand-stitched shirts with the same French cuffs Little Nicky wore. At Brooks Brothers, he bought me the finest Canali and Brioni suits. I didn't spend a dime.

In Chicago, we stayed in suites at the Ritz and went to the Water Tower Place shopping mall for expensive alligator, snakeskin, and ostrich shoes. We got me another Rolex, and now I was up to nine. And then came the cars. I was a Cadillac man, but I liked the look of what Zitani drove. All I had to do was say it out loud.

"I see you drive a brand new 560SEL, Vito. How come I don't have one?"

The next day, my new Mercedes 560SEL was waiting for me in the parking lot.

During this time, I met with entirely new crews than the ones I knew. In Chicago, I met an associate with the Giancana crew. Back in the sixties, the CIA reportedly enlisted the help of Chicago god-father Salvatore "Mooney Sam" Giancana—aka "Momo" or "Sam the Cigar"—to assassinate Cuban dictator Fidel Castro.

But I wasn't looking to get newly associated. I was still trying to extricate myself from the North Jersey crew. To help make that break, I decided to let go of my coke business for a while. Like the Jersey mob, the Philly and Cherry Hill mobs weren't keen on drug dealers so I hooked up some of my steady buyers to deal directly with my dealers and pay me a profit margin. That way I was still earning, but not getting my hands dirty.

Even though I wasn't selling it, I was still snorting it—more than ever before. By late summer of 1984, soon after I was promoted, it began to seriously affect my work. I was getting sloppy and reckless. After all-night partying at strip clubs, whorehouses, and nightclubs in Jersey, I started missing workdays in Cherry Hill because I was too wasted to get out of bed and plop myself into the limo.

The timing was bad because Zitani desperately needed me. The local papers had run an explosive article claiming that a soon-to-be-published report by a tri-state crime commission identified Cargo as a mobbed-up company and named Zitani as a mob associate. Even worse—the headline linked us with a prestigious government contract:

GOVERNMENT GIVES CONTRACT
TO FIRM LINKED WITH MOB

Zitani hit the roof. Some of my clients knew I had mob connections, but his were squeaky-clean types and didn't want to be associated with anything mob related, especially so publicly. It was the kiss of death.

Rival trucking firms began calling all of our clients to lure them away, warning them that we'd be indicted on criminal charges. In my hungover, drugged-up condition I finally dragged myself out of bed to fly to twenty-five cities all over the country and convince them the report was bullshit. Zitani's lawyers in New Jersey got to work filing lawsuits to block the commission from publishing his name in that report.

Zitani's lawyers called his inclusion in the report "false and defamatory" and the commission eventually agreed out-of-court to delete all mentions of organized crime in connection with Zitani or our company, the local newspapers reported.

That the information was leaked to the press beforehand was "inexcusable," said Zitani's lawyers, and demonstrated "a lack of professionalism which should be taken into account when considering the reliability of anything emanating from the crime commission."

Zitani had *really* good lawyers.

A few weeks later, I fucked up again and made everything even worse.

The Cabbage Patch doll craze reached epic proportions that year and desperate parents were fighting in department stores to get them for their pleading daughters. Lauren had at least fifty of them and was the envy of all her friends.

Which gave me a brilliant idea.

As long as I was arranging $21 million worth of dolls to be shipped to our warehouse in East Los Angeles, why not send a measly twenty-nine cases to my home in Jersey? Lauren could use a few more, I reasoned, and I could give away the rest as "gifts" to people I needed to impress (i.e., bribe) who had kids they needed to please. It wasn't ethical what I was doing, but it wasn't exactly illegal. As a higher-up in the company, I could technically ship the dolls anywhere I wanted. I'd tell Zitani about it later.

Instead of using our own company to transport them, I used another one that specialized in smaller loads so they'd get to my house faster. My impatience, coupled with my new sloppiness, massive ego, and drug-addled brain, caused the drama that ensued.

I'd forgotten that the damn dolls were so hot that dockworkers across the country were required by law to report any "suspicious" shipments delivered to private residences. People were so crazy for these dolls that trucks transporting them were being *hijacked*. Which would be laughable, if it wasn't for what happened next. Some sharp-eyed dockworker noticed the twenty-nine cases going to my Jersey home and called the cops, who called the FBI.

Back at the warehouse in East LA, I was in my office on the second floor. I'd flown there as one of the stops on my twenty-five city "the report is bullshit" tour and was looking out the window at the dozens of trailers lined up in the shipyard below, stuffed with Cabbage Patch dolls just off the boat from China. We had Cabbage Patch dolls coming out of our fucking ass waiting to be unloaded, moved, and stored into the warehouse.

I sat down and finished a bottle of Dom Pérignon, then cut up four grams of coke on a table. I had a hot-looking whore waiting for me at my hotel, naked under the sheets. I rolled up a hundred-dollar bill and snorted one line, then a second.

It's gonna be a helluva fantastic night, I was thinking, until my operations manager, Bobby, burst into the office.

"Tom, the warehouse is surrounded by police! There's a SWAT team out there!"

"Bobby, whattaya talkin' about?" I smiled, high as a kite.

"I'm serious! They got guns and . . ."

A second later—BAM! What looked like the entire department of the nearby sheriff's office and the LAPD Swat Team kicked open the door and came flying in, pointing guns at my head.

"Are you Thomas Giacomaro? Get up! Get against the wall, asshole!"

"I didn't do nuttin'! What did I do?"

They pulled me off my chair, slammed me against the wall, then wrestled me to the ground and handcuffed me. They barely glanced at the coke on the table.

"Everything in this warehouse is stolen goods," yelled one of them, "you're arrested for $21 million of interstate theft."

"What are you talking about? I got paperwork for all this shit!" I yelled, kicking and screaming. "Bobby, where's the fucking paperwork?!"

Bobby froze. He was so scared he couldn't move. He was also disorganized, drunk, and stoned. The paperwork was in the office somewhere, but he wasn't sure where.

The cops pulled me downstairs and threw me into the back seat of a sheriff's car. I spent the night in the LA County Jail. The next day I was the talk of the industry; everyone was calling me "The Cabbage Patch Caper."

Zitani flew in from Cherry Hill to post bail—one million dollars. He was not happy. After his lawyers sorted everything out, the charges for interstate theft were dropped but the damage was done. With the back-to-back bad exposure, it didn't matter how many times we tried to convince people we weren't mobbed up; it looked bad. The scandal was too much for Coleco, and we lost the Cabbage Patch doll account.

I went back home to Jersey for a few weeks to lie low and put it out of my mind, but Lauren's Cabbage Patch dolls all over the house were a constant reminder of how I fucked up. Lauren was overjoyed I was home and clung to me, following me around the house wherever I went. I put in some family time and cooked up Sunday night feasts—prime rib, stuffed peppers, penne and meatballs. At night, I lit the fire and put on *The Wizard of Oz* for Lauren—Tom Jr. and Nick were still too young for it. It was now her favorite film, too, she told me, so I'd bought a VHS tape of it and we played it over and over on the VCR. She wasn't afraid of the wicked witch or the tornado or the flying monkeys like some kids are. She had only one fear.

"I don't want to go far away from home like Dorothy and not see you, Daddy," she'd say.

"Never gonna happen, baby."

Debbie, however, couldn't stand the sight of me. She'd known about the other women for years, but learning I had a hooker with me in California was the last straw. When I pulled into the driveway after a night of partying a few days later, I saw what appeared to be snow on the oak tree in front of our house. *In September?* I got out of the car and walked over to take a closer look. *Early Halloween pranksters?* Nope. When I realized what it was, I exploded.

Chopped up pieces of sleeves, pant legs, ties, torsos, and French cuffs hung like dismembered body parts from the branches. Debbie had cut up my wardrobe and thrown everything out the window.

I raced upstairs, dragged her out of bed, and pushed her against the wall. The next thing I knew, she'd called the cops and they were in the house, hauling me down to the police station. I was let go a few hours later.

When I got home, the "body parts" were still hanging from the tree. I had to hand it to her, that Debbie was smart. She knew how to hit me where it hurt, like I'd done when I smashed my parents' organ long ago.

If I were the literary type, I'd say the ripped clothes symbolized my life at that time—tearing apart. What a perfect time for my father to show up and destroy me some more.

I was hungover, hollow-eyed, skinny, and in the garage wiping down the cars by hand just like he used to do. They were lined up on the driveway—three Cadillacs, a Sedan de Ville, an Eldorado Biarritz, a Seville, a limo, and four Mercedes-Benzes. Who the fuck needed all these cars? But god, they were beautiful.

Suddenly, the angry face of my father was among them.

"What do you want?" I asked.

"You're skin and bones, you look like a junkie, and you're fucking around on your wife. You're ruining your children! Look at you!"

"Mind your own business," I said. Was he seriously going to lecture me on how to be a good husband and father? He went on to tell me he'd had another neighborly visit from Captain Healy down the street (he'd been promoted since he last ratted me out in high school when he was a sergeant).

"Captain Healy said, 'Your son's in the Mafia and he's selling cocaine.' What are you doing to yourself?"

We all know what was coming next.

"You're no good! You're nothing."

My father had hit me hundreds of times in my life, too many times to count, but I never wanted to hit him back . . . until now. Maybe it was because I had a shitty month and I was hung over. Maybe it was because I blamed him for how I was. Maybe it was because he was right about everything he said about me. Both of us, Lauren would have said, needed to go to the Wizard to get a heart.

Whatever the reason, I stepped toward him and pushed him—hard. He lost balance and fell backward, hitting his head on the driveway. He lay there, hurt and in shock. I was in shock, too. He was a defenseless old man now; I wait until *today* to hit him? What the fuck?

"Dad, I'm sorry!"

I tried to help him up but he pushed me away. He got up and, with his hand on his head, marched to his car like a wounded Marine and drove away. I held back tears, which shocked me even further.

"I'm sorry," I kept repeating, as the car disappeared down the street. He didn't speak to me for a long time after that.

He hated me and he wasn't the only one.

Over the next year I continued my downward spiral. By the fall of 1986, Vito Zitani had reached a breaking point with me. He was angry because we were building a new truck terminal in Cherry Hill and he needed me there, but I was missing entire weeks of work. We set up a dinner together and I didn't show up for that either, leaving him waiting alone at the restaurant.

When I arrived at work two days later, I was summoned to his office. He dismissed his secretary, closed his office door, and went nuts. He moved toward me until his face was an inch from mine.

"Next time you don't show up when you're supposed to show up, I'll cut your fucking balls off!"

"Vito, I . . ."

"Shut up. You're doing drugs and you're all fucked up. And that's the last time you don't show up."

I got in my Mercedes and told Miguel to take me back to North Jersey. *Fuck everyone,* I thought. I was done with them all.

The next day at lunch, I drowned my troubles with $200 shots of Louis XIII cognac and lines of coke. I was with Teddy Duanno, one of my attorneys, and Patsy Giglio, one of my former coke suppliers.

Both were among the handful of guys I'd parceled out my cocaine business to. Teddy sold to highfalutin politicians and celebrities, and I knew both of them would love to have me out of the way so they wouldn't have to give me a cut.

They'd all like to see me dead. I poured myself another shot.

Joe, Little Al, and Streaky were still in a rage that I left and took my contacts with me, thereby killing Lone Star. Frankie still wanted to kill me because I'd pushed him out. Debbie and all the other women I'd wronged probably wanted to chop me up into little pieces like my clothes hanging from the oak tree. My father wished I'd never been born. I'm sure Zitani was about to sic Nicky Scarfo on me.

There were so many more, so many more. I poured myself another double and downed it. A minute later my new girlfriend, Lisa, called and begged me to come over. Yeah, maybe a naked broad would help. I staggered out of the restaurant and told Miguel I was gonna drive myself. I was speeding along the turnpike when a white van sped up beside me in the next lane.

What the fuck?

The side doors opened and three guys started shooting at me. I swerved, smashing through the guardrail and into the air before plunging downward into the Passaic River.

I hit the water like it was a concrete wall, then the car started to sink. My Mercedes went down until I hit the river's bottom with a thud.

It was dark and quiet; I couldn't see anything. All I could hear was my heart thumping against my ribs and the sound of water rushing into the car.

I had maybe a minute before the car would fill up and I'd be dead. My hip was smashed, I was drunk, in shock, disoriented, and passing out.

Then I heard a sweet little voice that jolted me to action:

Get out of the car, Daddy!

PART II

CHAPTER 11

ANGELS AND DEMONS

I couldn't figure out if I was cursed or blessed. All I knew was that in the eternal war between good and evil, the dark side inside me was winning.

I'm impossible to kill.

You can beat me, shoot me, drive me into a river, or throw me behind bars. It will never kill me; it only makes me stronger.

I found superhuman strength to shoot my way out of that car, a coffin in the water, using Frankie's stolen gun hidden under the front seat. With a smashed hip I swam to the river's surface. There was no way I was gonna fuckin' die in that car that day, no way, not like that.

The two construction workers who pulled me from the river—big-muscled Italian kids yanking a mob guy from the swampy drink—were locals who recognized me.

"We saw everything!" they said. They'd been putting up cement barricades and iron guardrails when my car sped right by them and shot into the water.

"You didn't see nuthin'," I told them, coughing water from my lungs.

Someone called an ambulance and they laid me out on the river's edge in my soaking wet Brioni suit. I reeked of rancid fish and garbage, the stink that would follow me around and haunt me forever no matter how expensive a suit I wore. My Mercedes was dead, swimming with the fishes. Above me, hundreds of motorists were standing along the curve in the highway cheering and clapping.

"Forget what you saw," I repeated to the two guys. "The police are going to come and ask questions. You say nothing, you understand me? Stay wit me. Don't let anyone come near me."

They did as instructed, even coming to St. Mary's General Hospital with me. I paid them well for their help and silence. I had to figure out myself who tried to kill me, without any interference or poking around by the cops.

Teddy my attorney was the first to arrive at the hospital, still buzzed from our shots of cognac and lines of coke. He immediately arranged for the top orthopedic surgeon in the area to be rushed in to tend to my shattered left hip, which had lodged into my rib cage in bits and pieces. I was bleeding from everywhere; it was pouring out of my ass and I was pooping it out. The doctors gave me blood transfusions, and they worried about toxic water I might have swallowed because the dye houses in the area all dumped their shit into the river.

"I'll find out who did this, Tom," Teddy said.

I didn't tell him that *he* was one of my many suspects. Teddy started making inquiries right away. The construction kids remembered the license plate number on the van but after checking, Teddy discovered it'd been doctored. Not quite enough, though. The stupid bastards kept it as a Pennsylvania license plate. Zitani must be involved, I decided. He must have reached out to the Nicky Scarfo crew to whack me.

Patsy, my coke dealer who'd been drinking with us, arrived at the hospital next, and he brought me a little something medicinal, for the pain, and all three of us got coked up together.

When Zitani arrived from Cherry Hill, the look on his face was a combination of shock (that I'd survived a shooting and near-drowning), disgust (that I was snorting coke into my bloodstream during a blood transfusion), and disappointment (that he was still stuck with me). I gave him a look like *You're one of my suspects, too, motherfucker.*

Everybody split when the priest got there. By that time, word had gotten out about my "accident" and my room began to fill with flowers. It looked like a fucking funeral, which was appropriate considering what the priest had to say.

"I've come to give you last rites, my son," he said, sitting down next to my bed.

Jesus H. Christ. "Whattaya talkin' about? Is there something the matter wit your brain?"

"Didn't the doctors tell you? You have massive internal bleeding. They're concerned you're going to . . . to pass away." He cleared his throat. "To *die.*"

"Look, uh, Padre. I *know* what 'pass away' means. But I don't need no last rites. I'm gonna be fine. I heard a voice. I saw the light. All that touchy-feely, near-death shit."

I knew that would get his attention. He moved his chair closer. I really did see a light when I was in the river, but it was a patch of sky when I looked up from inside the black water.

And there was Lauren's voice.

"I thought I was dead," I told him, "then I heard my daughter's voice: *Get out of the car, Daddy. I don't want to be alone. I don't want to be without you.*"

The priest ate it up. "She was your angel," he said, with confidence. "She was looking out for you. The police told me it was a *miracle* you got out of that car and out of the river alive." Or maybe I was just smart to remember about the gun.

He blessed me, said a few prayers, and left—certain that god had intervened to save my life that day and that I wouldn't be meeting my maker anytime soon.

"But keep saying your prayers and going to confession, my son"— he smiled, as my mother entered the room—"just in case."

When my mother saw the priest, she worried I'd taken a turn for the worst and had requested a deathbed confession. Ha! That's a confession that would have taken forever; I pity the poor priest who ever gets to me in the end. My mother had left the Catholic Church years earlier and became born-again, and now she believed in rites, miracles, and divine intervention more than ever. When I told her about Lauren's voice and what the priest said, she was elated. It was a new look for her.

"I told you, Tommy! You're special. Ever since your bike accident I've known this! God or something or someone watches out for you!"

The doctors were shocked that time when I recovered so quickly after I flipped over on my bike and smashed up my face. And they were baffled again this time when I woke up the day after my dunk in the river and was completely healed. My internal bleeding stopped and my hip—which had been too wrecked to replace, so they put me back together temporarily with bolts, screws, and a plate—had already healed enough for me to stand up and walk.

Maybe the coke? Or maybe I had a pact with the devil. Either way, I was back to my old self, terrorizing the hospital staff and demanding to be discharged.

News of my so-called accident hit the local papers the day after my plunge. The item was slugged "Man Overboard!" and it described me as an "unidentified motorist" who'd lost control of his car and went over the guardrails. My construction-worker heroes did good keeping things quiet, while my father walked around the house saying, in loathing disbelief: "My mobbed-up son's car was riddled with bullets."

The day after the attempted hit, I signed myself out of the hospital against doctors' orders and made Miguel drive me to the spot where I'd gone into the water. He parked on the highway, and I limped to the side of the road with a walker, hip cast, and an IV pole.

I looked down at the water and wondered: Was there really a force looking out for me? Did my daughter have something to do with it? I couldn't figure out if I was cursed or blessed. All I knew was that in the eternal war between good and evil, the dark side inside me was winning. The coke was starting to make me feel possessed. At the side of the road, with cars honking at Miguel as he blocked traffic, I made a vow.

"Nothing's going to stop me, you motherfuckers!"

I yelled it loud enough so they'd hear me in Philly. "Whatever I was before, I'm gonna be ten times *worse* now."

04/26/9· 11:30   z   ORTHO ASSOC   P.01

ORTHOPAEDIC ASSOCIATES *Orthopaedic, Spine, Hand Surgery and Sports Medicine*

15-01 BROADWAY, SUITE 20, FAIR LAWN, NEW JERSEY 07410-6003 • 201-794-6008 • Fax: 201-794-6190

PHILIP COHEN, M.D.
J. LEE BERGER, M.D.
ROBERT GREENBLUM, M.D.
PAUL D. PRAGNER, M.D.
MARK J. RUOFF, M.D.

Post-it™ brand fax transmittal memo 7671 # of pages ▷ (2)
To: Thomas Gia Comaro (Patient)
From: Isabelle Barbosa
Co.: Orthopaedic Assoc
Dept.:
Phone #: 794-6008
Fax #: 812-8313
Fax #: 794-6191

April 25, 1994

Confidential Insurance Company
P. O. Box 369
Piscataway, N. J. 08855

Attention: Chuck Burge
          Supervisor

                              Re: Giacomaro, Thomas
                              D/A: 9/25/86
                              SS#:   141-46-0396
                              CL#:   2708CC121
                              Our FL#: 7510

Dear Mr. Burge:

The following is a report on the above-captioned patient, who was seen in this office on 4/13/94.

Chief Complaint: Pain in the left hip, for 7-1/2 years.

History: This 41-year old male complains of left hip pain. He states that he was involved in a motor vehicle accident on 9/25/86, at which time he fractured the left femur. He underwent an open reduction/internal fixation of the left hip at St. Mary's Hospital in Passaic, on 9/26/86, performed by Dr. W. Altman (orthopedist). He has complained of left hip pain since the open reduction/internal fixation, left hip. He had no further treatment since Dr. Altman, however, he was seen by Dr. Stoffanelli (orthopedist) on 6/30/93, where he was examined, x-rays were taken and a left hip arthroplasty was recommended.

At the present time, the patient complains of left hip pain. He complains of occasional radiating pain to the left knee. He notes hip motions are painful. He notes squatting and stair climbing increase the pain.

Past Medical History:

General Health - Good.
Allergies   - None.
Medication   - None.
Operations   - Left hip.
Fractures   - Left hip.

Medical report eight years after my hip surgery, referencing the "accident"

A few months later, in January 1987, Nicky Scarfo was arrested on extortion and conspiracy charges and later that year, charged with two counts of murder and sentenced to life in prison. His own nephew ratted on him and had to go into witness protection or else he'd have been killed right away. We had no use for rats in organized crime. Rats should be dead, end of story.

If Scarfo and Zitani were the ones behind my near-death experience in the Passaic, I didn't have to worry about them anymore. If they weren't, the damage had already been done in my mind. I didn't trust Zitani now, and I started giving my leftover freight to a company called A-Z Passage. They gave me monthly commissions of $100,000 while I kept working with Zitani and figured what my next move would be.

I did do one last big favor for Zitani, because he'd been good to me.

Zitani had bought a hundred computers on the cheap from a company in Cincinnati to update his office equipment, but like a *stugatz*, he didn't read the fine print in his contract. When the shipment arrived, he realized why he only paid $1 million instead of the $3 million other computer companies asked for: the computers were secondhand.

The vendor refused to give Zitani his money back, so he called me to get it for him. He knew I could come up with a creative and devious plan, but he had no clue how truly devious that plan was.

First thing I did was hire a bunch of private investigators who were former FBI guys that I knew (I once hired them to follow an ex-girlfriend) to go to Cincinnati and trail this computer guy for a month.

"Take pictures of every move he makes and every place he goes," I told them, "his home, when he takes his kids to school, where he goes on Saturdays and Sundays. I want pictures of the kids getting on the school bus in the morning. I want pictures of the kids getting off the school bus, pictures of his wife when they go to the movies. I want you to fill up a pretty photo album, like a wedding album, and I want to know everything he does for a thirty-day period."

They asked for fifty grand to do the job and I doubled it to a hundred. I was going to need them again later, I told them.

Then, I called up Frankie Cam to help.

I crossed Frankie off my "suspect" list soon after the accident when we saw each other again and made up. We were in the same crew, he and I, and that was for life. Even if I did business with another mob family, I'd always be an associate of the Genovese crime family in the Gatto crew because it's where I started. Later, when Frankie married Kim in the late eighties, I was there, stuffing money into the money box and draining all the champagne at the reception.

So I called Frankie to be my muscle on the Cincinnati sitch because I knew it was an assignment an ex-boxer with a temper would love.

Frankie's assignment was to pretend to be a customer and tell the computer asshole he wanted to spend $1 million to set up his company with new computers. The computer guy came to Jersey to see Frankie's Camway warehouse and confirm he was legit, then they set up an appointment to meet in Cincinnati two weeks later.

Frankie, Miguel, the private investigators, and I flew to Cincinnati for step three. I told the investigators to bring their old FBI badges and a bunch of walkie-talkies, and after we arrived, I sent Frankie out to Toys "R" Us to buy plastic guns that looked real.

Frankie was to meet the guy in our hotel lobby for breakfast, then bring him upstairs to the penthouse suite to go over the pretend deal points. I posted two PIs in the hotel lobby to let us know when they got in the elevator and two on the penthouse floor to let us know when they got out.

Miguel and I were in the hotel suite waiting. I gave Miguel one job:

"As soon as the guy gets in the room, shut the door. *Make sure* you shut the door."

He nodded, scared to death. Miguel was a driver, after all, and this was way above his pay grade. He reminded me of Enzo the baker in *The Godfather*, standing watch outside the hospital with his hands trembling in fear.

I was sitting in the big dining room with two toy guns on the seat next to me and the walkie-talkie beside me when Miguel let in Frankie and a goofy-looking, geeky guy, whom he brought to my table.

"This is my assistant," Frankie said.

I must have looked really, really evil because the guy took one look at me and turned to run. He bolted out the open hotel suite door and down the hall.

"Miguel, what the fuck? *The door! Frankie, get him!!*"

The guy ran down the hallway yelling for help as Frankie and Miguel ran after him—tackling him to the ground just as the elevator door opened in front of a group of astonished hotel guests. Frankie and Miguel dragged the guy back to the room, punching and kicking him along the way. Back in the room we duct-taped his arms to his body and stuffed a washrag in his mouth, then sat him down at the dining room table and slid the photo album in front of him.

"I'm going to tell you something, you motherfucker. I'm a friend of Vito Zitani's. See this photo album?" I started flipping the pages.

"Oh, look! Here are your kids getting on the school bus in the morning. And here's your wife taking the kids to a baseball game. And here you are with your wife going out to the movies. Look how pretty she is in that dress. How's she look under there? Nice?"

I waved around my toy gun for emphasis. The guy paled and gagged on the washrag.

"Let me tell you something. You see your kids? You see your wife? You can leave here and call the FBI, but my crew already has a copy of this fucking book. If Frankie or I go to jail, the first person we kill is your wife and then your kids. And you're last, so you get to watch everything. You understand?"

Like I said, the dark side inside of me was winning. The monster inside of me that I kept down for a while was busting out, worse than ever.

I told the guy to get a cashier's check for $1 million—plus $100,000 extra to pay for the PIs I hired—and bring it to me by

2 PM that day, which he did. The next day I flew to Cherry Hill and handed the check to Zitani.

———————

In a way, it was my parting gift to him before I fucked him for good.

Soon after the Cincinnati incident, Frankie closed down Camway and we started up another trucking company together—City Lines Xpress—in direct competition with Zitani. I even gave it nearly identical call letters—CLX—just to fuck with him. All this because he *might* be the guy who put out the hit on me. Or maybe I had to destroy anything good in my life.

Why go into business again with Frankie Cam? It's better to do business with the devil you know than the one you don't know. I put my new girlfriend, Tina, in charge of the City office. She was an actress friend of Frankie and Kim's whom I nicknamed "Spacey" because she was into New Age spiritual stuff, a real upside-down cake, and she claimed to be psychic. I didn't believe in that shit, but I told her about hearing Lauren's voice as the car filled with water.

Lauren, a few years after she saved my life

"I think Lauren protects you," Tina said, "but it was also a warning for the future." She looked worried, but wouldn't say why.

City, like all my new businesses, went through the roof in sales, and Zitani was enraged. He knew it would take away from his company and figured I'd start stealing his clients, and he was right. One night as Tina rode with me from Cherry Hill to North Jersey, she asked me why I hurt people. She saw what I was doing to Zitani, whom she liked, and didn't understand my unquenchable need for revenge.

"You're an intelligent man who could have everything," she said. "Why must you do this to Zitani? Why must you lure people into your web like this?"

"Because," I told her, "the student must overcome the master."

"What does that even mean?" she asked.

"You'll see."

By the end of 1988, Zitani had had enough of his student. I was to be the honored guest at his holiday party, and he had a speech ready to give his guests, about how we'd built up the company together, praising my talents. He was paying me a $1 million salary at that point, and for Christmas that year, he bought me two new Mercedes-Benzes. My help with his computer fiasco had given him renewed hope about me.

But I never showed up at his party. The night before, I got all fucked up on coke and booze in Jersey and never got out of bed the next day, never mind to Cherry Hill. Zitani was humiliated. When I made it to the office a week later, he had a few muscle guys around him when he told me that we were breaking up, and he was throwing me out of the company for good.

I didn't care. I was already luring other new victims into my web.

In early 1989 I hooked up with a crew I'd had my eye on for a while, a crew more powerful than any I'd been with before. I was already providing A-Z at least half of their business—they had a gross revenue of $50 million—and my contribution caught the attention of one of the company's owners, Alberto Lido.

Alberto was a Genovese associate, like me, and a big, powerful guy. Which didn't impress me much 'cause I'd seen plenty of big, powerful guys. It also didn't impress me that they were late paying me half a million in commissions, and that their last check bounced at the bank. They were in financial trouble, my favorite kind of company. My plan was to be their savior, as I'd done with Zitani, and bring them back to life.

We set up a sit-down at Alberto's office to discuss how I could help them, and I took Frankie along to vouch for me as a made man, and to be my muscle in case I needed any. Miguel drove us to their offices hidden behind tall, electric iron gates in Newark. Alberto's office inside was a dark cavern of carved wood, and at the center was a giant replica of an old-fashioned ship under glass.

Alberto introduced himself. Standing next to him was a good-looking guy in a black suit with dark slicked-back hair and biceps that gave Frankie a run for his money.

"Hi," he said, putting out his hand. "I'm Sal Gigante."

Frankie's glance met mine for a fraction of a second. Sal, we knew, was the son of Vincent "The Chin" Gigante, the capo of the Genovese crime family and the *Capo di Tutti Capi*—the boss of all bosses—for all five New York crime families. The Godfather. What we didn't know was that Sal and his brother, Andrew, worked with Alberto. We got the required handshakes, hugs, kisses, and *How youse doin'?* out of the way, and I went straight into my pitch.

"Here's the problem," I said. "You owe me nearly half a million dollars. I did some research on you and I know you got Teamsters problems because of their high rates. Well, I got a good connect there and I can make your union problems go away. There's just one thing. I want to take over your company."

Alberto looked shocked. "You want to *buy* it?"

"Yeah. I'm already booking half your freight and there's more where that came from. I can fix all your money problems and make you richer than you've ever been in your life."

Sal shifted in his chair. Frankie's hand went to his pocket.

"How are you going to buy it?" Alberto asked. "How much are you going to come up with?"

"Why do I have to come up with any money at all? Youse owe *me* money and your company's a failing mess. How much money are you going to pay *me* to take this disaster of a company off your hands?"

Alberto and Sal were so offended they didn't say anything.

"First, I'll take over as president," I said. "And after I show you what I can do, you're going to sell me the company."

They needed time to think about it, Alberto said, and we set a time to meet again two days later with Alberto's board members. Frankie came with me again, and we met a dozen guys in a boardroom a mile long. Sal's brother, Andrew, was there and so were some New York mob guys I recognized. I sat on one end, Alberto sat on the other, and Frankie positioned himself in the middle.

I stood up and Golden Tongued them.

"I'm going to stuff this business with $200 million to $300 million in revenue from major Fortune 500 companies," I said, "and it will be the most successful trucking company in this country. By far."

I explained more and when I was done, Alberto asked us to step out of the room while the board members talked. In the hall, Sal pulled Frankie aside to tell him something and soon we were summoned back to the boardroom.

"I made my decision," Alberto said from across the long desk. "Tom, you are the new president of A-Z Passage. Congratulations! Let's take the minutes accordingly. *The board appoints Tom Giacomaro as president of the company.*"

Because when you're a big earner, everybody wants you. And when you're a big talker, you can con most of the people most of the time, especially when they're desperate. In the car on the way home, I asked Frankie what Sal wanted with him alone.

"He said, 'You know who we're wit. You know who our father is. You better make sure Tommy don't fuck nothing up or he's going off a fucking bridge.'"

Frankie and I looked at each other and started laughing our asses off, and so did Miguel up front.

Not the fucking *bridge* line! Holy shit, ain't these mob guys ever original? That was *our* fucking line!

And didn't they already know I'd been there, survived that? You could throw me off any bridge in the world and I'll rise up through a river of toxic shit and reach the surface, stronger and more ruthless and determined than ever before.

CHAPTER 12

BUYING, BLEEDING, BUSTING

The corporate bank accounts were overflowing with millions in front of our eyes. Not touch it? Out of the question.

Jimmy Hoffa predicted I'd be big one day in the trucking business, but he didn't plan on me destroying it. Neither did I, but that's exactly what I did.

After Alberto named me president, I sent Miguel to one of those places that sold movie theater equipment to buy a long red carpet and a velvet rope, the kind they use for Hollywood galas and premieres. The main area of A-Z Passage was an open space, and I needed to mark my kingdom within. I unrolled the red carpet and put up the rope to lead up to my office door.

"What do you think you are," Alberto asked, when he saw my setup, "a king?"

I was moving up the ranks for sure. At the Apple Ridge Country Club they even gave me the original locker that belonged to my Uncle Petey when he was capo of the Gatto crew in the seventies.

My first task at A-Z was to go through the company's paperwork to see how badly it was failing. It only took me a week doing the numbers to realize it was dead on arrival; the company was hemorrhaging badly. Even with me adding the business I would steal from Zitani, it wouldn't be fast enough to bail it out. *Unless . . .*

"I need an injection of at least $2 million to save it," I told Alberto. "Or $3 million." I might as well ask for extra that I can play with. "What you really need is another $5 million and I can save your company."

Alberto invited a bunch of wealthy types to the office for me to do my dog-and-pony show and convince them to invest. Alberto was a typical mob guy; he had a lot of money, but he had no intention of putting it into the company even though he was personally responsible for the millions of debt it was in. He wanted someone else to put in the money.

That's when Enzo Camino glided in, smooth as silk.

Camino was a brash hotshot real estate developer who divided his time between Cherry Hill, New Jersey, and a gigantic mansion in Coconut Grove, Miami. When he wasn't there, he leased his manse to the *Miami Vice* TV show to use. He was a charmer who looked like Tony Bennett, drove a Ferrari, and co-owned a famous five-star hotel in Los Angeles. He was described in a *Business Week* article in 1989 as a *workout specialist.*

Alberto had heard that Enzo was looking to buy trucking companies, so he brought him in for a meeting as a potential investor. As soon as I met him, I recognized my own kind: scam artist. Alberto thought he was a rich goose who'd lay a golden egg for us, but I knew he was going to fuck Alberto and everyone else and all the horses they rode in on. I also knew it was only a matter of a little time before I'd join him at it.

Enzo promised Alberto he'd invest $2 million to save the company even though he was secretly in debt up to his eyeballs. He spent the eighties borrowing from people and banks and buying new companies, then Ponzi scheming them into each other to pay for his lavish life-style. He'd move from one company to another and "bust out" the previous one by letting it go bankrupt. He got away with it for a long time, but the stock market crash in the late eighties hurt the hotel industry, and now he was looking for a new area to rape and pillage.

Enzo was a brilliant thief, even better than me. And now that he had his eye on the trucking industry, he was about to teach me everything he knew about buying, bleeding, and busting out companies.

I watched with amusement as Enzo convinced Alberto that instead of giving him the $2 million as promised, he wanted Alberto to give *him* money—nearly half a million—so that he could buy *other* trucking companies. He could save A-Z this way, he insisted, by making money with the other companies and taking Alberto and his partners along for the ride. Enzo was good and Alberto was desperate. *Here comes the mousey into the little housey*, I whispered to myself, as I watched Enzo set him up.

"We're going to build the biggest trucking company in the country!" Enzo said. "Don't worry about A-Z. We'll stuff that over here. We'll have all these other ones. We're gonna go worldwide!"

Enzo was smart enough to see that I was smart, too—*scary* smart, he called me—and that he'd need me in on his plan to bait the other companies with my trucking experience and credentials. Within a few months of his arrival, Enzo and I began buying up companies all over the country. I gave City to Frankie so I could focus on my Enzo business—his ideas and ambition were humongously huge, like mine, and the two of us together were a lethal combination.

Being a South Jersey guy, Enzo was connected to the Nicky Scarfo crew. The New Jersey State Commission of Investigation had already categorized him as a "key organized crime associate," and I'd heard he was friends with Nicky Scarfo's nephew, the one who ratted on Nicky. His two right-hand guys were Tyrone DeNittis and Tony Palma, both also reported to the Scarfo crew. DeNittis even broadcasted it on the business cards he handed out, which said, "Tyrone DeNittis, a Nicky Scarfo Entertainment Company."

Enzo taught me how to read balance sheets and showed me how to buy companies using leverage buyouts, purchase agreements, and private placements. We walked into trucking companies like bandits—two stinking-rich businessmen arriving in stretch limos—convincing the owners to sell to us on promissory notes. They trusted us because of my rep in the business and Enzo's in Miami. In the age of no internet, there was no Google search to prove otherwise. We robbed them with a smile; we were the Butch and Sundance of the trucking industry.

"Listen," I'd say to the trucking CEOs. "Your company's not worth very much, but I'll pay you ten times more than it's worth over the next two years if you sell it to me."

It was easy because most of them were doing shitty business anyway and were desperate. A deregulation in the late seventies caused eventual rate wars (which I used to my advantage as a salesman) that slowly killed a lot of companies and now Enzo and I had arrived to put the nails in the coffins and profit from their deaths.

We bought them dirt cheap because we promised big back ends. One failing company, which we bought on April Fool's Day, was Global Shipping, based in Los Angeles. Enzo convinced them to sell to us for the astounding price of twelve dollars cash. Nineteen days later we ran it out of business by not paying the bills when the receivables came in and took the money and ran, leaving four thousand employees out of work.

One prominent trucking company exec wouldn't budge, so I gave him the old, reliable dumpster-bridge offer.

"You have a choice," I said, with a smile. "We'll bring you to New York and throw you offa the George Washington Bridge, the Brooklyn Bridge, or the Verrazano Bridge. You decide. Or you can choose the dumpster of your favorite restaurant and we'll put you in there. What the fuck do you want to do? I'm offering you a fucking giant offer for your company, why wouldn't you sell it to me?"

We bought up the nation's largest trucking companies this way.

At the same time, I started a whole other scam on my own with Tommy Barnetas in Long Island and Harry Kapralos in Brooklyn (not to be confused with another unfortunately named guy in Jersey with the same name), two Mafioso trucking guys I gave extra freight to when I was with Zitani. Whatever Enzo taught me I did with them, too, only we did it with both trucking and the airfreight business. Everything we bought, I put in Harry and Tommy's names because they were the official owners. Yeah, sure, that's why I did that. One of the first companies we bought was Majestic Carrier in Newark. I appointed Barnetas, who must have weighed over five hundred pounds, as the trustee of their near-$2 million pension fund.

So now, I was working it all over the place, juggling Alberto and the Genovese crime family in Jersey, Camino and the Nicky Scarfo crew in Philly, and Tommy and Harry with the Barnetas crew in Brooklyn and Long Island.

The coke kept me going, and going fast.

In a six-month period, I bought at least thirty trucking and airfreight companies and merged them together into two groups.

By late 1989 my rolled-up trucking companies with Enzo were worth $2.5 billion, and my consolidated airfreight companies with Tommy and Harry were worth $1.5 billion—a total of $4 billion. Within the year, Enzo and I had the largest privately held trucking company in the country and produced $250 million per month in receivables.

And now, as we entered a new decade, it was time to steal every dime of it. We'd done the buying, now came the bleeding and busting. The corporate bank accounts were overflowing with millions in front of our eyes. Not touch it? Out of the question. They were like giant pussies waiting to be fucked. A man in my position never turns down pussy or money.

Suddenly, Majestic Carrier mysteriously "went out of business," and its juicy near-$2 million pension fund disappeared.

On the Enzo side, he started wiring millions to numbered bank accounts in the Cayman Islands, then he'd fly down there on his private jet, clean out the money from the bank accounts in cash, and fly back to Philly or Miami with the dough.

Almost all the companies we bought went bankrupt—including A-Z Passage.

I didn't care about the thousands of people out of work or without their pensions. I just didn't care. I felt and saw nothing except dollar signs and a ravenous need for more money. And coke.

"What is happening to you?" Tina asked one night. By now, I'd separated from Debbie and was seeing Tina full time—along with the dozens of other girls I was fucking. Lauren was distraught that I left home and Tina was worried, she said, because I was "dancing with the devil."

"You're getting so dark," she said. "Your eyes are like black olives. I'm afraid to be around you anymore. It's like you're possessed."

My mother had given Tina a Bible as a gift the previous Christmas, and Tina's spiritual side had been on overdrive ever since. She noticed I was lighting red candles at home and at the office, which she said symbolized a lust for power.

"Why are you causing so much chaos, Tommy? Are you trying to fuck over the mob? Why do you want to take everyone down? This is not going to turn out well. It's going to blow up in your face like napalm."

Tina was certain dark forces had taken me over. The day after we talked, she opened the ashtray in her car to get some change—she only used it for coins and no one had ever smoked in her car—and the ashtray burst into flames. That was confirmation to her that something evil was happening, she said, and she had to stay away from me for a while.

She was right about one thing; I'd set off a bomb and created a $4 billion mess. By the middle of 1990, the collateral damage began to crash around me. I'd taken down more than two dozen companies, put about twenty thousand people out of work, stole people's pensions, and was overdue on all my promissory notes. Enzo and I were single-handedly ruining interstate commerce and transportation. No one wanted to ship goods anymore; we'd virtually wiped out the industry.

It wasn't like no one was gonna notice. People started calling the FBI screaming "fraud."

Alberto was beyond raging; he wanted to kill us. He took Sal Gigante with his slicked-back hair and popping biceps with him to the five-star hotel to either get his $400,000 back from Enzo or kill him, one or the other. Enzo paid back Alberto in full.

It was around this time that I started to feel like I was being watched.

The FBI had been slow to figure out something was going on, but once they did we were goners. The government created a Senate subcommittee to investigate who the hell was behind all this. The heat was on.

One of my restaurant-owner friends pulled me aside. "Tom, the FBI came to see me. They want to wiretap my tables to listen to you." Someone else tipped me off that the FBI planned to wiretap my house. I'd been checking my car for bombs ever since my Passaic plunge, and now I refused to leave my car alone unless it was in my garage. I made Miguel stay with it at all times and wouldn't allow valet parking.

It was a good time, I decided, to get outta Dodge.

I flew down to Miami, and Enzo set me up in a beautifully furnished hotel suite nearby and I started dating a friend of his, Kate Davies—big tits, tight ass, the usual. But down there, the heat was on Enzo. The FBI was trying to nail him for the stuff he'd done before we met, and by the end of 1990, they'd gathered enough to get him. In February 1991 he was indicted on fifty-four counts of wire fraud and one RICO count. That August, he left Miami for Philly to get sentenced. There was a chance he wasn't coming back.

"If that happens, Tom, the rabbi will take over my end of Apex Systems and be the president. Okay?"

Apex Systems was the last consolidated company we owned that we hadn't looted yet and Enzo was in charge of it. Enzo wanted a rabbi friend of his to keep it going for him if he went to prison, and when we looted it, the rabbi would keep Enzo's share safe for him.

"Sure, Enzo, sure," I told him.

Enzo got twenty-four years for wire fraud and racketeering, and they took him away on the spot, ordering him to pay $6.8 million in fines and restitution.

Three weeks later I called up Enzo's boys, Tyrone and Tony, and staged a sit-down with the rabbi in Detroit, where Apex Systems had its office. Enzo's boys were more than happy to force the rabbi out after I told them I'd make them fifty-fifty partners with me in the business. The three of us showed up at the Detroit office, where the rabbi was preparing to take over but hadn't yet. I stayed in one room while Tyrone and Tommy met the rabbi in the conference room. There, they put some papers in front of him that awarded me 100 percent control of the company and told him to sign. He hesitated.

"Sign the fucking paperwork," Tony told him, "or we'll blow your fucking head off."

A few minutes later, the rabbi emerged from the room looking as pale as the pope and left the building, never to return. He didn't even go back to his office to get his things from his desk. Tony and Tyrone came out looking proud of themselves.

"The company's ours!" said Tony.

We went over to the rabbi's office and I took a seat at the desk—the chair was still ass-warm. Tony took the office next door and earned a new nickname that day, "The Enforcer." We celebrated that night by going to a car dealership in the area and buying ourselves three new Cadillacs.

That September, I moved from Miami to Detroit to take over the company just before Lauren's fourteenth birthday.

"All I wanted for a present," she cried on the phone, "was for you to be here."

"I know, baby, I know," I said. "But Daddy had to come here to work. Please understand."

That kid was the only one who could get some feeling outta me. Now that she was a teen, I could see she was becoming the same OCD mess I was. And just like me, she liked to steal money and deny it. I still had cash hidden in shoeboxes in the basement where she lived with Debbie, and Lauren knew where they were. She'd loosen the duct tape when she wanted to go shopping with her girl-friends at the mall and take a handful.

"I didn't do it, Daddy," she'd say, when I confronted her.

She was a chip off the ol' block, that girl, stealing from her old man. It kind of made me smile.

In Detroit, I once again had a whole new crew around me.

Because Apex Systems was a Teamsters company in the Motor City, a lot of them had known Hoffa in the day. But much had changed in the twenty years since I'd picked him up at the airport, and in the early nineties, the players everywhere were coming and going.

Streaky was sentenced to a sixty-five-year term in federal prison for racketeering, and John Stanfa became the new boss in Philly. They even got Frankie Cam, who went to prison that November for run-ning his gambling rings.

I was getting nervous. I'd now moved to three different states in one year, but I still felt like I was being watched and followed. My bookkeeper for the previous year, Maggie, called to say the FBI was breathing down her back. Maggie was the one person who knew everything about all my businesses—how much I made, how I got it, and where I hid it. In the same way that Ponzi schemer Bernie Madoff had his one bookkeeper who knew everything, shut away in a little room for decades, I had my Maggie.

The kids came to spend Christmas 1991 with me in Detroit and I had a nightmare—at least, I think I was asleep. I heard Lauren's voice just like when I was sinking into the Passaic and about to drown. Once again, her sweet voice said, "Get out, Daddy!"

The next day I got the phone call.

"Mr. Giacomaro, this is the US Attorney's Office in Newark." They were investigating the disappearance of the Majestic Carrier pension fund, he said, and they wanted me to come in.

Fuck!

"You're in a lot of trouble," the man said. "We've been watching you and we have enough evidence to indict you. But first, we'd like you to come into the office and talk to us about cooperating."

Cooperating? Turn myself in? Those weren't words in my vocabulary. But at my lawyer's urging, I was sitting on the hot seat in their Jersey office the following week, surrounded by guys in cheap suits— two assistant US attorneys, one FBI agent, one guy from the Department of Labor's racketeering office, and an IRS agent.

"We want to know what you did with that pension fund," asked one.

"I don't know what you're talking about," I said. "I had nothin' to do with it."

"We know the money got transferred to you and your partners, Tommy Barnetas and Harry Kapralos."

"Like I said, I don't know what you're talking about."

"You don't know what we're talking about?" another one asked, standing up and moving closer. "Well, let me refresh your memory. We know you're mobbed up and doing business with the Genovese family. We know you were associated with the Nicky Scarfo crew in Philly. And we know you've been doing three billion in trucking nationally with Camino. *And we don't like it.*"

"And"—a third one pointed a finger inches from my face—"then you go and loot a pension fund for one point three million? We really, really don't like that. You're going to cooperate with us or you're going down big-time."

They knew too much.

"All right," I said.

"We want you back here at the end of January to turn yourself in."

"I'll be here," I told them.

Instead, I listened to my Lauren. I packed twenty-one suitcases and boarded a flight from Detroit to Amsterdam, then connected to Nairobi, Kenya—one way. And I took Kate, Enzo's friend, with me.

As I told Tina, the student must overcome the master. She didn't know what I meant when I said that, but I did: You had to one-up your teachers—you had to be smarter, faster, better. There was no way I was joining Enzo, Frankie, Streaky, and Nicky in prison. I was smarter than all those dumb-as-shit mob guys put together, and unlike them, I'd prepared for this day in advance.

I was going to a land far, far away, where the clouds were far behind me. And South Africa was a place as far away as I could think of to go.

CHAPTER 13

LIFE ON
THE LAM

South Africa had no extradition laws or treaties with the US,
so I could disappear there forever behind my walls of stone.

Outside the gates of my villa near Johannesburg, hundreds of homeless squatters slept in urine-soaked, rat-infested cardboard boxes. Behind the gates, I was living like an American king.

My seven-bedroom, palazzo-style home had a tennis court; a 50,000-gallon cascading waterfall swimming pool; two brand-new 750Li BMWs in the driveway; and a stone fortress surrounding it. At the snap of my fingers, maids dressed in pink, ruffled uniforms brought me vodkas by the pool.

I arrived in South Africa on Valentine's Day 1992, a wanted but filthy-rich man.

Half the twenty-one suitcases I packed were stuffed with hundred-dollar bills. And there were the millions I'd been secretly moving out of the country for years. I was The Worm, but I was also prepared just in case my ass was ever nailed to the wall. I had set up my exit strategy as soon as I started making shitloads of money selling coke, when I'd returned from Michigan a decade earlier.

Back then you could waltz into any top bank in Manhattan with your ID and without filling out reams of paperwork, open up numbered bank accounts in international branches in Sweden, England, Germany, Italy, France, and Switzerland. It was all so easy, *so* easy. In the years leading up to South Africa, I moved out $600–$800 million in total, the government wrote in their files later. Give or take ten million. Once I knew Kate had friends in South Africa and that's where we were headed, I wired money there from my European banks. South Africa had no extradition laws or treaties with the United States, so I could disappear there forever behind my walls of stone.

Kate and I landed in Amsterdam from Detroit, then boarded a flight to Nairobi. When we arrived in Kenya we had to go through customs. The airport was swarming with security guards armed with machine guns, and there was the matter of my suitcases full of cash. I slid my Rolex from my wrist and dangled it in front of the security guy in charge. His eyes lit up.

"Come with me," he motioned with his hand, quickly pocketing the watch. It don't matter where you are in the world, the language of money is universal. In Swahili, he ordered several guards to transfer us with our luggage directly to the plane to Botswana, bypassing customs and security checks. From Botswana, we took a small plane to Johannesburg. Within a few days we were lounging by the cascading waterfall in the backyard of my new villa, downing Absolut on ice and sitting pretty under the hot sun.

My first few weeks there, I tried not to think about the giant fucking mess I'd left behind in Jersey. I distracted myself from the disaster I'd made of my life and everyone else's by staying drunk and playing tennis with Kate's friends, Mitch and Dina, a couple who owned the a chain of restaurants in South Africa.

Meanwhile, back home in the dead of winter, all hell was breaking loose.

I finally called my mother after two weeks to let her know I was alive, and she was relieved, but panicked.

Passport stamped at Jan Smuts International Airport
in Johannesburg, February 1992

"Tommy, the FBI are all over the place turning everybody and everything upside down," she whispered. "They're investigating all of your friends. They're watching me and your father."

I wasn't sure if she was whispering so my father wouldn't hear, or because she thought the phone was tapped. I'm sure my father was beating the shit out of her more than usual because of the new, even bigger shame I'd brought on the family.

In the year leading up to my Valentine's Day massacre, I'd left those 20,000 people out of work and billions of dollars missing from all over the place. Now, the FBI descended and grabbed anyone associated with me—asking questions and gathering testimonies. All my friends and colleagues were calling my mother, she whispered—Teddy Duanno, Patsy Giglio, Stevie Moretti, Tina, Miguel the driver, Maggie my bookkeeper ... the list went on and on. I hadn't told anyone I was leaving; I just vanished. After I left, any business I was still connected to collapsed.

Like Tina said once, it was like a napalm bomb had detonated.

Everyone was looking for me and screaming at each other: *Is he dead? Where is he? What is going on?*

But mostly, my former colleagues and the FBI wanted to know: *Where the fuck was all that money?*

"I don't know!" my mother answered, over and over, to every question. "I don't know, I don't know!" And it's true, she didn't. Except for the suitcases of cash I'd hidden in the basement.

I sat back in my subtropical paradise eight thousand miles away, drunkenly looking at my waterfall, and for the first time in a long time I felt regret—mostly for myself. I'd been on top of the dog-shit pile with Zitani and I'd let it all collapse. Why?

Then I worried that everyone was gonna rat on me and fry me. I had set up Camino, Barnetas, and Kapralos to do the dirty work, and their names were on all the official paperwork. But by now, after a year of surveillance, the FBI would know I was, as always, the mastermind behind all the bullying, buying, looting, and busting. Enzo taught me, but I was a student who surpassed his master. I manipulated them all, and that's what they're all gonna fucking say when they rat.

Maggie was the only one who knew about my overseas accounts and where I kept the file with my meticulous, handwritten records. When the FBI brought her in and interrogated her, she wasted no time telling them where all the money was and, yes, she'd show them everything if it meant saving her own ass. But when she went to look for the file in the Clifton office, it wasn't there—I'd cleaned everything out weeks before I left. Now Maggie looked the dummy and she made the FBI look like dummies, too. Humiliating the FBI was the worst thing you could do. They fried her for it.

By the time Maggie and the FBI saw that my files were missing, I was liquidating into diamonds all the money I'd wired and carried with me. In South Africa, they let you bring in millions of dollars—they encouraged it as an investment in their economy. When I wired my money, I got a 1:4 ratio conversion for every US dollar to the South African rand. Once the money was in the country, though, they didn't want you to take it out. They had a $20,000 limit to how much money you could leave with.

But they didn't mind if you bought a few of their homegrown trinkets to take away. South Africa was rife with underground and open-pit diamond mines and had been diamond crazy ever since the largest gem-quality diamond—over three thousand carats—was found in one of their mines in 1905. It just so happened that De Beers had its world headquarters in Johannesburg. And it furthermore just so happened that Kate's buddy, Mitch, knew a VP there at De Beers who'd help me buy more diamonds than your average tourist.

I didn't consider myself a tourist; I planned to stay in the country and make a fresh start. After a few weeks of drinking and tennis, my brain couldn't stand being idle anymore and I was ready to get back to work plotting and scheming. I was going to take over the trucking business in South Africa, I'd decided.

I was delusional, of course. Thinking I could re-create my life with a new company, a new country, another big house, another beautiful girl, another expensive car—and not have to go back and answer for the mess I'd left behind. Extradition treaty or not, there was no way someone wasn't gonna come after me sooner or later.

But for a while at least, I was able to convince myself I was safe behind my walled-in paradise.

———

The reality outside my mansion gates was a whole other chaos.

After twenty-seven years in prison, political revolutionary Nelson Mandela had been released, and two months before I arrived in Johannesburg, he'd given a speech at the Johannesburg World Trade Center in front of 228 delegates from nineteen different political parties to denounce current president de Klerk's regime. South Africa was shifting from an apartheid government to a democratic one, and I saw the country transform before my eyes.

One afternoon I was doing some banking downtown and I left the building using the wrong door. I stepped into the street and into a crowd of thousands of South Africans marching. I was swept up, engulfed, and pulled forward with the throng and couldn't get out.

Military trucks were moving in, and men with swords and shields started hosing people with water to get them to disperse. It was a matter of minutes before the guns would come out and shooting would begin. I got soaked, but was able to slip into an alleyway and run.

Thinking as I do, I intended to use the political upheaval to my advantage and got to work wooing the people around Mandela. It didn't take much to lure them. The black people in South Africa would finally be free to make money and attain positions, and they were about to take over the banks and the economy. I was a white businessman with millions of dollars to spend, ready to start up my company and pay them more money than they'd ever seen. What was not to like? Again, since this was before the internet, they couldn't go online yet and find out about my past in America.

I zeroed in on the black guys prepping to be in Mandela's administration and did my usual—took them to expensive dinners, got them drunk, partied with them, promised them big salaries and VP titles, and I slipped them cash. One of the guys, Magabi, later became a big official in South Africa. I could see his potential and made it a point to get especially friendly with him.

Every few weeks, I called home to Jersey to talk to my mother and Lauren and check in with my lawyer in DC. The calls were always the same: Lauren would cry and beg me to come home; my mother whispered about strange cars parked outside the house; and my lawyer warned me I was in big, big trouble. The FBI was issuing arrest warrants, he said, and he strongly suggested I come back and do damage control. Enzo Camino was all over the newspapers that month trying to get a new trial and get out of prison. There was a chance, my lawyer warned, that they'd find out where I was and come get me.

"It's better if you go to them, Tom," he advised. "You'll be in a position of more power."

I didn't want to think about it.

Kate and I took off to Botswana for a few days with Mitch and Dina to have some fun. The capital city, Gaborone, was like Vegas. It had a long strip in the city's center bustling with restaurants, casinos, and tourists. To get there, we drove along dirt roads through a maze of thatched grass huts, thorn trees, and donkeys roaming around the city's outer edge—real backward, third-world stuff. As Mitch drove, I stared out the car window, and people stared back at me as we passed. Some had painted faces and wild eyes and they looked stoned out of their minds. I heard faint snippets of chanting coming from the huts.

We stayed at a casino-hotel owned by an American hotelier, and in the bar the next night over dinner I knocked back vodka after vodka, nervous about the FBI at home. I was also jittery because it had been three months since I'd snorted coke and I was jonesing for the devil's drug. I didn't take the chance of bringing any with me and hadn't found a local drug contact yet. I thought about the wild-eyed, stoned-looking tribesmen we'd passed. From the casino window, you could see the tops of the thatched roofs.

"What the fuck is going on in those huts?" I asked our friends.

"That's the Bakgatla tribe," Mitch said. "They do ceremonies and rituals to get the evil spirits out of you."

"Exorcisms?" Kate asked, interested. Tina and my mother weren't the only ones who'd told me I was "possessed"—Kate had said it, too.

Mitch and Dina nodded. The exorcisms performed in the huts, they explained, were common practice in the country and part of the natives' religion and culture. Everyone did it, tourists too. The belief was that everyone was possessed in some way or another and the only way to get unpossessed was through one of these exorcisms.

"There are evil spirits all around us," Mitch said, ominously.

"You fucking believe in that shit?" I asked him, laughing, while downing another vodka. All three of them looked at me, dead serious.

"All right, let's fucking go." I stood up, unsteady. "I wanna do it."

My whole life I'd been hearing there was something seriously wrong with me, from a lot of people. Maybe they were right; maybe I was possessed. Maybe a tribal ceremony on the other side of the world with people dancing around chanting mumbo jumbo would cure me of who I was. Or, maybe it was the six straight vodkas talking.

Mitch and Dina stayed behind, and Kate and I drove along the dirt roads until we reached a hut that seemed like the kind of place that gives a good exorcism. It looked creepy, silhouetted by the moon. I looked up. *Great. A fucking full moon.*

Kate waited outside and I paid a woman $500 before she led me inside.

The hut was decorated with candles and masks that sprouted grass and leaves— "They are gods," said the woman, with a heavy accent. She pointed to a straw mat on the floor and told me to lie down. Another woman entered the room carrying something that was burning and stank to high heaven. At first I thought it was incense, until I felt that familiar high school feeling of being stoned. Ha! It had been so long! A few minutes on the ground and I was high as a kite.

The two women, black as night, were smoking something on their own as they painted me with a mixture of . . . did she say *chicken's blood*? Oh, yeah. This oughta scare those evil spirits out of me. Jesus Christ. I let my mind drift as my two exorcists started dancing and chanting. I saw images all blurred together of Lauren crying and homeless people in cardboard boxes and piles of stolen money falling from the sky and my father's demented face.

The image of his face made me vomit, literally. I puked into a bucket by the mat, and puked and puked so much, I thought I was gonna choke on the regurgitated vodka and steak coming out of me.

Then came the sweats and hallucinations, in which I thought I saw a black shadow leave my body, slide along the dirt floor, and slip under the wall of the hut to the outside where Kate was waiting for me, smoking a cigarette. I passed out.

When I woke up, I was out of the hut in the cool night with Kate. She was shaking me and trying to get me into the car.

"Bad Tom is all gone," I slurred, as I lay down in the back seat and Kate drove us back to the house. "We're safe now."

———————

But we weren't.

A few days later at the start of the US Memorial Day weekend, I was sitting by the pool still recuperating from my exorcism when one of my three-hundred-pound maids in pink handed me the phone—it was my lawyer. The FBI put a trace on Debbie's phone and knew where I was because of my calls to Lauren.

"Tom, you gotta get out of South Africa—*fast*. You've got to come back. They're coming to get you with a burlap bag. Never mind extradition papers. They'll kidnap you and smuggle you back to the United States. You've got about eight hours to get out of there; they're on their way."

I knew all about that burlap bag. They throw a potato sack over your head, handcuff you, and suddenly you're in the cargo area of a US Air Force plane chained to the wall. It's what they did to former Panama dictator and drug lord Manuel Noriega. These people don't play around.

I had a plan, but I had to move fast and be efficient.

I ran upstairs into the bedroom with a needle and thread, a pair of white Ralph Lauren dress socks, and a small mountain of flawless, sparkling 2.5- and 5.5-carat diamonds—worth $10,00 to $100,000 each—on the bed. Kate was running around emptying drawers into suitcases. She was a pampered princess; she wouldn't know how to use a needle and thread to save her life. But I did, thanks to my mother. "You never know when it's going to come in handy," she used to say, when she taught me how to baste and cross-stitch when I was a kid.

I chopped off the elastic tops from three socks and carefully poured in my diamonds, evenly distributing them among the socks. Then I expertly sewed the tops of the socks back together until I had three, perfect, two-inch-wide balls lined up on the bed. They looked just like a plate of fresh mozzarella. In the bathroom, I shaved my thighs, then slid on two pairs of briefs and *ever so carefully* placed the three diamond balls into my briefs, under my privates. That made five balls, I noted—I was a numbers guy, after all.

Over that, I slipped on a third pair of underwear and, using surgical adhesive, taped down the bottom edges of my briefs onto my hair-free thighs. Unless someone slipped their hand under the waistband to spontaneously gave me a hand job, those diamonds weren't going fucking nowhere. I practiced walking back and forth in the room, trying to look like I didn't have millions of dollars in my crotch. I was known for having big balls, but this gave a whole new meaning to the phrase "family jewels."

Within hours of my lawyer's call, Kate and I pulled up to Johannesburg's Jan Smuts Airport (as it was called at the time) where I parked my BMW and tossed the keys into the trash.

I left everything—the house, the cars, the new company I was building, and at least $7 million in the bank I didn't have time to clean out. My government friend, Magabi, called in a favor at the airport and arranged for our luggage to be checked in ahead of us so we wouldn't cause suspicion, and booked us on a 2 AM flight to Nice, France. Our next hideout destination: Saint-Jean-Cap-Ferrat, where Kate had a "very rich and very crazy" friend.

"The FBI could land on the tarmac and pull you off," Magabi warned. "There might even be a passport hold on you. We won't know until you get to the airport and try."

I got through security and onto the plane, but until it took off, I was as nervous as a whore in church. During the ten-hour flight I barely moved. All I could think was: *You can cut glass with diamonds and I'm sitting on a small mountain of them under my balls.*

I didn't breathe until we landed in Nice.

Not only had we eluded the FBI, but I found out soon after landing that we narrowly missed one of South Africa's most brutal, bloodiest outbreaks of violence during the revolution—the

Boipatong massacre, in which forty-five people were murdered in a township twenty-five minutes from my house.

In Nice we crashed with Kate's hottie heiress friend, Karen, in her villa overlooking the Mediterranean. She came from a billionaire family that made money in newspapers and copper mining and gave her a $40,000-a-month allowance. She was into pot and coke and knew the hottest clubs and the most powerful people in Europe—my kinda girl.

For the next month we lived the good life with Karen in the little fishing village—one of "the pearls on the French Riviera," as people called Saint-Jean-Cap-Ferrat. It was my first time in France and I loved walking along the cobblestoned streets and bartering with the butcher, the fishmonger, the fromagerie guy, and the florist. Soon I knew everyone in the outdoor markets and cafés.

Every morning before the girls woke up, I'd walk to the boat docks at 5 AM and sit with "Frenchie," the owner of a little café. He'd be drinking wine with his two red poodles at his side and arguing about politics and soccer with his friend Pierre, a French-Lebanese arms dealer who sold contraband weapons to the Arabs. Pierre had a 110-foot Ferretti yacht in the marina worth $9 million and guys on deck guarding it with machine guns. He was a real bad dude, but no one bothered him about it because he was so rich. That's what money can buy you, the freedom to do whatever bad thing you want and people will still suck your dick in Macy's window.

He was just the kind of guy I was looking for to help me liquidate my diamonds and the twenty-five Rolex watches I'd brought with me. Frenchie made us omelets and brought us wine and cheese, and we argued and laughed and I gave him jewels and watches for money. Karen also had a jewelry contact a twenty-minute drive away in Monaco that I made use of.

In Monaco, we'd visit Karen's friend and the heir to a famous hotel fortune who also had a villa overlooking the sea. We'd speed around in his new Bentley on the Circuit de Monaco, a street-racing circuit laid out on the streets of Monte Carlo, where the Formula One Monaco

Grand Prix had been just a few weeks earlier. We raced while smoking joints and doing coke; how I'm still alive, I have no idea.

But I figured those weeks were my last taste of excess and freedom for a long time, maybe forever, so I lived them to the hilt. My days were numbered. Soon I'd have to go back to Jersey and when I did, I'd go to prison or get whacked by the mob to shut me up. This time, they wouldn't miss.

On July Fourth weekend, Kate and I went on the run again—to London. We rented a three-floor apartment behind Harrods and spent another month living it up, until the day Lauren's voice jolted me once again, ripping my heart to shreds.

It was mid-August and her fifteenth birthday was coming up, and she desperately wanted me to be there, especially since I'd missed the last one. But there was more. The FBI went after Debbie for the money I took and seized their house and Debbie's bank accounts.

"Daddy, everything's gone," Lauren cried on one of our phone calls. "We're in a little apartment. I want to see you! Please come home!"

Tina once called Lauren my protector; maybe she was my conscience, too.

Fuck. I hung up the phone and agonized about what to do. I'd rather be in prison or dead than to have Lauren suffer that much.

I called my lawyer.

"Make a deal with the government," I told him. "Tell them I want to come in and talk. I'll turn myself in."

We arranged for me to fly into Miami at the start of Labor Day weekend and get picked up by federal agents at the airport there. My lawyer gave them my flight number and I gave Kate the kiss-off, telling her that I'd be in touch soon. We both knew that was a lie.

I didn't fly into Miami. Instead, I flew home. I boarded a plane with those same three socks stuffed in my crotch, but significantly reduced. In September 1992 I returned to my parents' street in a silver limo and showed up at their door unexpectedly. My mother threw her arms around me and cried, and my father glared at me as the driver unloaded my luggage into the garage.

"You lost everything, stupid! You disgraced the family name," was the first thing he said to me. He looked older and tired, and so did my mother. I ignored his words.

"Dad, I need to hide out here for a little while until my lawyer makes a deal with the government."

My mother looked at him pleadingly.

"You're not going to be here very long," he said. "Everyone's looking for you. You're going to jail for the rest of your life. You're a thief and a mob guy. Like I always predicted, *you amounted to nothing.*"

My parents in their later years

I put my suitcases in the basement next to the accounting/ cocaine-smashing table and called my lawyer to let him know I was there. I slept that night in the basement, but barely slept at all. I was trying to make a plan. First on my list was to go see Lauren. Then I had to deal with the FBI.

The next morning bright and early, they found me first. My mother picked up the phone during breakfast and I could hear the serious voice on the other end.

"Hello, is Tom Giacomaro there?"

"No."

I almost laughed out loud. While I was gone, she'd turned into a well-trained Mafia mother.

"Look, we know he's there," said the voice, insistent. "This is Harry Mount from the FBI."

I motioned to her to give me the phone. It was time. I got on the line and introduced myself.

"Hi, Tom, this is Harry Mount from the FBI."

"Oh yeah? How do I know you're really the FBI?" I was going to bust this guy's balls from the get-go.

"Because, Tom, the FBI doesn't lie."

"Oh, I didn't know that. That's beautiful."

"Tom, you have yourself a nice holiday weekend. I'll be at your mother's door ringing the bell Monday morning to pick you up and bring you in."

"Yeah, well . . . Harry? I'll be wanting to see your badge before I get into that boring, unmarked car of yours."

He laughed. "I'll have it ready."

I had the FBI guy laughing already. That was a good sign, I thought, as I hung up. Already things were looking up.

CHAPTER 14

INFORMANTS

*All those years I dodged being a made guy in the mob and
the joke was on me: I was now a made guy for the FBI.*

The following Tuesday, Harry pulled into my mother's driveway in a Chevy Impala with US government plates. Ah, the
Chevy Impala. Reminded me of the secondhand, metallic
blue beauty I drove in high school.

Piece of shit car, I laughed, watching from the window and inspecting Harry's clothes and shoes as he walked to the door—khakis,
cheap loafers, rumpled sport coat. *Piece of shit clothes.* When Harry
knocked, I opened the door an inch.

"Hold up your ID," I ordered. I was going to make this badly
dressed asshole work for it. He held his badge up. My next move was
classic Giacomaro, meant to take him off guard. I swung the door
open wide, threw my arms open, and smiled.

"C'mon in, Harry! Hey Ma, come meet Harry!"

It was priceless; you shoulda seen it. Harry—a stocky, stoic-
looking Fed shaking my tiny mother's bony, overwashed hand. She
even managed to blush. How could he be a cocksucker to me now that
he'd met my mother? As we drove to the FBI office in West Paterson,
I entertained Harry, telling him about my youthful misadventures in
the warehouse section as a teen and made him laugh about playing
Christmas music in September until I drove my father nuts.

In the witness interrogation room—an empty office with a desk, four metal folding chairs, and no phone—Harry introduced me to some other agents involved in the investigation of Camino, Barnetas, Kapralos . . . and me. They'd been watching us for *two years*, they said.

"Thank you for coming in," said one, politely—too politely. "You did the right thing, coming to the good side of the law." He was obviously playing the "good cop."

"Look, we know everything you did," said a second agent, "and we could put you away for twenty years if we wanted." Bad cop. Got it.

"But we don't want to put you in jail," Harry continued. "We want to put Kapralos and Barnetas in jail and especially Camino. We want to keep him there for a long time. But we don't want that for you. With you, we want to make a deal. Cooperate with us and help us put them away, and we'll recommend to the judge that you get minimal or no jail time."

I sneered. "You want me to *rat*?"

"It's not ratting," Harry said. "It's making an alliance with me, it's helping me."

"It's helping the FBI!"

"No, it's helping me *personally* get this case done. You wouldn't have to testify to the grand jury, just talk to me. No one would know. I want those other guys."

Truth was, I had no allegiance to those other guys. I found out when I was in South Africa that all three had fucked me out of millions of dollars doing shit behind my back. Putting them away was justice in my mind—they deserved it, they hung themselves. Harry and the others already had enough information to take them down, they explained. I'd just help push them over the edge. In exchange I'd get minimal jail time and negotiate a plea agreement that covered me for all my past crimes.

"What about everyone else, the people I worked with? My friends? You've been interrogating them."

"We'll leave them alone," Harry promised.

"We don't need them now that we caught you," said one of the others, with a smile. "You're The Big Fish!"

Well, wasn't that the truth: hook, line, and sinker.

"You got a deal," I said.

———————

As soon as I could, I saw Lauren. She came to the house and threw her arms around me, crying. I was home in time for her birthday, and with the money I got selling more diamonds (I'll get to that), I bought her a new car, her first—a white Nissan Altima with a beige interior.

For the next six months, five days a week, Harry picked me up in the morning and took me to the FBI office in West Paterson for the "debriefing" phase.

Part of my deal was that I'd live with my parents during this time, which I assume was meant to keep me on the straight and narrow, and made it easier for them to keep tabs on me. Living at home again was like living in a twisted 1950s *Twilight Zone* episode. My fuckhead father had taken over my childhood bedroom and wouldn't give it up—he liked having his own room and having my mother make his bed every day, taking care of him like a little boy. He liked to give her the coin-drop test every morning. My poor mother.

I set up a bed in the basement with racks of clothes lined up perfectly from my twenty-one suitcases. A week earlier I'd been shopping on Savile Row in London and chewing cigars in front of Kensington Palace, and now this? It gets worse. As an early Christmas present that year, my mother bought me a set of green-and-white Hess Toy Trucks like I was still a little boy, and artfully displayed them on the cocaine table. It was so fucked up.

At Harry's request, I gave his phone number to my parents in case there was ever an emergency, like, if I got shot coming in or out of the house or something. The Feds weren't after me anymore, but others were. It was the beginning of the nineties and the decade would not be a good one for the mob. John Gotti was all over the news that autumn and everyone was nervous. In December, he surrendered to federal authorities to serve a life sentence in prison. Over the next several years, the Mafia would lose its power as one by one, the big guys would go down.

But apparently, I was on the good side of the law now!

For five to seven hours a day, Harry and I and another agent sat in that bare interrogation room in West Paterson and I talked. And talked. He wanted to know everything about me, about all my criminal activities from the start. Poor Harry, he had no idea what he was asking. He hauled an electric typewriter onto the table and typed what I told him onto FBI 302 forms.

I told him about stealing money from my father's wallet on Saturday mornings, and stealing steaks from the A&P and suits from Larkey's in high school. I described Whitey Bulger's thick wrists and Hoffa's fateful prediction for my future. I told him about the evolution and brilliance of Golden Tongue, and how I fucked up my brilliant future forever with one snort of cocaine on a bad night. I describe how I crushed it with a machete in my parents' basement, two feet from where I'd be sleeping that night.

I told him about putting people's arms in the triggerfish tank until the water turned bloody, and putting bodies in dumpsters, and how Streaky wanted to kill me at Vesuvius that time. I told him about Nicky Scarfo's French-cuffed shirts and nose-diving into the Passaic—I even stood up and pulled down my pants to show him the scars on my hip from surgery. I told him about how I fucked over Vito Zitani and the Cabbage Patch dolls and taping up the computer geek in Cincinnati. I told him how everyone thought I was possessed by the devil and about Alberto Lido and the Gigante brothers and hiding the diamonds under my balls, inside my Superman underwear.

And of course, I gave him the information he needed on Barnetas, Kapralos, and Camino. For the pension fund and the trucking companies, I pointed him in the direction of incriminating paper trails and filled in the blanks on information dozens of other people had already given him.

And I made Harry laugh. He typed page after page and he laughed. That was my MO and even the FBI agents couldn't resist. I'm not a gansta, I'm a pranksta. I made it a point to charm everyone in that building, from the receptionist in the foyer ("Hey, how ya doin', beeeooootiful?!") to the FBI guys I passed in the hall as I came and went with Harry.

"Hey, Giacomaro, ain't you locked up yet? We hear you came over from the Dark Side."

"Take it easy, I'm one of youse now," I'd say.

"Nah, you'll never be one of us. It's all right, though. Who'd want to be?"

Thirty years of confessions that should have gone to Father Stanley went instead to Harry Mount, my official FBI wrangler, in one six-month mother lode of a confession.

I told Harry *almost* everything, but not quite. I held a few choice tidbits back. And in the telling, I baited him and set a trap. As I listed my criminal activities, I described my high lifestyle, big money, best drugs, and hot women, all the while keeping an eye on how Harry reacted. I knew what those descriptions could do to a certain kind of man who made an average wage and worked in a drab office every day drinking crappy coffee, but wanting more in life. Like that other agent in the hall said: Who'd wanna be them?

I was showing him The Dream and reeling him in, for later. You'll see.

In the car on the rides home, I asked Harry about himself. I asked about his family and found out he'd been a history professor and a Marine before joining the FBI. Even though I had ulterior motives, and so did he, I couldn't help but like this Harry Mount. We were two guys on opposite sides of the law but we clicked. In another time, in another world, we might have been friends.

At the end of the day, Harry dropped me off at my parents' or at Tina's. My mother called Tina the morning after I got back to let her know I'd returned, mindful of any taps on the phone.

"Tina?" she whispered, "remember that package? You know, *the package*? Well it arrived from out of the country last night."

Tina came right over and just like that, I was seeing her again. We'd go out drinking and partying and get fucked up like old times— something I wasn't supposed to do while under the auspices of the straitlaced FBI and my parents' watchful eyes. My behavior was an emergency, my frantic mother decided. So she called up my FBI handler and snitched on me.

"Harry, this is Yolanda Giacomaro, Tommy's mother. Tommy's out at a party with Tina and he's drinking and taking drugs and yelling at me and causing trouble and he doesn't get home until 4 AM."

Give her a few drinks and my mother would blab to anyone. The next morning, I got the business from Harry.

"I got a call from your *mother*," Harry smirked, when he picked me up. He gave me a speech about boozing and drugging and told me to quit it. Later that day, I made sure my mother would never call him again.

"Ma, are you fucking kidding me?" I yelled, when I got home. "This is an *FBI guy*. He's not your *friend*. What are you thinking? He could put me in *jail*, you stupid fuck! Next time you call Harry Mount, I'll twist your fucking neck!"

I sounded just like my father, and I hated myself for it.

Besides partying with me, Tina performed two other crucial functions those first few months I was back. She gave me a job and helped me liquidate the rest of my diamonds and other valuables I had hidden in the house.

Before I moved to Detroit a few years earlier, I'd hidden $100,000 in cash and jewelry in my mother's basement, plus a dozen Rolex watches, cuff links, and a set of antique pens. I'd wrapped everything in towels and stuck them in the rafters. And I had the diamonds I came back with, too. I left South Africa with about $20 million worth in my Superman underwear, and after liquidating what I could in France and London and depositing the money in banks there, I came home with at least half.

Every Saturday and Sunday, Tina drove me to the diamond district on Canal Street in Manhattan to get rid of them. She double-parked and waited while I took my diamonds and Rolexes to the little booths just off the Holland Tunnel, a stone's throw from Little Italy and Chinatown. I went back to Frankie Cam's old connect, the guy who sold me my checkerboard diamond ring ten years earlier, and laid out my diamonds for him. At $8,000 per rock, I usually went back to Tina's car with about $160,000 cash in my pocket, plus whatever I got for the watches and cuff links.

As for the job Tina gave me, it was the kind of place a guy like me goes undercover in some screwball comedy. Three times a week after debriefing was done, I logged in a few hours office work at Tina's acting studio for kids to fulfill the "work release" program the Feds had me on as part of my deal. I worked as Tina's office manager, answering phones and managing the books, surrounded by girls in tutus and boys in pirate outfits playing pretend. But I organized that dingy little office impeccably, even if I did scare the shit outta the mothers in my mob shirts and a cigar dangling from my mouth. It was a little different from my usual line of work.

Harry had bigger plans for me.

I was already considered a "cooperative" federal informant, delivering information on the cases I was involved in. But after a few weeks with me spilling my guts in the interrogation room, Harry sensed a gold mine. He saw I was smart—*scary smart*, he said, just like Enzo had. The more I told him about the dangerous but genius tales of Tom "Golden Tongue" Giacomaro, the more he realized how in-depth my involvement was in the trucking-and-looting schemes and how far-reaching my hand was in the mob world. He wanted to be the guy to bust everything open, and I was the guy to help him be that guy.

Harry, as I suspected from the start, did not want to stay a $50,000-a-year shmuck slurping bitter coffee from Styrofoam cups. And if there was something I knew about human nature after years of being a salesman—of drugs, of dreams, of trucking companies, and of people's souls—it was this: people were motivated by two things, greed and fear.

Harry feared being mediocre and he was ambitious. Greedy for more. So it was a double whammy.

What was I to Harry?

I was a golden fucking goose, that's what.

I had my Alberto Lido–Enzo Camino–Gigante crew in New York and New Jersey, tied to Vincent "The Chin" Gigante. I had my Philly link with the Nicky Scarfo–Tony Palma–Tyrone DeNittis family. I had the Tommy Barnetas crew in Long Island and the Harry Kapralos crew in Brooklyn. I was smack in the middle of a $3 billion trucking operation that was interwoven with three factions of the Mafia.

As he saw it, I could offer him and the FBI limitless insider information over the long run about top organized criminals in the Tri-state area and beyond. How the hell, Harry wondered, was I able to move back and forth from one mob family to another, to yet another, as I had done? Bringing someone like me in on a more extended, in-depth basis would be a feather in Harry's cap.

I had a feeling something was up. He was preparing to make me a new offer in our quid pro quo agreement, just between us. A few months into our talks, as we finished for the day, Harry gave me one of his serious looks from across the table.

"Tom, I want you to continue on as a special confidential informant," he said, pausing for emphasis—"for the government's crime syndicate operation."

He wanted me to feed him information on the mob guys. And if I helped him, he said, not only would he keep me out of jail, but he'd let me "carry on my businesses as usual." It would be part of the job, he explained, but also (he implied) he'd be looking the other way somewhat.

I sat back in the cold, creaking chair and thought for a minute. There was no way I'd ever really rat on the main mob guys—*that* I knew for sure. But could I string the FBI along and make them *think* I was, in exchange for my freedom?

My old Maislin regular, Whitey Bulger, had done something like that. The following year he'd go into hiding after his FBI handler tipped him off that agents were coming to arrest him when the jig was up. A few years after that, we'd read in the *Boston Globe* that Whitey had been an FBI informant for decades—something he denies to this day. I'm sure he conned his FBI handler, just as I was about to con mine. Guys like us weren't informants, I once heard Whitey say, we were "opportunists."

I for sure was an opportunist.

"Deal," I told Harry.

A few weeks later Harry took me before federal judge Harold A. Ackerman to get me approved as an informant for the covert crime syndicate operation. Judge Ackerman put Streaky away, and he had recently presided over a two-year trial involving twenty members of the Lucchese crime family charged with gambling, loan-sharking, drug dealing, and fraudulent credit card operations. He approved me and also approved funds if I ever needed to go into the witness protection program.

"That's so very reassuring," I said to Harry, when he told me.

Also approving me was Michael Chertoff, New Jersey's US attorney at the time (who would later be appointed by President George W. Bush to head the Justice Department's Criminal Division and after that, as Secretary of Homeland Security).

As we all stood in the judge's chambers, the court order that I was now working for the government as a confidential informant, plus my plea agreement, was officially sealed and put away—for ninety-nine years.

After that, strange and wonderful things began happening.

Like . . . oh, remember all that money I ran away with that everyone was screaming about while I was in South Africa? I was under

FBI protection now and an important informant. There was no need to bother about such details. I wasn't supposed to tell anyone about my surprising turncoat of events, but I had to rub it in my father's face over dinner that night.

"Dad, looks like you were wrong," I said, sitting across from him at the same old kitchen table. "Looks like I'll be here for a while and I won't be going to jail for the rest of my life after all, seeing as I'm now a special informant *working for the FBI.*"

My father looked like he was going to choke on his meat loaf.

"So you talked your way out of another jam once again," he said, with a scowl.

Deep down inside, I think he was impressed. And maybe even a little bit jealous. But there was no way he'd ever admit either.

———————

My special informant training started a few days after my fortieth birthday in February 1993, at the FBI Academy near Quantico, Virginia, population 480.

It was a huge complex hidden away on 385 acres of woodland and monitored like the Pentagon. The complex housed different kinds of schools—CIA school, DEA school, and (added after I got there) Homeland Security school. If you attempt to fly a plane or anything near it, you'd be shot down.

"You're already dangerous smart," Harry said, before sending me off for training, "and now we're going to make you worse."

I slept in a little dorm room on site and took classes all day. The instructors were FBI agents at the top of their fields, teaching us about martial arts, government law, racketeering law, computer technology, and how to use an F-Bird—a Federal Bureau Investigative Recording Device.

One week a guy came in to teach us how to handle covert instruments; another week it was weapons. I learned how to shoot and discovered I was an unbelievable marksman. Every day, a new guy came in who was an expert at something else. The curriculum was so organized and the teachers so smart, it was like an army for geniuses—and I loved it. I was good at it. I thrived there.

One of my favorite classes was how to escape potential deadly encounters. First tip: never get into a car if a guy is sitting in the driver's seat and another guy is in the back seat.

"It's a setup," the teacher said. "Remember in *The Godfather* when Carlo gets in the car and Clemenza's in the back and he garrotes him around the neck with a wire cord and Carlo kicks at the front windshield until he's dead? Like that."

If you're sitting at a table and someone goes for their gun, but you forgot to hide a knife in your sock, "What do you do?" the teacher asked the room of thirty students. He had set up mock scenarios that mimicked diners, coffee shops, and the inside of cars so we could act everything out.

"Hopefully you thought to order a steak for lunch, because now you have the big steak knife. You grab it and stick it in their eye," he said, going through the motions. "Their mission is to hurt or kill you, so you have to hurt or kill them first."

The teacher asked me to come up to the front of the class and sit across from him to help illustrate the lesson.

"Okay, Mr. Giacomaro, I'm going to go for my gun and I want you to . . ."

In one swift move I grabbed a plastic knife off the table, lunged my entire body across it, knocked the teacher off his chair, and pretended to stab him repeatedly in the neck.

"Good, good!" he told the class, red-faced, as he got up off the floor and regained composure. He was impressed.

"As you can see, Mr. Giacomaro stabbed me in the side of my neck to hit the jugular! Very smart! The eye, the neck, the cheek. Don't go for the body or the chest because you have to go through clothes. *Always try to hit the skin.* Stick a knife in their hand like when Luca Brasi gets it in the bar in *The Godfather*."

Not surprisingly, I was adept at tactical and situational awareness and escape. The instructors taught us how to read the room and move fast, and I excelled at watching people's eyes to recognize the fraction of a second before they went for their gun. The eyes will always tell you what the person is going to do, where they are going to go. And they'll blink first, so you have a split second to make your move. All my years trying to guess when my father was about to hit me trained me for this one.

Every day I sat in class, I looked around in amazement. *This is fucking fantastic. I don't believe where the fuck I am. How did I pull this off?*

When I left the compound eleven weeks later I was a fully trained government informant. They even gave me my own code name: Aquamarine. They should have just outfitted me in a white cowboy hat and white steed and stamped on my hat: "Good Guy."

Back at the office in West Paterson, Harry explained the power of my new alias.

"If you ever have a problem," he said, "you can call the office twenty-four–seven and say, 'Aquamarine down,' and we'll come running to help you."

In a matter of months, I'd gone from being hunted by the FBI to being their newest ace in the hole, their tactical maneuver guy on the street against the bad guys.

"You were a weapon before," said Harry, as he poured us a cup of that shitty coffee, "but now the difference is you're *our* weapon."

I was a hunk of meat that was stamped "USDA approved." My ass now had "Department of Justice" tattooed on it, and that made me laugh.

All those years I dodged being a made guy in the mob and the joke was on me: I was now a made guy for the FBI. It wasn't so different.

"So Harry," I asked, trying to sound nonchalant, "just out of curiosity, how long am I going to be your weapon?"

Harry gave me his serious face.

"Forever."

CHAPTER 15

A LICENSE TO STEAL

It was a sweetheart setup—I had the protection of the FBI as I broke the law.

When I got back to Jersey in May of 1993, Harry gave me my official assignment: "Get yourself back on the street," he said, "and be a bad guy."

That was easy, no training required there. He and Newark's assistant US attorney, José "Joe" Sierra, had only two caveats before I headed out to, basically, be myself. Seeing as I'd just demolished the trucking industry and ripped if off by $2 billion, "it would be good if you don't go into trucking right now," said Joe.

"And," Harry added, "don't *kill* anybody."

Got it. No trucking, no murder; I could do that. Anything else, I took their conversation to mean, was fair game. *We won't look, just don't get caught.*

So I went back to my old ways and started a new company, Cambridge Investment Corp.—taking the name from an area in London where Kate and I used to walk south of Hyde Park. I convinced a businessman I knew, David Lardier, to be "acting" boss and put the company in his name while I took the title of chairman. I assured him that because of my sealed plea agreement, no potential investors would ever know I was a convicted felon. But because I was still awaiting sentencing, it was better I stayed a bit under the radar.

Still, I ran the meetings, made the decisions, and everyone reported to me and called me "Boss." Failure to disclose a de facto ownership was fraud, I knew. But Harry and Joe never said anything about not committing fraud. We found office space in Wayne, sandwiched between a strip joint and the Department of Motor Vehicles.

For two years, Cambridge would be the umbrella for a number of companies I'd acquire involving cars, software, buses, couriers, funeral homes, and hotels. If there was a business I thought I could make a lot of money from or steal a lot of money from, I took it.

I was embarking on a double life, like a secret agent, and to keep my lives straight and worlds separate I bought three cell phones—two Motorola 1993 flip phones, one for my businesses and one for personal; and a nonflip Unisonic "Bat Phone" for my FBI calls. I Scotch-taped little labels on the back of each so I wouldn't mix them up.

One of the first companies I bought was a group of funeral homes from a nice middle-aged couple, Richard and Alida Quirk, in Bergen County. When I say "bought," I don't mean I actually paid for it. In fact, I convinced them to give *me* money—just like I'd seen Enzo do with Alberto Lido.

The Quirks' company was in financial trouble, and I was like a shark spying a wounded fish and going in for the kill. I went to meet them in my new Mercedes, designer suit, and Rolex to tell them that they'd be rich beyond their wildest dreams if they'd follow my instruction: invest $1 million in Cambridge and sell me their funeral homes using a $3 million promissory note. Not only would they get their $3 million owed plus $1 million invested back but they'd make another $20 million from their investment in Cambridge that first year!

"We're going to make a *lot* of money together," I promised. "You're going to get money from all my big deals!"

Promising people everything and seeing their eyes light up never got old for me. I loved a fresh, new conquest, when nothing bad had happened yet—like the honeymoon phase of a new romance.

I took over the funeral homes and proceeded to immediately loot them the usual way, by not paying the bills and stealing the receivables. That always takes a few months to do, so I had a lot of wakes and funerals to contend with in the meantime—which was another way I made money. Those caskets cost up to $10,000 each; why not reuse them and pocket the money each time someone bought a new one? It only made sense.

I showed the corpses in their caskets at the wakes and at the cemetery, even going so far as to lower them into the ground at the cemetery. But after everyone left the grave site, we'd take the embalmed bodies and caskets back to the funeral home, stow the bodies in cardboard boxes in the garage, and recycle the casket for the next dead guy.

Bad, I know. Crossing-the-line bad. Sacrilege bad. But they told me to go out there and be a Bad Guy, so I was.

We were supposed to bury or cremate the stowed bodies, but we fell behind. After a few months we had at least sixty embalmed bodies stacked up on top of each other in piles until one garage was completely filled, so we had begun using our second garage for the bodies.

I didn't know that when I took Brenda there one afternoon for a quickie, after-lunch blow job. I'd spotted Brenda's great ass in a store months earlier and hired her, purely based on her magnificent tush. One day after a boozy lunch we returned to the funeral home to fool around and I backed into the second garage.

Cruuuunch!!! It was the sound of bones smashing under my Mercedes tires.

I got out of the car to find I'd run over at least twenty bodies— broken bones, scattered limbs, and busted up cardboard was everywhere. It looked odd with no blood, like someone had committed a mass murder in a wax museum. *Way to spoil the mood*, I thought. I looked over at Brenda who was so drunk she didn't even notice and was busy unhooking her bra. *Maybe not so spoiled.*

I whipped out one of my Motorola flips.

"Rob! I ran over all our dead clients! Call up the crematory people and tell them to get a U-Haul over here to load up the bodies and take them away!"

Harry said not to kill anyone; he didn't say anything about *after* they were dead.

But I do want to point out that I stuck to the thou-shalt-not-kill commandment, as promised. During my first year back, I heard from my on-the-lam girlfriend, Kate Davies. She tracked me down at my mother's and came to see me with her new, young, rich boyfriend in tow. He apparently had a problem. Kate's boy toy was one of the heirs to a European shipping conglomerate, and he wanted me to make his sister disappear so he could inherit all the family money.

"Kate, I can't help," I told her. I wasn't sure if the boyfriend was kidding or not.

I felt bad. She helped me when I needed to get out of the country, and I'd dumped her in London. I made a referral—it was the least I could do.

With the $1 million from the Quirks, I paid cash to buy a Porsche-Audi dealership and convinced Freddy Minatola, my Cadillac guy for fifteen years now, to leave his longtime sales job and be my general manager at Somerset Hills Audi.

This is how it worked: Volkswagen Credit gave us cars on credit, we sold them, and they trusted us to tell them how many we sold and give them their share of the money. So if they gave us one hundred cars in one month worth $50,000 each, that's $5 million credit. At the end of each month they sent an auditor to pick up the inventory information, and we reconciled how much we owed them and paid up.

Freddy was so good at selling cars that we quickly went from selling a hundred a month to selling seven hundred per month. And because I knew trucking people who loved a good kickback, I was able to bring in imported Audis on tractor-trailers from all over the country that other dealerships in the area didn't sell.

Three months was all it took for us to become the largest Audi dealership in the country. I'd already been stealing for two of those three months.

The auditor who did the inventory once a month did all the figures and paperwork manually because we didn't have computer systems yet. As our sales doubled, then quadrupled, it got harder for him to tabulate everything. It got especially more difficult after Freddy took him out to bars and got him shitfaced. That guy returned back to the lot so toasted, he could barely see straight, never mind count cars or numbers. So he signed off on whatever Freddy wrote down. Within those first three months, I'd taken $5 million. We also had used cars that came in each week from customers who traded up, cars we were supposed to return to Volkswagen. Instead, Freddy sold them and brought me the cash—I made at least $100,000 per week that way, too.

By month four, Volkswagen Credit was onto us. The hapless auditor came in with his boss and went through all the numbers. The next day, they closed down our dealership. I got a call from Harry on the Bat Phone and he was furious. They had to investigate me now, he said, and he had to recuse himself and put another agent in charge, a friend of his.

I met them both in Harry's office a few days later and explained in a fifteen-minute monologue exactly what happened, the god's honest truth this time.

"Listen," I said, "I hired my friend, Freddy Minatola. He used to work at Brogan Cadillac, see. But listen, Freddy does a lot of drugs and he gets all fucked up and I think he took a lot of the money because he's got his bad drug habit, you know? I don't know what happened exactly. That fucker, Freddy. I tried to help him with his problems and he fucked me over real good, that motherfucker Freddy!"

I looked over at Harry, who was stone-faced. His agent friend had fallen asleep in his chair and started to snore. They didn't give a fuck, it was all for show. A few days later Harry called again.

"The agent said there's nothing to investigate," he said. "Case closed."

I slowly closed the Bat Phone with a smile. This would be the first of many FBI cover-ups of my illegal actions, and it was a beautiful thing to behold. There was no way they were gonna get rid of me on account of a few million dollars—they trained me and needed me! It was a sweetheart setup—I had the protection of the FBI as I broke the law. You might even say I had a license to steal.

But, there was the matter of what I owed the FBI in return. "Quid pro quo, Clarice," as Hannibal Lecter says.

After I returned from Virginia I made one attempt to bring the FBI recorded intel on the mob. After a failed try to sew a recording device into my suitcase, the tech people gave me a one-inch-by-one-inch self-transcribing F-Bird that could record for eight hours. I put it in the breast pocket of my suit and went to a confidential meeting with some mob guys at a social club in Manhattan. I was shitting bricks the entire time, so worried someone would frisk me. When we checked the recording the next day, it was all muffled and unusable.

"Harry, I'm never doing that again," I insisted. "This thing is going to get me killed."

Harry agreed. And soon, he didn't even need me to bring in that kind of intel anymore. New developments had occurred on the Camino front that completely changed my assignment. Camino's lawyers had successfully appealed his 1991 verdicts and now he was headed back to Philly for a new trial facing those same charges. Added to that, the Feds brought new charges against him for crimes committed in New Jersey and he was going to have a whole separate trial for that in Newark.

Which meant that Harry would now spend the next two to three years preparing for the Newark trial because it was such a massive case involving so much money—$3 billion. Camino had the best lawyers in the country, and they planned to shove the US attorney's dick in his mouth, but Harry wasn't about to let that happen. He knew that if he could nail Enzo's ass to the wall, it would make him a rock star at the FBI.

And he had just the person to help him do it—his ace in the hole, me.

Harry and Joe needed to absorb every bit of detail and data I had in my brain about Camino as if it were their own.

Now it was my turn to train *them*.

I started meeting Harry and Joe twice a month at the FBI office in West Paterson or at Joe's office in Newark. Within the first few days I'd already memorized the secret push-button front-door codes for both buildings after deciphering the tones while listening to Harry and Joe punch them in.

At our meetings, I taught them all about the creative, inner workings of trucking fraud that Camino, Barnetas, Kapralos, and I employed. As I talked, Harry sat mesmerized. They'd been investigating the looting of trucking companies for years and couldn't figure out the machinations. Now I was giving him the combination to unlock it.

"But I couldn't find the trail of money. How were they able to take so much cash out?" Harry asked.

"Truck stops," I said. "They used truck stops to launder it."

"How?"

"They'd write checks to different truck stops all over New Jersey that were cooperating, and the truckers would take in the checks and get cash from the cashiers."

"Smart," Harry said, nodding. "The truck stops don't need to report the checks they cash."

"Right," I said. "And the truckers were already cashing their pay-checks at these truck stops all the time anyway when they stopped for fuel on the road. It was a perfect way to do it because the check-cashing agencies would also get a big fee for cashing the checks, much more so than the banks. So everybody was getting something."

"And the cashiers just agreed?"

"They were taking orders from their bosses. They were told to just cash the checks."

"They would have enough money?"

"They were prepared. Tommy Barnetas would walk into a truck stop with $20,000 to $30,000 worth of checks every day and cash them. It was like a bank. They were cashing up to $100,000 to $200,000 a day in total using various truck stops."

Harry was floored. And hungry for more information as I doled it out to him. In exchange he kept FBI higher-ups off my back about not bringing in new mob info. Not only was I indispensable for the Camino trial, he told them, but I could be essential for ongoing help with other cases other agents couldn't crack.

"The guy has an accounting background and he's fucking brilliant," Harry told the US attorney. "He can look at paperwork and follow the trail of money faster and better than anyone we got."

Harry already had a notch on his belt for bringing me in. Sharing me with others gave him another.

They put me in a little room in the West Paterson office where, once a week, agents hoisted stacks of "live" files involving corporate mail fraud, money laundering, drug running, and accounting onto my desk. I reviewed cases on white-collar criminals moving money all over the world and politicians in trouble—well-known mayors, senators, and governors.

"What do you think?" the agents would ask. "How do I prosecute them?"

I'd show them the trails of money. Look here and look here, I'd say. I saw the numbers the same way I saw the squares and pieces on a chessboard: as a whole story all at once, from beginning to end, and I instinctively knew all the moves and motives in between.

During these years it didn't escape my notice once again that I was being followed. But the question this time was by whom?

Kapralos and Barnetas were by now in prison after I'd helped Harry with their cases, but Camino was out on bail awaiting his new trials, so he was around and I'm sure worried I was talking. And if anyone in the mob heard I was an informant, they'd want to make sure I kept my mouth shut about them, too. And lastly, the FBI could be following me to keep tabs on whom I was seeing and what I was up to. It was enough to make a guy paranoid.

I was watching O. J. Simpson's white Ford Bronco chase live on TV at the Cambridge office on a Friday in June 1994 when Freddy came rushing in, panicked.

"There are four agents in two cars in our parking lot watching the building!"

Fuck. Enzo sent guys to clip me. Yeah, I was paranoid. Freddy, Dave, and I went outside to beat the shit out of them. I forgot about calling the Fed hotline and telling them, "Aquamarine down!"

"Who the fuck are youse?" I asked, banging on one of the cars and causing a commotion. Two big guys looking really pissed off got out and slipped their hands under their jackets. My expert, Quantico-trained spatial awareness went into high gear; they were going for their guns. Instead, they pulled out government badges. *Oh, shit.*

"Who the fuck are *we*?" asked one of the guys. "Who the fuck are *you*!"

They were US treasury agents staking out the strip joint next door, waiting for Russian mob guys to show up. Not only had we blown their cover, we'd blown months of man-hours and thousands of dollars of investigative work. I should have noticed their Chevy

Impalas and casual khakis! Did these guys all shop at the same shopping mall outlet?

I explained to the agents who I was and gave them Harry's name to verify me and they let us go. After they left, Freddy and Dave and I went into the strip club to get drunk and watch naked girls. We needed to de-stress. And Dave wanted to see what Russian mob guys looked like.

The next day, I was summoned to Joe's office so he and Harry could ream me out.

"You blow their cover," Joe yelled, "and then you go into the strip club they were staking out and get smashed? Are you kidding me? What the hell is wrong with you?!"

Seems there was a Treasury guy inside, too, who ratted me out.

"Hey, it was youse guys who trained me to keep my antennae up," I yelled back, "and now you're mad 'cause I was trying to protect myself? I thought those guys were sent to clip me!"

Harry sighed. He knew I was right. He didn't want anything bad to happen to me, either. Which is why the one time I did call in my emergency code name, Harry came running.

In the fall of 1994, just before Whitey Bulger fled Boston and went on the lam, Tina got a warning in the mail for me. It was a paperback book on the Philly mob and inside some words were underlined in pen:

Omertà

Tyrone DiNettis

And in the margin, a handwritten note:

Tommy better keep his mouth shut.

She brought the book to my office, and I called FBI headquarters right away: "Aquamarine. I got a problem."

Harry showed up fast with another agent to make sure I was okay and they carefully put the book into a plastic bag and took it back to headquarters for fingerprinting. If something were to happen to me it was evidence of a threat, he said. DiNettis was one of Camino's right-hand guys, you may remember, and both were associated with the Nicky Scarfo crew in Philly.

Not long after Tina got the book delivery, one of Scarfo's capos, John Stanfa, was indicted for conspiracy to commit murder. Among other charges, he'd arranged for the drive-by shooting of Joseph "Skinny Joey" Merlino a year or two earlier. Merlino was about to become the new boss of the Philly crime family when the attempted assassination took place—from a *moving white van on a bridge*. Which confirmed my gut suspicion a decade earlier that it was the Nicky Scarfo crew who tried to kill me when I went into the Passaic River.

Tina was worried about me, warning me that treating the mob and the FBI like a human chess game would lead to a bad end.

"Sooner or later, Tommy, if you play with fire," she said, "you're going to get burned."

It was a lesson I still hadn't learned in so many areas of my life— business, money, drugs, and with women, too.

I told myself maybe Tina was jealous because I'd dumped her and was about to marry another woman. Before I left Detroit and went on the lam a few years earlier, I met a gorgeous twenty-year-old blonde, Dorian Hayes. She was one of those rosy-cheeked, Michigan State college girls I told you about, working as a cocktail waitress in a strip club called The Landing Strip in Romulus, Michigan. I was sitting at a table getting all fucked up when she slithered past in a little bikini, balancing a tray on her arm. Just like when I met Debbie, I reached out and grabbed Dorian by one of the strings and pulled her in.

"Sit down here with me," I said to her, putting her onto my lap. "You're not going anywhere. You're mine now."

Dorian and I lost touch while I was in South Africa, but when I was in Virginia getting trained, she tracked me down at my mother's address (everyone seemed to find me there) and sent a perfumed love note for me to my lawyer's office in DC. When I got out of training, I invited her to Jersey for a visit and she never left.

We had a lavish wedding in September 1994 in Dearborn, Michigan. Did I love her? What did I fucking know about love—nothing. She was young and beautiful, and so I married her. I was stinking rich again and chartered a jet to fly everyone in and put them up in suites at the Ritz Carlton—my parents, the Quirks, David Lardier, Freddy Minatola—the whole cast of characters came for the big event, everyone except Lauren.

Now seventeen, there was only a five- or six-year age gap between the two, her and Dorian, and they were like siblings vying for my affection and attention. I couldn't blame Lauren. She'd lost a year with her father when I was in South Africa and was desperate to make up time with me.

Lauren as a teenager, around the time I married Dorian

"Baby, we'll have plenty of time together," I promised. "You'll see."

I think it broke her heart a bit when I announced Dorian and I were engaged. She had been hoping I'd get back together with Debbie and refused to come to the wedding. I wish I had known then how to talk with her about it, but I didn't. I wish I had known how to assure her that no one could or would ever replace her in my heart.

In the summer of 1995 our daughter Alison was born. Once again, I was in the delivery room and I kissed her forehead and followed her as the nurses took prints of her hands and feet, never taking my eyes off her. Lauren loved little Alison and the feeling was mutual, and that love became a bonding thread for Lauren and Dorian as well.

That year, Cambridge was finally going to shit after I looted and busted too many companies. But I didn't care, because I always had another great idea up my sleeve.

Instead of going into trucking, I was going to try my hand in the courier business. I'd simply do there what I'd done in trucking—consolidate and roll up dozens of companies, which had never been done before in the courier business. Business was business, it didn't matter what the product was, it was all the same.

I was told by a friend to get in touch with New Jersey businessman Pauly Russo—aka "Fat Pauly"—because he could open up the doors for me in the courier business. He was a successful entrepreneur who owned one of the biggest privately held courier companies in the country. For my genius deal to work, I needed Fat Pauly's help to lure the others. Over lunch, I explained the millions we could make if he pounded the drum and led the way for us.

He was a short, round man with twinkling eyes and a smile as honest as the day. He was also straight as an arrow and wary to work with me at first, until I laid out the numbers in front of him.

"It's a function of economics," I told Fat Pauly. "There's no way this deal won't work. It's mathematically impossible."

It took a few months to convince the other fifteen companies to join us and another year to put the deal together on paper, but by November 1995 we were doing an initial public offering on the stock exchange. I was home making potato leek soup when I got the call from one of my crew:

"Tom, we pulled it off! We just raised $250 million in one hour on NASDAQ!"

The courier deal was one of Cambridge's biggest bona fide success stories against the other looting and stealing ones. Fat Pauly made a cool $20 million profit, I made $25 million, and the owners of the other companies were deliriously happy because I sold them for ten times what they were worth and now they were stinking rich, too.

I had a knack for selling, for putting deals together, ever since I was a kid. I just didn't know how to do it without the stealing part; they were two sides of the same coin to me, two sides of myself that I couldn't reconcile.

The following year, Harry had his own long-awaited success that he'd worked so hard for. In the fall of 1996 it was showtime for Harry and Enzo Camino in court. Harry got up on the stand and repeated what I'd taught and trained him to say perfectly. After a grueling six-week trial, the jury convicted Camino of all fifty-four counts of conspiracy, money-laundering, and embezzlement in his indictment.

Harry was a star at the FBI, and they promoted him to a top position at the main office in Newark. I had helped him nab the bad guy.

Over the years people have called me a career maker or a career breaker, depending on which side of the coin you got from me when you flipped it.

That year, I was a career maker for Harry.

The breaking was yet to come.

CHAPTER 16

TWO (OTHER) NICKYS AND A FUNERAL

I was a numbers guy and I was never wrong about them or this:
companies could be bought and sold and so could people . . .

Even on his deathbed, my father was a monster.

He was diagnosed with colon cancer around the time of my wedding to Dorian, and during his final months, I set up twenty-four-hour hospice care in the Gerhardt house next door. I bought it after Midge died a few years earlier to keep my parents away from each other and more importantly, to lessen the amount my mother got hit.

Midge lived a long time after Charlie died, well into her nineties. She eventually went into a nursing home for her final years and my mother was the only one to visit her.

"They're not taking proper care of her," she told me one day. "It's horrible."

This was my chance, I realized, to make up for the heartless way I treated Charlie before he passed away. I drove to the nursing home in

Passaic and found Midge drugged and parked in a wheelchair in the hallway with a row of other sickly patients, sitting in her own shit.

"Take me to the doctor in charge," I said to the head nurse. "NOW!"

I had to hold myself back from choking the guy as soon as I walked into his office. Let me cut to the chase: Midge was taken care of like a queen after my visit that day. And I hoped that for all the love Charlie and Midge had given me, this was giving just a little bit back.

Buying their house later and separating my parents was the best thing to ever happen to their long-suffering marriage. She was safer, and he watched TV all day in peace.

A week before my father died, I took Dorian—eight months pregnant at the time with baby number two—with me to my parents' home to say our goodbyes. He knew he was dying and I was hoping he might have a word of regret or apology or kindness for me— something, *anything*—before it was too late. It was our last chance.

We stood at his bedside in the living room where he was hooked up to a bunch of tubes and oxygen.

"Dad, we're going to name our son after you," I told him. He glared at me and hissed, then looked at Dorian.

"Get away from him . . . as quickly as you can," he said, laboring for breath. "He's . . . no good. He's . . . *the devil*."

Those were pretty much my father's last words. He died in September 1996, one month before his namesake, baby Joey, was born. He left this world hating and abusing his own son until the end, certain I was a failure and even worse—evil. I guess my full-moon Botswanan exorcism didn't take.

At his funeral, no one got up to speak about him. What could they say? Everyone knew he'd abused his family for years, and they were all glad the motherfucker was dead. As for me, I felt sick as I saw his coffin lowered into the ground. I both hated him and loved him, and I had no idea how to make sense of those conflicting feelings.

I spit on his grave.

The irony was that my father died believing I amounted to less than nothing. But that year, I was about to make the biggest, most lucrative deal of my career.

Cambridge went bankrupt after I looted the funeral homes and Audi dealership, but I immediately started a new investment company, Wellesley (another London street I used to frequent with Kate), and I took my cast of loyal and unusual suspects at Cambridge—David, Rob, and Freddy—with me.

My new brilliant idea? Garbage. Garbage!

What I did with the courier companies and trucking, I could do with garbage! It was a highly profitable industry already and my approach—packaging small companies together to sell to a larger, strategic partner that was already public—had never been done before, either. When you think about it, my entire life had been about doing things that had never been done before. I knew the deal would be a winner because my hands got itchy just thinking about it, and I could smell the stench of the Meadowlands dump. I took that as a good sign.

To pull off my deal, I was going to need more than my usual Golden Tongue touch. Garbage was even more mobbed up than trucking, and no company would consider cooperating with me unless I had the power of the mob behind me.

Fat Pauly—still flush from his $20 million windfall from the courier deal—was eager to help and make more money, so we met at the Tick Tock Diner to discuss it.

He knew the top two people in garbage in the Tri-state area: Bruno Paglia, also known as "the king of New York garbage," and Marco Benelli, also known as "the king of New Jersey garbage." Like me, they were both Genovese-associated, so we were already family. Both had sold their companies to a big conglomerate, so they couldn't be part of my deal. But they knew everybody who was anybody in the garbage industry and would talk me up to all of them for a price.

Before we even did that, though, I had to get approval from the big, *big* boss of all of us.

In the winter of 1996, I made my way down a dark staircase to the basement of Angelo's of Mulberry Street in Little Italy to "go to the well." I went to meet with Vincent "The Chin" Gigante—the head of the Genovese crime family and capo of all five New York crime families.

It was months before the mob boss's dramatic trial the following summer in which he'd be convicted of racketeering and conspiracy and later sentenced to twelve years in federal prison. With a waiter standing lookout at the top of the stairs, he and I met in the bathroom, then stepped into a little "office" down the hall. I wasn't nervous. His sons, Sal and Andrew (whom I met at A-Z Passage with Alberto Lido), already told him I was one of the family's biggest earners who could make him a lot of kickback dough with this garbage deal.

He wore regular street clothes—not the bathrobe and pajamas tourists hoped to catch a glimpse of when he did his "crazy" act in the West Village—a performance he kept up for years to appear unfit for trial and stay out of prison. Our meeting lasted just a few minutes; we didn't even sit down.

"How you doin'? I'm Tom," I said, and we did the mob-guy hug.

"I heard all about you," he whispered.

He was known for his whisper, and I found out later that he talked like that all the time in case anyone around him wore a wire, or in case a place was bugged. We didn't intend to talk much, anyway. I was there so he could eyeball me. And so he could tell me that if I didn't kick back to him, they'd fucking kill me.

"Make sure you give my sons the envelopes. Don't make us come and look for you."

"You'll be well taken care of," I promised.

"That's good, Tom," he said. "You go ahead and do this thing and good luck. You got my blessing to go forward with the garbage deal. Make sure you do the right thing."

It was the same thing Hoffa said to me once. With The Chin's support, no one could stop me; I would turn garbage into gold.

Wellesley's first office was in one of the Quirks' defunct funeral homes in Bergenfield. I'd been stringing the Quirks along for a few years at this point, and they were still waiting for their money to come in. They lost big money in the Cambridge collapse and took back their funeral homes after that. But I was able to convince them to invest half a million in Wellesley and loan me one of the funeral homes to use as an office.

How did I convince them to invest *again*?

Easy. I didn't *own* Cambridge, so it wasn't my fault they lost money, I told them. I wasn't the official owner, David Lardier was.

"David did it. David fucked it all up," I explained, as we sat in the parlor of one of the funeral homes. I could smell traces of formaldehyde in the air. "I was busy doing the courier deal and I put David in charge of the funeral homes."

Harry had kept the Feds from investigating the downfalls of both the Audi dealership and the funeral homes, but that didn't stop the Quirks or the Volkswagen Group from filing a lawsuit against David. I thought it best not to mention that David was now working with me at Wellesley, too. Because he took the fall, I put David on the payroll and gave him a company BMW for his troubles, then kept him out of sight.

Meanwhile, I took the Quirks out for expensive dinners at Valentino's restaurant and got them to invest another half a million into Wellesley, and pledge more as collateral on loans to the company.

"You're gonna make millions of dollars with the new deal," I promised. "Come on over to this deal over here. I'll get back all your money—and more. You can be fifty percent owners."

I did the numbers for them with pen and paper right there at the dinner table, as the waiter poured champagne, and handed them the pages.

"When we take it public"—I pointed to my scribbles—"you'll make *$27 million.*"

Do ya understand yet? I break into people's lives, that's what I do.

The official owner and president of Wellesley was Keith Moody, a former investment banker at Smith Barney and a neighbor of mine at the townhouse complex where Dorian and I lived. His best qualification for the job? He came with built-in investors, which was beautiful.

For chief financial officer, I recruited my cousin Anthony Bianco—the nerdy, smart bookworm I used to play with as a kid. He was now a CFO at Panasonic in Secaucus. Like my father and me, Anthony was a crackerjack with numbers and had it in his DNA. He had a double master's degree in finance from Fairleigh Dickinson University. Anthony had a very specialized role in the company; I needed him to do the books and checks exactly as I told him to. In other words, I needed someone I could trust to launder money out of the country for me, like Maggie had done years earlier. Every money guy needs another money guy like that.

Our managing director was Mario Sisco, and to handle our insurance, we got Luca Bastone, the son of underboss Pasquale "The Pipe" Bastone, who was in prison at the time. Luca called his father in prison to get dad's approval before joining us. Luca had an insurance agency, and his clients included all the garbage companies in New York. How'd he get them? The Pipe put pressure on everyone. I was about to use that same tactic.

At Wellesley, I was the "consultant." I lined up all the good people with honest faces and squeaky-clean reputations, and I stood behind them, a convicted felon, with the power of the mob behind me.

———

As soon as I had my key infrastructure in place, I got to work bringing in investors and putting together the garbage deal. Our qualifications to be an investor? You had to have a pulse. Fat Pauly was my

biggest cheerleader, telling everyone about the $250 million I'd mas-
terminded with the courier companies and the $20 million he made.
He was the first to invest a few million into Wellesley and after his
lead, the other courier guys from our previous deal followed.

Now I had to convince dozens of private garbage companies to
sign "notes of intent" so I could sell them to a bigger, public company.

Fat Pauly, Marco, Bruno, and I started meeting up with garbage
guys for dinners to get them excited and convince them to cooperate.
We ate too much, drank too much, yelled across the table, and shoved
each other around. And by the end of the dinners, they usually said
yes. If it wasn't the money that convinced them, it was something
else: one look at Marco and Brunou at the table and they knew I was
mobbed up the ass. The understanding was: sell me your company or
I'm gonna fucking break your fucking legs.

When some garbage guys still hesitated to take our meeting or
do our deal, I brought in guys—the Two Nickys—who had ways of
making them say yes.

Nicolas Ola was the son of a high-ranking Colombo underboss,
and Nicolas Calo was the son of a high-ranking Gambino underboss (and had recently worked as bodyguard for a major mob boss). I
nicknamed them Big Nick and Nicky Glasses, respectively.

I met Big Nick after Dorian found a beautiful stone house for us
in Saddle River, one of the wealthiest suburbs in New Jersey. When
the owner and builder came to meet me at my funeral home office,
I didn't recognize the name at first. I hadn't had many dealings with
the Colombo family. His father had gotten out of prison while I was
in Quantico at the FBI Academy.

Big Nick was a good-looking monster of a guy—about 6'7" with
shoulders like a linebacker.

"How much do you want for the house?" I asked.

"Two point five million."

I could have taken that out of the petty cash.

"I ain't got it," I told him. "But here's what I do got—$50,000. I want to buy your house but I won't have the money for another six months, until I do my big deal. I want to give you $50,000 now to hold it for me."

His face fell. "You want me to take my $2.5 million house off the market for fifty grand?"

"Yeah," I said. "And while you're at it, go check around and see who I am. I don't know you from shit."

He looked surprised. "I'm also in the trucking business," he added calmly. "And I do business in the garment center."

That was all I needed to know to tell me he was plugged in with the Colombos. Big Nick returned the next day to tell me I had a deal.

"My father asked around about you," he said, "and he was told 'Giacomaro's mobbed up and he's got the right people behind him. But he's more than that. He's a *sophisticated thief*. Give him the house.'"

The Saddle River house I bought from Big Nick

I liked the big lug right away. Three days later he brought around his business partner, Nicky Calo, who was just as big. He wore dark shades all the time, rarely talked, and even if you were standing close to him and could see his eyes, he looked right through you.

The Two Nickys were good enforcers when I needed to lean on someone. They were calm on the outside and vicious on the inside. I took them with me to Valentino's the time I had to convince two brothers who did garbage in Jersey to sell us their company. We were in a private dining room upstairs, and the brothers were being stubborn.

"It's a family business, you understand," said one.

"This deal really isn't for us," said the other.

"Listen to me," I told them. "One way or another, you're going over the goal line with us. Maybe it's with a broken leg. Maybe it's in a body bag. But either way, you're in the banana boat."

Without saying a word, one of the Nickys (does it really matter which?) grabbed one of the brothers and dragged him to the fire escape door. It was a winter morning after a heavy snowfall, so to get the door open he had to kick it against a two-foot snowdrift on the other side. Once he got the door open wide enough, he threw the brother out the door and down the metal staircase. We heard him bounce against the steps and hit bottom. Nicky slammed the door shut and came back to the table.

"Now," I said to the other brother, who was frozen in his chair, "are you gonna sign the letter of intent or what?"

"Absolutely," he said. "And if my brother is still alive out there, he'll sign, too."

I could pretty much do anything I wanted and get away with it.

After Harry got promoted following his Camino-trial success, the FBI gave him a new, huge corner office with a view in Newark and made him the head of a new division they would develop especially for him. He was a big shot now.

But he was still my official "handler"—I was the only case that he kept. So any time the US Attorney's Office asked about me, which wasn't often, they reached out to him for an update.

"He's still feeding me ongoing information," he'd tell them, buying me another year of time. I was supposed to get sentenced for the pension fund money after the Camino trial was over, but I completely fell through the cracks. In the process of covering for me in furtherance of the greater good (my feeding them information), what happened next was against all the ethical rules: Harry and I became friends.

Once a month we'd meet at his new office and walk to a nearby Spanish restaurant for lunch—always making sure he paid for his and I paid for mine, so we followed at least one rule. Harry wouldn't even take a bottle of water from me.

"I want you to be alert, Tom," he said, in one of our first post-trial lunches. "Be vigilant. Enzo's been convicted now—they're all going to point the finger at you. He might come after you, or send someone to."

I didn't tell Harry that some of the connected garbage guys were so nervous about me that they were frisking me before meetings to check for a wire. One time I had to take my pants down in the bathroom to prove I wasn't hiding a gun.

Harry was worried about me; he liked me. After we got shoptalk out of the way, we talked about our families, history, politics, and his hopes for the future. I'm sure he was the one who pulled a few strings for me to keep my eleven handguns (under Dorian's name) and cases of double clips of ammunition at the house. I made her buy them soon after we got married even though a convicted felon out on a plea agreement was not supposed to have them. But Harry understood. He knew what I was doing made me a target and was very dangerous, so he wanted me to protect myself.

Harry was biding his time and running the clock until he reached twenty years with the Feds and could retire with a high-level pension for the rest of his life. I had an ulterior motive, of course. I didn't want him to retire at all.

"Harry, I want you to be my Director of Security and Human Resources at Wellesley," I told him. "I'll start you at $150,000 a year salary and a new Porsche Boxster."

Every time I made my offer, he laughed. But he didn't say no.

Two of my loves—Lauren and one of my Bentleys, 1999

As my official handler still, Harry tried to keep me somewhat in line when and where he could. When I started living too lavishly again, I got an angry call from the US Attorney's Office, yelling about the pension fund money I still owed.

"Are you crazy!" they said. "You've got Bentleys in your driveway, and the pension fund people are waiting for their money back!"

Harry had to talk me into giving the money back. I had tens of millions of dollars in the bank, but it hurt me to part with one penny of it. We set up monthly payments of $88,000 for a year and as it turned out, returning that money didn't hurt as much as I thought it would; I took the money out of the Wellesley bank account.

———

By the end of 1998, as Harry was preparing to retire, my humungous garbage deal was ready to happen.

After two years of convincing, luring, threatening, and bribing, I rented the entire twenty-second floor at the Hilton in Bergenfield, New Jersey, at the end of November and gathered a group of fifteen garbage company owners. I had set up multibillion-dollar contract with the garbage conglomerate Allied Waste to buy a hundred smaller, private companies over the next year in groups of fifteen, and this would be my first group.

At the hotel I had fifteen rooms set up next to each other. In each sat the CEO, lawyers, and accountants of each company with pens in hands, waiting to sign contracts. Everyone would be signing all at once in what was called a "simultaneous closing"—kind of like an orgy where everyone climaxes at the same time, but more fun.

They were all ready and willing, pens poised, until Allied Waste found a contract problem an hour before our start time and we had to delay a day.

"No one is leaving this hotel!" I told them all, after gathering them in the hallway, "not even to go to fucking McDonald's! You're on lockdown!"

I couldn't risk anything happening to anyone, or someone changing his or her mind. I sent out my bodyguards to buy pajamas, toothpaste, whatever they needed to stay the night and got everyone rooms. One day led to a second, and a third, until finally the day arrived.

On December 4, 1998, each group returned to its appointed meeting room on the twenty-second floor, and I ran up and down the hallway with a clipboard, darting in and out of each room. I was like a doctor, running in and out of patients' rooms in a hospital. At this point, we were more like a loony bin.

One room had Mr. Rotundo and next to him was Mr. Appolito. Down the hall was Mr. Solano, then Mr. Pisanno. Next to him was Mr. Garofalo, Mr. Nicholas, Mr. Aiorielli. For hours I went in and out of the rooms, prepping everyone, until it was time to take the Allied Waste team around for the monumental signing of the contracts and shaking of the hands.

In one hour, we signed the fifteen contracts. The next day $100 million magically appeared in the Wellesley bank account— $25 million of it was all mine. It was like an injection of heroin into the bloodstream. And there was so much more to come.

It was cause for a celebration.

A week later I threw a massive party at the Stony Hill Inn with a twenty-one-piece orchestra, three hundred guests, and all the caviar, oysters, and champagne they could eat and drink. The party tab was $150,000, but to the victor go the spoils.

All the garbage company guys who'd done the deal were there, and so were the ones lined up for 1999. My Wellesley crew mixed it up with my mob crew, and even though it was against the rules, Harry was there. He was two weeks from retirement; what were the Feds gonna do, fire him?

Keith Moody gave a tipsy speech and thanked the garbage guys and me, his humble consultant: "To our special advisor, Tom Giacomaro!" he said, lifting his glass of champagne.

Everyone cheered as I lifted my glass and the band struck up one of my favorite non-Christmas Sinatra tunes—"I've Got the World on a String."

That's exactly how I felt. That December, I received two Christmas gifts I'd wanted all year. First was the genius deal I pulled off, which was going to make me rich beyond my sickest, most indulgent dreams and imagination.

And my second gift was Harry, who was across the room toasting me with his champagne flute in the air.

I was a numbers guy and I was never wrong about them or this: companies could be bought and sold and so could people, if the price was right. That month I hit the jackpot on both. I really did have the world on a string.

What could possibly go wrong?

CHAPTER 17

OTHER PEOPLE'S MONEY

On the driveway I lined up my symbols of success:
Rolls-Royces, Bentleys, Mercedes-Benzes, Ferraris,
and a new addition—a big black Hummer.

Everything was gold.

The interior of our new 8,000-square-foot house on Fox Hedge Road in Saddle River was bathed in $500,000 worth of twenty-four-carat gold-leaf paint on the moldings, in the wallpaper, and running up and down the spiral staircases. Even the carpet was gold. It was like living inside a fucking jewelry box.

I had ten people on staff—nannies, housekeepers, groundskeepers, and an official shoe wiper who handed visitors a pair of hospital booties to wear after taking their shoes to be cleaned and buffed. I had someone to do every little thing for us, except move the kitchen utensils, dishes, appliances, and expensive chef knives from our previous house. I personally hand-wrapped those and drove them to the new kitchen, where I carefully unwrapped and put them away in the organized way I required. None of my kids ever did a chore in their lives, not like me having to make my bed like a Marine. I gave the staff walkie-talkies so I could reach them immediately if I saw anything amiss. This wasn't a house; it was a gilded compound.

I had a putting green in the front yard and a 70,000-gallon swimming pool, more like a lake, in the back, filled with New York State spring well water and industrial-strength heaters to keep the temperature at ninety degrees Fahrenheit in December. Next to it was a pond filled with twelve Japanese koi at $3,000 per fish. On the driveway I lined up my symbols of success: Rolls-Royces, Bentleys, Mercedes-Benzes, Ferraris, and a new addition—a big black Hummer. Inside the perimeter of the wrought-iron fence that circled the five-acre lot, I ordered a tulip to be planted every three inches—*exactly.*

The backyard pond in Saddle River: $3,000 per fish

Then I bought the mansion next door, and then the one across the street—recently seized from a Colombian drug lord—and paid for both in cash. After that, I bought a mansion in Delray Beach in Florida. I just kept buying and buying, the bigger the shinier the more expensive, the better. Big Nick (whom I paid in full for his house six months after we shook on it) took care of all our house renovations, skimming a few million off the top for himself, as expected—as any mob guy would.

Baby Stephanie, my third with Dorian, was born in January of 1999 soon after we moved in, and I asked Big Nick to be godfather. That spring, 45,000 red and yellow tulips bloomed around us. Who knew garbage could smell so sweet?

Oh yeah, I was back. *Again.* Bigger, crazier, and richer than before. My need for other people's money was my sickness; stealing it was my cure.

Thanks to $200 million of investor money and Allied Waste deal money, my checkbook balance on an average day was anywhere from $600 to $800 million. Seeing those numbers in my bankbook made me feverish—I needed to spend it. So what if I was using other people's money or money I didn't have yet to bankroll my lavish life of luxury—I'd pay everyone back when the money came in later that year. Of course I would.

"Who makes all the money, Rob?" I'd ask my assistant.

"You do, Boss!"

"And who *spends* all the money, Rob?"

"*You* do, Boss!"

*Wearing my Wellesley jacket at the mansion
in Delray Beach, Florida*

Damn right. I moved Wellesley out of the funeral home and into a $5 million, 87,000-square-foot office in Montvale, where my weekly cost for upkeep was $1.2 million. I hired 160 new employees in the first three months and fed them well.

Every day I gave my staff free breakfast, lunch, and dinner from the gourmet kitchen. Fridays were extra special—that was "Mob Day" at Wellesley, inspired by Mr. Alex and his Friday "Police Day" lunches. On those days, I arrived at the office at 1 AM wearing my monogrammed TJG chef outfit and met Freddy there to open up the kitchen. The crew arrived close behind with the goods—tomatoes, corn on the cob, ground sirloin, basil, sausages, garlic, peppers, onions, fresh pasta, filet mignon, prime rib, turkey breasts—and we'd start chopping, peeling, marinating, simmering, and seasoning. Fat Pauly and The Nickys would arrive around 6 AM with fresh mozzarella and thirty loaves of Italian bread fresh from the oven and start on the pizzas. I had four Bakers Pride pizza ovens brought in special from the Bronx. Cooking dinner, whether it was on Sundays at home or Fridays at the office, was one of the few moments I felt a sense of family happiness—a leftover from my childhood.

Wayne, my newest muscle-bound driver-bodyguard, drank coffee and stood guard as we worked. A former Newark cop, Wayne was my kinda nuts and had a temper, a good combination for a bodyguard but not so much for a sous-chef. The one time I asked him to stir the sauce he told me to go fuck myself. Say it a second time, and I'd be forced to kill you with my best Suisin high-carbon-steel Japanese Gyutou chef's knife. And that would be a waste of a good knife.

By 10 AM, as the tables were being set to seat 150, I went out to the parking lot to inspect the company cars. I had an outside service come in once a week in panel vans to hand-wash them—thirty BMWs, thirty Mercedes-Benzes, thirty Lexuses, and ten Lincolns.

At noon, before we served, my kitchen help and I started on the Grey Goose vodka before the staff, cops, and mob guys arrived to eat— they came in from Staten Island, Brooklyn, NYC, and Connecticut.

The final touch was to outfit my guys in white chef jackets for serving. A few more shots of Grey Goose and we put on Sinatra over the sound system. The setup was *spectacular.*

By 3 PM everybody was stuffed and ripped-up drunk. The cafeteria turned into a social club with all different factions of the Gambinos, Genovese, and Colombos—many of them packing guns—playing poker and blackjack. The music turned from Sinatra to disco, and the pretty receptionists from upstairs danced on the tables. On a Friday afternoon, it was *the* party of the week to be at.

And you know who else was there on the sidelines, quietly watching the mob guys play poker and the pretty girls dance? Our Harry.

As soon as he retired from the FBI, he got permission to join me at Wellesley as my Director of Security and Human Resources, with a starting salary of $150,000 and a brand-new Porsche Boxster, as promised.

At first glance, his job was to protect my crew and me.

He set up an off-duty, plain-clothes police officer to sit in the Wellesley lobby from 6 AM until I left the building at night. He installed closed-circuit TVs throughout the building and watched everyone who came and went on monitors in his office down the hall from mine, making sure no strangers approached me. I was a "high-security risk," he reminded me, because of all the enemies I'd made, past and present. That garbage guy we threw down the fire escape at Valentino's, for example, was one of many who didn't have warm, fuzzy feelings for me.

"I'm sure a lot of people want you dead," Harry said. He beefed up my security at home, installing a camera system and hiring two off-duty cops—one a lieutenant—to man the two front gates twenty-four hours a day and a third to sit in an unmarked car in front of the house. Anybody arriving for a business meeting was scanned with a metal detector to check for guns or knives before stepping in.

On the human resources side, Harry vetted and did background checks on the hundreds of job applications coming in. I was hiring twenty new employees a week to build up the accounting, due diligence, and legal departments in preparation for all the garbage deals to come in the year. I hired a lot of people to populate my chessboard; everybody had something I'd need and use at some point, even though I wasn't sure when I hired them what that something would be.

Harry worked harder for me than he ever did for the FBI, he said. But it seemed to agree with him.

In late spring I threw a Hawaiian luau for three hundred in my backyard, complete with a twenty-one-piece band, propane tanks cooking Lomi Lomi salmon and kalua pork, waiters in white gloves, and a whole lotta poi and leis, all going on under a big tent. I was standing with The Nickys drinking vodka when we saw Harry arrive. After parking his Porsche out front, he came around back and was ordering a scotch at the bar when we spotted him, looking sharp.

"Get a load of the highfalutin Fed over there, banging down scotches," Big Nick said, with a smirk.

"Yeah, he's traded in his JCPenney rags for Bloomingdale's," I said. We watched Harry hang a lei around his neck and mingle with the crowd.

The pool in Saddle River in progress

"Now there's a guy who was suppressed for twenty years working for the government," Big Nick said.

"And now he's wit us," said Nicky Glasses.

"See what you done to this guy, Tommy?" Big Nick said. "He always wanted to be bad and you brought it out in him. You ruined him. You turned him out like making a nice girl into a whore."

To me, Harry never looked more beautiful.

Because having a former FBI agent on my payroll gave Wellesley rock-solid credibility and looked so good in our portfolio, investors flocked to us. That was the real reason I wanted him. *If this FBI guy's on board, Giacomaro must be clean and legit!* They opened their wallets. The more money they gave, the more I spent—on house renovations and expanding the office.

Having Harry on staff also meant he'd continue running interference for me with the US Attorney's Office. Every few months he'd get that call. Lately, it was from Joe Sierra.

"Jesus, Harry. I got another call from the judge today. He says it's time to sentence Giacomaro."

"Nah, not yet," Harry would say. "He's still giving us information."

I had it made. An FBI guy in my pocket, money flowing like Niagara Falls, and my cousin Anthony hidden away in his office laundering it for me—we had more than 117 bank accounts at Wellesley and at least fifty of them were out of the country. I was so bigheaded and self-important about who I was and what I could do, I thought I was invincible. And I was, for a very long time.

Until it all came crashing down.

After the simultaneous deal in December, we continued to close them in groups of fifteen in the same way, at that same hotel, until March. That's when I helped broker a massive deal for Allied Waste in which they bought the Houston-based waste and disposal company Browning-Ferris Industries (BFI). It was an unusual "reverse merger" because BFI was the bigger company, doing $4 billion a year, while Allied only did $1.7 billion. But I knew a way to get it done, and the move made Allied Waste the second largest company of its kind, giving it annual revenues of more than $5 billion and assets of close to $14 billion—they were instantaneously gigantic, and it was because of me.

So it didn't make sense when my deals with Allied slowed down after that. By July, the president of Allied wasn't returning my calls. In August, after they fully merged with BFI, I finally got him on the phone. Now that they'd gotten so big, he explained, they didn't need my hundred garbage companies anymore.

"We're reneging on the deal," he said.

"What? That's a breach of contract!" I yelled. I actually said those words. Me, the guy who never fucked anyone over, never.

"You're leaving me no choice but to sue you," I said.

Although Allied Waste was a legitimate, publicly listed New York Stock Exchange company, behind the scenes they were also mob linked and had no problem playing dirty. Problem was, I couldn't just send The Nickys over to beat them up as I normally would. With my sentencing looming precariously, any attention to me would raise a red flag and could get me in the kind of trouble Harry might not be able to fix.

"If you sue us," the president continued, "you'll be showing up in court in shackles."

My hands were tied.

Losing that deal left me with my dick in my hands and up my ass, totally fucked. I owed investors well over $250 million and they had to be paid yesterday, but I'd already spent their money. I went to see Joe Sierra at the US Attorney's Office to explain.

"I got a problem," I told him. "They broke the contract."

"Well you better figure it the fuck out," he told me. "You did this to yourself, you've got to undo it. You're smart—think of something. Diversify."

And that's how I got back into trucking. Even though Harry had told me not to, a massive trucking deal could get me out of my mess; I was sure of it. I knew the industry and I knew the guys.

Big Nick knew the owners of the largest trucking company in the Garment District, Dynamic Delivery Corp, because it was Gambino owned.

"I want to buy it," I told him. There was no time to waste. "Get me a meeting." He made a few calls and days later a black Mercedes arrived at Wellesley carrying Tommy Gambino Jr., the son of Tommy Gambino Sr.—owner of Dynamic Delivery Corp and longtime capo of the Gambino crime family.

My managing director, Mario Sisco, got to work wooing the Gambinos in a series of meetings, while I researched and came up with another one of my never-been-done-before brilliant ideas.

Overnight Transportation was a nonunion trucking company based in Richmond, Virginia, that did a billion dollars a year business. They spent $100 million per year to keep the union *out* of their business while the Teamsters spent $100 million a year trying to *unionize* them. What if, I thought, I got the Teamsters to lend me the $100 million they would have spent anyway and I would take that money and leverage it into $300 million and with that, buy Overnight Transportation and unionize it. That way, the Teamsters would add tens of thousands to their membership and I'd have money to pay back my investors. It could work. And there was only one person who could help me make it happen—someone irrevocably linked to my past by way of his father.

I sent Mario Sisco to Detroit to meet with Jimmy Hoffa Jr., who had taken over as Teamster president a year earlier and already had the reputation as a leader who wanted to build and unite the union. That summer of 1999 he held solidarity rallies and created 2,000 full-time jobs for his union members. He also met with a team of investigators and lawyers to form an official probe, manned by former FBI agents, to stamp out the mob's influence on and infiltration of the Teamsters.

I didn't let that stop me. His father and I went way back; he was the reason I was there.

Mario met Hoffa Jr. at a hotel in Detroit to pitch him my idea. From his father, he'd heard about the scrawny kid with the baseball cap who used to bring him suitcases full of money. Since then, he'd heard my name around. Hoffa Jr. loved the idea, but there was the problem of this new legal team watching over any mob influences.

"I got another idea for Tom," he said to Mario. "The Central States Pension Fund is worth $22 billion and I can lend you $50 million from there. Then I'll hook you up with my guy in Chicago, and he can give you the second $50 million you need."

His guy in Chicago was the president of one of the Teamsters Union Locals, who was mobbed up with the Giancana family.

"Mario, I want those union memberships and I want to help Tom out of his mess," he said, "but there's one other thing I want in return."

"Anything you say, Mr. Hoffa."

"I got five guys in Kansas City, and I want you to put them on your payroll as consultants for two grand each," he said.

"You got it," Mario said, and they shook on that.

———

With the $100 million expected to come in, I started to quickly put together the Overnight Transportation deal, and just in time. By the end of 1999 my beleaguered investors were losing patience and the lawsuits were piling up.

The Quirks finally filed a lawsuit against me and so did a New York businessman, Michael DeBlanco, who'd complained to Joe Sierra three years earlier about me and nothing was done about it. I wasn't worried about those two suits. I knew I'd have my money soon and could pay them.

The lawsuit that did derail me that year was one filed by Reme, one of the garbage companies in my first Allied Waste deal in December 1998. The owner of the company, Ray Esposito, was a mob guy I knew from the Bronx. He was a big guy, about four hundred pounds, and he'd become one of my best friends during the year I was putting together that deal. He loved me—*loved* me—like a son, even more. He'd also become one of my biggest investors in Wellesley, to the tune of $6 million. His businessman son, Neil, had invested $5 million.

After that December deal, I paid Ray the $100 million that I owed him for his company, fair and square, but Neil insisted I owed $20 million more. I had made Neil a verbal promise, he reminded me, that he was a partner in Wellesley—a promise I'd made to so many. I didn't mean it, of course. But it was the only way I could get his father to agree to be in my deal.

Like Mr. Maislin, I demanded loyalty. But that didn't mean I gave it myself.

I reneged on my promise and Neil sued me in federal court in Hartford, Connecticut. Harry was trying to get me out of it, but the Espositos were a prominent family in Connecticut and my FBI guys had less pull there.

Plus, Neil was sneaky. He had friends who worked at Wellesley and got them to sift through my garbage and piece together shredded documents to build a case against me—confidential papers about bank wires and movements of large blocks of money. His lawyers used them to convince a federal judge in Hartford to order an injunction against me to stop all Wellesley activity, and they put a monitor on the company.

I wanted to break the guy's fucking neck.

I went up to Connecticut to meet with Ray to discuss the situation.

"Ray, your son is jeopardizing my future acquisitions here in Connecticut," I told him. How was I supposed to pay back investors if I couldn't work?

"I don't know what to do, Tom," Ray said. "I can't control him."

"Tell him that if he doesn't get off my back, there's gonna be a problem."

Two weeks later on the night before Halloween, Neil was hosting a grand opening party at the new Henri Bendel boutique he'd just bought in Hartford. I sent The Nickys to make him sweat. They showed up looking like two goons on a casting call for *The Sopranos*—which had premiered on TV that year and was a big hit with my crew—and plopped a case of Cristal champagne at Neil's feet.

"Tom Giacomaro wanted you to have this," one Nicky said. Neil's face went white. The Nickys hung around for a while, long enough to make him so nervous that he drank too much booze and did too much coke. But they were long gone by the time Neil hopped into his silver Mercedes 500SL (with a black interior) with his girlfriend and sped home. As he took an exit off the highway, he lost control of the car and went off the road into the woods, hitting several trees before overturning. Neil went flying through the sunroof and ended up in little pieces in the woods. At 4 AM my phone rang. It was Carmine Esposito, Ray's cousin.

"Tom, Neil's car went off the road tonight," he said. "He's *dead*."

"What?" I was truly shocked.

"The word on the street is that you did it."

"No, no way. I swear to you."

And I didn't, I really didn't. At the same time, I couldn't help but think: *No more lawsuit!*

The Connecticut State Police arrived at my gate on Fox Hedge Road early the next morning. After a lot of phone calls and pulling rank, Harry was able to convince them I had nothing to do with Neil's death and to back off. The lawsuit disappeared.

But I don't think Ray was ever convinced I had nothing to do with his son's death. At the funeral, I sat at the family table and saw how he looked at me. His grief-stricken eyes said: *You killed my son.*

After that, the garbage companies in Connecticut started spreading the word that Wellesley was mobbed up and had financial problems, and it messed us up even more. I started working from home because there was too much heat on me.

The cocaine arrived just in time to ease the tension.

That year, Big Nick brought in his sister-in-law's husband, businessman Eric Reichenbaum, as an investor. He'd just sold the family company (they made those Christmas tree air fresheners people hang inside their cars) and made $100 million in profit. Eric was liquid and a good "mark," but also heavily into coke, which was not good for me. I'd been staying away from it so I could stay sharp for my business deals, but with the year I'd had, I didn't need much encouragement to start up again.

At least once a week Eric and I drank too much and got coked up and rented a bunch of top-of-the-line hookers. Wayne set up the girls for us—their rate was $1,000 per hour—and we'd pick them up in a limo along with any other Wellesley investors who wanted to party with us.

The girls were nicknamed for the cities they grew up in—Albany, Berkeley, Chicago, and Cincinnati—Berkeley being my personal favorite. At the Plaza, an apartment/suite would be waiting for us. We'd do more coke and champagne before we each took a girl into a private bedroom.

In the morning, we'd meet for eggs Benedict in the suite's dining room like a little family, go shopping at Bergdorf's, then go back to the Plaza to do it all over again. My bill at the end of two days would be $150,000. If it was winter, we'd take hookers and strippers to my house and drink in the hot Jacuzzi while Dorian and the kids were away.

Fat Pauly had an office down the hall from me (next to The Nickys, who were next to Harry), and he was not so happy watching me stumble down the destructive path with Eric. He was a family man, a "good Catholic," and well respected in the community. And as of late, he'd become my *consigliere* of sorts.

"You've got to calm down," he'd say to me, after I'd drag myself into the office following two days of boozing and coke with the hookers. "This behavior is going to lead to disaster."

Several times over the next few months, Fat Pauly would find himself at the Plaza, banging on the door of my suite because I hadn't shown up for work.

I was spinning out of control again like I'd done years before. Even The Nickys were appalled at my behavior. As a rule, mob guys didn't get involved with hookers or drugs, but I convinced The Nickys to come to a strip club with me around that time. I was so fucked up that night that I let a stripper suck my dick right there in the strip club in front of them, in front of everyone.

"You're fucking repulsive, Tom!" said Nicky Glasses. "Look what you're doing! What the fuck is *wrong* with you?"

He was so disgusted that he got up and left. I zipped up my pants and put my head in my hands. I didn't know how to explain to them what was happening to me. I didn't know how to tell them I was panicked that I wouldn't be able to fix the mess I'd put myself in this time.

That New Year's Eve, I stayed home with Dorian and the kids as we entered a new millennium. Every tree and shrub and the swimming pool were lit up with white lights; it was so bright it looked like daylight.

My mother came over to sit through midnight with us because she was paranoid the world would be plunged into chaos. She was caught up in the Y2K mass hysteria that everything was going to crash, and computers and clocks would go haywire, so she withdrew all her money from the bank and stored cans of food and bottles of water in the basement. She arrived at the house with a Bible.

On TV, we switched channels back and forth between the crowds in Times Square wearing funny hats, and the news that Boris Yeltsin had resigned that day and Vladimir Putin, a longtime KGB foreign intelligence officer, was the new president of Russia. He was a corrupt killer, an enemy of our country, and my mother shuddered when his face appeared on the screen.

As the clock struck twelve, my mother clutched her Bible closer to her chest and braced herself for doom and the impending apocalypse.

"I have a feeling," she said, shivering, "that something terrible is about to happen."

CHAPTER 18

THE MAN BEHIND THE CURTAIN

*I liked to verbally beat my workers in the head over and over again
about what I wanted them to do and how I wanted them to do it.*

A t Wellesley we had a curtained off cubbyhole in the nurse's quarters on the second floor that we called "the crying room." It's where employees retreated after I roughed them up too much.

I liked to verbally beat my workers in the head over and over again about what I wanted them to do and how I wanted them to do it, and if they didn't do it fast enough or right enough, I yelled at them in front of everybody until they were red-faced or sobbing.

If an employee really got on my bad side, I'd toy with him or her like they were a pawn on a live, interactive chessboard. I'd pit staff members against each other by saying one bad-mouthed the other and sit back and watch the drama and chaos play out.

I was bad, but the coke was making me worse.

I called my managers and directors "Smurfs" and before board meetings I'd line up a dozen Smurf dolls (left over from my Coleco days) on the leather chairs around the boardroom table and when everyone arrived, I'd say, "Okay, everybody! I'm taking the Smurfs to the Super Bowl!"

And then, suddenly and for no reason, I'd lavish praise on all of them.

I was like a tyrannical director of my own reality show.

It really messed with their heads. A week rarely went by without someone running to the crying room, which was equipped with plenty of tissues. Any employee who couldn't withstand my methods got whited out. I hired twenty people a week those first few months and fired about ten per week. This is how you knew you were about to be fired: I'd put a little piece of masking tape on your office door and write "Endangered Species" on it with a Sharpie.

The loyal ones, they stayed. Loyalty was more important to me than smarts because if the shit hit the fan, as it was doing now, I wanted to know that my loyalists would cover up and lie for me.

After the Neil Esposito sitch I had to lie low for a while and started working from home. The company needed money and my backyard in Saddle River was overflowing with wealthy celebrities, so it was a perfect location to find my marks.

By the spring of 2000, world-celebrated suspense novelist Mary Higgins Clark was already a big investor in Wellesley—to the tune of $20 million, which is a spit in the ocean compared to the billion she's made with her books. Keith "White Bread" Moody got her as an investor early on through his connections at the local country club. I used to call him "White Bread" because of his pull with the upper-class elite. He hooked up with a lot of high rollers at the club who invested early with us and made high returns right after the Allied Waste deal.

I never met Mary Higgins Clark, but I had every intention of buying her.

That spring, I pressed Keith to get more money from her, but she wasn't budging. She'd heard the rumors that Wellesley wasn't as squeaky-clean as she thought it was, and that Keith, whom she'd been dealing with for two years now, wasn't really the guy in charge. Rumor was that the man behind the curtain was a convicted felon. Clark was demanding a full payout of her money unless she met the hidden mastermind face-to-face.

She was married to a former chief executive at Merrill Lynch and lived less than a mile away from me. I'd seen her at Valentino's, where our eyes had met across the room. I even sent her drinks anonymously, telling the waiter to say it came "from a fan." But the looks and drinks were mere foreplay for what was to come.

Clark arrived with her son, David, and parked her Mercedes at the top of my circular driveway as I stood outside waiting to greet them. *Here comes the mousey into the little housey*, I thought to myself. I was setting a trap.

One of the entrance gates in Saddle River

Photo by Aris Economopoulos/*The Star-Ledger*

She looked like your typical rich Upper East Side socialite with her Chanel bag, teased blonde hair, and Jackie O sunglasses that covered half her face. She was in her early seventies at the time, but some nips and tucks made her look younger. I wore my usual mob clothes and had a cigar in my mouth.

"*Howyadoin'?!*" I said, pumping up the mob accent.

If she liked characters, then I was gonna give her one. I'm sure she prided herself on knowing the psyches of the criminal minds she wrote about. But while she'd written about guys like me, she'd never met one.

In the foyer, Mary slid her sunglasses down the bridge of her nose and scanned the house, looking impressed. I led them through a pair of etched-glass doors and into my oak-paneled office and seated them across my $350,000 Italian mahogany desk. If Clark wanted to know where her money was, she need only look around—she was surrounded by it. My designer lake in the backyard, my Jags and Bentleys out front, the Rolex I was wearing, and the $25,000 leather chairs she and her son had just parked their asses on.

I was going to convince her to keep her $20 million invested in Wellesley, and I intended to clip her for more.

"Mrs. Clark," I said, "I want you to know that I've put in $20 million of my own money into Wellseley, too. That's how much I believe in it. And I'm about to invest more. The returns are going to double in a year."

She shook her head in doubt.

"You're a *felon*," she said. "What if other companies find out about your past? Who will want to do business with you?"

I didn't tell her that most of the companies I dealt with employed criminals worse than me. I'd save that juicy tidbit for another time.

"I am so sure of Wellesley," I said, leaning forward, "that I'll give you the mortgage on my house if we lose a single nickel of your money."

That made her pause. It was a great tactical maneuver I'd used in the past and it always worked. With Mary, it still wasn't enough. She was a tough girl from the Bronx; she wasn't easily pushed around by smart-talking bad boys. Now it was her turn to intimidate. She had connections at the very top, she told me. She was about to become a White House regular as George W. Bush's new literary committee chairperson.

In front of the Wellesley office

Photo by Aris Economopoulos/*The Star-Ledger*

"So if you lose my money," she warned, "it's not going to be pleasant for you." She removed her sunglasses, narrowed her eyes, and looked at me directly. "You better think carefully about screwing me."

I thought about it, for a millisecond, and kept going.

I told her I wanted to donate $10,000 to the FRAXA Research Foundation, an organization for which she was chairperson. I'd done my due diligence and discovered that her grandson suffered from the illness, Fragile X, a genetic syndrome that causes autism. When I saw her eyes soften, I made a move that always worked on women, whether you want to get into their pants or into their pocketbooks. I walked to her side of the table, took her hands in mine, and looked deeply into her eyes.

"Mrs. Clark, I'm going to make you an offer you shouldn't refuse," I said squeezing her hands. I was practically kneeling now.

"If you stay with me," I promised, "I'll give you twenty percent of the business. We'll be partners."

It was the same lie I told Neil Esposito, who had died five months before in the car crash. Mary smiled and blushed. Bingo; I'd hit the mark.

"Dear," she said, returning the hand squeeze, "please, call me Mary."

(Years later, Mary would indeed write about a character fashioned after me in her book *The Christmas Thief*: "He had a smile that inspired confidence and trust," she wrote of her character, Packy Noonan.)

I released her hands and told her and her son to think about everything I'd said, and I gave Mary a hug and a kiss on the cheek before walking them to their car. Early the next morning, son David telephoned.

"We're in," he said. "We're keeping our money with you, *and* my mother wants to give you five million more."

Rolex and an unlit cigar, circa 2000

I hung up and sat back smugly in my ridiculously priced armchair and chewed on an Arturo Fuente Maduro cigar. I had them. In fact, I had them so good that in the following months David would come on board at Wellesley as Vice President of Investor Relations with a salary of $5,000 per week for a no-show job. All he had to do was continue to get his mother to invest, which he did.

I breathed a sigh of relief. With Mary's money and the upcoming Hoffa Jr. money and the trucking deal I was working on, it was all going to work out.

I chewed on my cigar some more, then saw Rob at the glass doors and waved him in. He'd just come from the bank with my daily take of $20,000 to $30,000 in cash. On a credenza in my office, I had a big automatic cash-counting machine.

"Put the money in the machine and count it, Rob!"

He put the money in and the machine went *brrrrrrrrrr* just like an ATM. Then he handed me the cash and I hugged him and kissed him on the cheek, too.

"Rob, who takes all the money?"

"You do, Boss! You take all the money!"

———

I did follow through on some of my promises and gave Mary signed paperwork for a $3.7 million mortgage on one of my fully paid homes. By then I had Mary's new money and more coming in from other investors.

That Christmas, Mary invited me to her "Deck the Halls" kickoff party at the New York Athletic Club as her guest of honor. When I got off the elevator, she hugged me and introduced me to the crowd: "This is the man who's going to make me rich and famous!"

Besides mingling with wealthy neighbors like Mary and hitting them up to invest, working from home had other perks, too. The house I bought across the street was now a vacant piece of property after I had it bulldozed, but I kept the pool house in back intact as my own mob hangout, so we could play poker day and night.

The Nickys, Fat Pauly, Wayne, and I drank vodka while we played, and when I got a hand I didn't like, I pulled out a loaded gun and started shooting in the air around the room—*boom, boom, boom, boom!* God knows what the neighbors thought.

On Memorial Day weekend, the Saddle River police discovered my guns after Dorian and I got into an argument and she called them, saying I was violent. The cop on my payroll, stationed out front, was away that weekend so he couldn't run interference, and the cops hauled me into the station. When they saw on their computer that I had eleven guns in the house, they charged me with unlawful possession and confiscated them. Harry intervened and "took over the case" and it went away.

Problem was, the incident put up a red flag. The new judge who now had my case, Federal District Court Judge Alfred M. Wolin, called my attorney and said, "Tell Giacomaro the next time he gets caught with guns we're going to put him right in jail!"

But Harry made sure my guns were returned to me; he was a real friend in a world where, as I said, guys didn't have true friends.

My theory on that was tested, though, when I went to visit Frankie Cam that September at Hackensack Medical. My first Mafia "friend" and Lonestar partner had been diagnosed with a very aggressive intestinal cancer weeks before, and his doctor, a friend of mine, gave me the bad news.

"We've got him for about thirty days," said my doctor friend. "There's nothing we or you can do for him."

When Frankie got out of prison, he'd gone to Kim's stepfather, the head of the Gambino Assassination Squad, "Murder Incorporated," for help on trying to go straight—he wanted out. Everyone tries to go straight when they get outta the joint, but it never sticks. After a few months of trying, Frankie went back to doing numbers and sports like always. I hadn't seen him in six months but last I'd heard, he was selling fur coats that had fallen off a truck.

At the hospital, he was in a hospital gown and robe but was his usual healthy-looking, strong self. He still looked like he could chew a guy up and spit him out sideways.

"I don't even *feel* sick," he said, as we walked through the wing of the hospital together. "But they tell me this is something that's gonna eat me up fast."

We reminisced about old times and our first meeting twenty years earlier, and we laughed. Then we got sad. Frankie couldn't believe he was going to die.

"I mean, Tommy, what the fuck? Is that it? It's over?"

What was I gonna tell him, that he'd be going to a better place? That I'd see him in heaven (or hell, for that matter)? I didn't believe in those made-up places Father Stanley use to brainwash us about. I believed in the here and now. But I still wanted to give him hope even though the doctor said there was none.

"Frankie, I'll find you a specialist in Europe. They're doing all sorts of experimental stuff there. Money is no object, I'll take care of it."

"Thanks, Tommy," he said. But we both knew this was goodbye. I hadn't cried since I was a kid, but when he gave my shoulder a boxer's right hook and then we hugged, I had tears in my eyes.

"Take care of my boy for me, will you, Tommy? Watch over Chris." He had a son with Kim who would have been about ten years old at the time.

"Sure, Frankie, sure I will."

Wayne drove me home and I was quiet. Frankie died two weeks later; he was only forty-eight. For a mob guy with no feelings, I was broken up about it.

Several months after Frankie died, my fourth child with Dorian was born—daughter Kristina, in June 2001. It had been nearly two years since Allied Waste pulled out of our historic deal—two years of convincing, conning, diverting, hiding, deal making, and scheming to make up for the money I'd lost—and it looked like I was approaching the end of my worries.

Mario Sisco was invited by Hoffa Jr. to attend the big Teamsters convention in Vegas at the end of June and while there, he was asked out to dinner with Hoffa, his Local 705 president from Chicago, and the Kansas City guys who'd be our new "consultants."

Our deal had been in the making for over a year and everyone was ready to go. Some of the delay was because the special FBI monitors watching over the Central States Pension Fund did their research on me when Hoffa Jr. told them of his plan, and explicitly told him *not* to invest in my trucking idea.

"But we're going to do it anyway," he told Mario, over dinner at the Bellagio. "The deal's gonna happen."

(Three years later, the twenty-one-person team of investigators and lawyers quit en masse from the probe, claiming Hoffa wasn't willing to back them up to get rid of continued mob influence, reported the New Jersey *Star-Ledger*: "He veered off course.")

But now, after one year convincing Overnight Transportation to do the deal and another year setting up the paperwork, Hoffa Jr. and his Chicago connect were ready to send the money so I could buy the company and everybody would be happy. We set up the documents to be signed and money to be transferred after Labor Day weekend that September—a hundred million dollars to buy a billion-dollar company. Hoffa Jr. was ecstatic and so was I. Who knew that nearly thirty years after his father told me I'd go far in trucking, I'd be doing it with his son?

That July, I threw a big blowout party in the penthouse at the Ritz-Carlton in Chicago to celebrate. The fete was originally planned to cultivate more investors in the area, but when Mario returned from Vegas with the great news, we went all out and partied the night away with booze and coke brought over state lines for us by our favorite city-named hookers—Albany and Berkeley. The tab was $100,000, but if there ever was good cause to celebrate to the max, this was it. I was about to clean up the biggest mess I'd ever made.

No one was happier to hear this than Harry, whom I told as soon as I got back to Jersey. Harry and his FBI crew had been fending off, containing, and covering up the lawsuits and angry calls that had come in for me ever since Neil Esposito's death, in hopes I'd square things away with my investors before they'd be forced to do something serious about it. He was beyond relieved that he could now tell everyone I'd taken care of it, and they'd be getting no more alarming calls about me. Or so we thought.

Me in 2001, just before my life was over

Photo by Angela Jimenez/ *The Star-Ledger*

A month later, I got a panicked, early morning phone call from Joe Sierra.

"A reporter from the New Jersey *Star-Ledger* called Washington, asking to speak to Michael Chertoff for a comment," he said. "The reporter said they're publishing a big investigative story about you in the Sunday edition on the front page. Do you understand what's going to happen to you if this article comes out? You're going straight to jail, directly to jail. Do not pass go; do not collect $200. You're *done.*"

I hung up the phone, ready to shoot myself. *A reporter?* I'd spent years dodging investors, cops, FBI agents, mob guys, drug dealers, girlfriends, and businessmen. And all along I should have been worried about some nosy journalist somewhere, taking notes?

That Saturday night The Nickys and Fat Pauly came over to sit by the pool with me and drink vodka. I had my loaded gun handy, which made them nervous. At 3 AM on Sunday August 21st, we sent an assistant to pick up the early edition of the New Jersey *Star-Ledger* from outside their newsroom, hot off the presses. When he got back, he plopped a bundle on the grass in front of us.

We tore it open and each grabbed a copy.

"Holy shit," said one of The Nickys, "you're all over the front page."

FBI INFORMANT STILL FREE AND, SOME SAY, STILL SWINDLING

We opened it up. I was all over the second page, too. And the story continued on the third page. Someone started reading aloud by the pool light:

> *Bergen con man cut a deal 8 years ago but has yet to be sentenced.*
>
> *For two years, authorities say, Thomas J. Giacomaro and his partners in crime soaked up cash.*
>
> *A half-million here. A few million there. A banner score in Florida— more than $30 million, by one estimate . . .*

I looked at The Nickys and Fat Pauly and swayed in my bare feet. "You think anyone will see this?"

No one answered; they just looked at me. They knew how much trouble I was in and so did I.

I opened up another bottle of vodka and started pouring.

My life was destroyed. I was finished. It was over.

CHAPTER 19

UNBREAKABLE

*The room had a cement slab to sleep on with four posts on it,
in case they needed to chain you down.*

They try to break you in prison.

They try to destroy your mind until your sense of self shatters into a billion pieces. If you're especially obstinate, they give you a dose of what they call "Diesel Therapy."

It goes like this: For a month they move you from prison to prison every two or three days—pulling you from sleep in the middle of the night or pulling you off the toilet when there's still shit coming out of your asshole; they don't care. The goal is to keep you moving and never let you feel settled in any one place.

They stick you in a holding area before they move you, and all you have is the orange jumpsuit you're wearing; you can't even take a toothbrush. You're a number, not a person—you don't *own* anything. Then they shackle you and put you on a bus, chaining you together with a dozen others like animals, and drive you for five hours, seven hours, eight hours; you can't be sure how long and don't know where you're headed.

No food or water. Two guards stand watch in the bus with shotguns. The toilet is in a little cage out in the open but most guys end up pissing and shitting themselves before they can get to it.

When you arrive at your new temporary prison, you're thrown into another holding area. You'd be lucky if, at that point, they toss you a moldy cheese sandwich. After a few hours, the correctional officers (COs) take you to a new cell or bunk that you're sharing with a 6'6" savage named Bubba, whom you've just woken up and he's really mad. He wants to kill you. He probably has a shiv under his dirty blanket. I learned early how to handle guys like Bubba:

"Listen, you fat motherfucker," I'd say right away, giving them a crazy-eyed look as soon as the officer left.

"Maybe your arms are as big as my legs. But don't fuck with me. Because eventually you'll fall asleep, see, but I never sleep. And you'll wake up with me on top of you biting your ears and nose off, biting your entire face off. So leave me the fuck alone."

"You're the craziest white guy I've ever met in my life," they'd say.

I got the nickname "the Italian Hannibal Lecter" without ever having to actually chew off someone's body part. They were scared of me, and that kept me safe.

But let me back up a bit.

Three weeks after that New Jersey *Star-Ledger* article was published, terrorists flew planes into the World Trade Center.

It was exactly thirty years earlier that I made secret money deliveries for Mr. Alex there, while the towers were being built. My career was on the rise as those towers went up, and my world collapsed as those towers fell down. Years later, Tina would describe the fall of the Wellesley empire very much like the tragedy across the river: "There were so many dead bodies," she said, "it was catastrophic."

The news article in the *Star-Ledger* that August was instigated by several of my beleaguered investors and scorned partners, including the Quirks, who got zero help or results after trying to sue me and after reporting me to the FBI. So they went to the press.

The story detailed everything—my looting and bankrupting of the trucking industry, the lawsuits against me, the millions I stole from Wellesley, the questionable ethics of the FBI and US Attorney's Office, the pension fund, Cambridge, Allied Waste, and more. It named names—Camino, Kapralos, Barnetas, Frankie Cam, David Lardier, Michael DeBlanco, Michael Chertoff, and Keith Moody.

The reporter called me a "con man" and "quintessential salesman" who "used Wellesley bank accounts as a personal slush fund to pay his family's prodigious bills, from lawn care to electric service to the $87,000-per-month mortgage on a Bergen County property . . ."

On the way to court, January 14, 2002

Photo by Aris Economopoulos/*The Star-Ledger*

Not only was I in hot water but so was the US Attorney's Office and the FBI—who were bombarded with furious calls from Washington: *What do you mean he was on the docket for six years and you didn't sentence him? What do you mean he was scamming and looting while working as our informant? What do you mean Harry Mount now works for him?*

Joe Sierra was immediately asked to resign and so were a few others. In a hasty attempt to do damage control and save face in front of the public, Judge Wolin quickly set my long-awaited sentencing date.

"Giacomaro is going to get fried for this," he told my attorney, Cathy Waldor, in chambers before my sentencing. "I've had hundreds of calls about him from people insisting we open up a new investigation, which we are. I knew all along that he was just playing us. The *government* let this happen," the judge told Cathy, "not *me*."

No one wanted to take any blame, but they were all willing players in my con game—all of them.

———

In January 2002 Judge Wolin sentenced me to eighteen months for the embezzlement of $1.2 million from the Majestic Carrier pension fund, the sentencing I'd been ducking for ten years. It didn't matter that I'd already paid the money back (thanks to Harry's urging).

Three days after my sentencing, Mary Higgins Clark—who still held a mortgage on my Saddle River home—gave an interview to the *New York Post* about my con artistry: "I was shocked," she said. "Shocked is the only way you can describe it. I may have a great imagination, but I never could have invented [Giacomaro]."

I took that as a compliment.

I started my prison term at the end of February at Fort Dix camp in Jersey. Camps were the lowest security you could get in a prison—it was a sissy-la-la camp full of white-collar criminals and kids caught with pot. It had little "out of bounds" signs around the perimeter, and you could come and go from your unit all day long, twenty-four hours a day.

Still, it was a shock to my senses. I went from sleeping in a $25,000 canopy bed to sleeping on a dirty mattress in a metal bunk bed. From dining on filet mignon and champagne to white rice with soy sauce, which I had to stand in line for hours in the cold and snow to get.

From wearing $2,000 Canali suits and Bruno Magli alligator shoes to prison khakis and ten-dollar boots with steel toes. From having maids to clean every speck of dust to me mopping the barrack floors.

I had no idea how to do jail. I was in complete denial and pissed off and had no intention of adapting. I refused every program offered to me on how to "better" myself and wouldn't look at the TV or read newspapers because I didn't want a reminder of the real world. It made my new reality too impossible to endure. Besides, why do I need to change? *It's only eighteen months,* I kept telling myself. *As long as I don't fuck up I'm out in six!*

The sleeping quarters at Fort Dix were like military barracks, a giant room with bunk beds lined up against the walls. I had my own locker near the bed, which I kept perfectly organized. I made my bed until it was coin-toss Marine tight. I washed my hands on the hour in the dirty communal bathroom. Every morning, I borrowed an iron and ironing board from the COs so I could press my cheap, used, stained khaki uniform and crease the sleeves and slacks. With commissary money that my mother deposited every month for me, I was able to buy some extras like pasta, sweat pants, socks, a pair of sneakers, and instant ramen noodle soup that everybody called "crackhead" soup because at ten cents a cup, it was the cheapest item at the commissary.

Three days after I arrived at Fort Dix, I got a collect call from Dorian. Before going in I'd found a way to secretly leverage $25 million to her so she could take care of herself and the kids while I was gone, but it wasn't enough to keep them.

"You just lost your beautiful wife and your beautiful family," she said. "I'm divorcing you." *Click.*

Lauren and my mother were the only two who visited me the first few months, coming together every Saturday. Lauren was comforted to learn that I'd probably be home for Christmas, and we tried to cheer up my mother, who was skinnier and more nervous than ever, with that. Now that Dorian and the kids had left me, I wasn't sure where I'd be.

"With me, Dad," Lauren said, giving me a reassuring hug.

But as the days and weeks went by, I was less reassured.

In April and May 2002, the New Jersey *Star-Ledger* published two follow-up features on me:

EXTRAVAGANCE GONE UNCHECKED

THE MAN WHO STOLE $80 MILLION WHILE WORKING FOR THE FBI

One afternoon at that time when I called my mother from the prison pay phone, she sounded frightened.

"There are people here. A lot of *people*."

It took some time to figure out what she was trying to tell me; the FBI was there and they were searching the house and taking everything.

"Ma, did they go downstairs?"

They did. And when they opened the air-conditioning ducts in the ceiling, they got hit in the head with my falling suitcase filled with a million bucks.

———————

One by one, and quickly, I lost everybody.

Everyone I knew except Fat Pauly stopped taking my calls—advised by their lawyers to have no contact with me. I mailed Fat Pauly a note of gratitude; he was all I had left:

June 11, 2002

Dear Pauly,

I always knew you would be there for me, as I would be there for you.

I'll look forward to seeing you every month—I'll call you every week.

Thanks, Tom

6/11/2002
Tuesday

Dear ▓▓▓▓

I always knew you would
be there for me, as I would
be there for you.

▓▓▓▓▓▓▓▓▓▓▓▓▓▓▓▓▓▓▓▓▓▓▓

I'll look forward to
seeing you every month —
I'll call you every
week

Thanks,

Tom

Keep Confidential Our Conversations

Writing to Fat Pauly from prison

But soon after, even Fat Pauly had to go. He came to visit me the third week of June and told me his attorneys had said the same. Sitting on the plastic chairs in the visiting room, he also gave me a warning:

"A few of the guys worry they're targets in the investigation on you because they haven't been spoken to yet," he said. "They said to tell you that you better keep your mouth shut."

"Who told you to say that?"

"It doesn't matter who." He cleared his throat and looked away, then met my eyes with worry. He was scared. "They said to remind you that your daughter and your mother are still out on the street *so you better be careful.*"

Fat Pauly and I both knew it was a real threat. I was being reminded to follow omertà, or else.

Lauren visited a few weeks later by herself on July 3rd. She was bubbly and pretty in her pink jogging outfit, excited that my mother had bought her a new Chevy Blazer from money she'd taken from the basement suitcase before the Feds got it.

"But baby," I said sadly, "they're probably going to take away the townhouse I bought you." It was a gorgeous half-million-dollar townhouse she was sharing with her best friend.

"It's okay, Dad." She smiled. "I'm going to move in with grandma. Don't feel bad."

I thought about Fat Pauly's warning and told her to be careful on the roads with the holiday drivers. She and her best friend were going out that night to celebrate Memorial Day. And for the first time since the article came out and I fucked up my world and hers, I apologized to her about what I'd done.

"I'm sorry," I told her. "I'm sorry for being so stupid and for letting this happen to us."

"Don't worry, Dad," she said. "Everything will be back to normal at Christmas, after you get out."

We made plans to see each other the following week and hugged goodbye.

The next afternoon I was in my barracks readying for four o'clock count when a CO ordered me to report to the counselor's office. I walked in to find a group of people waiting for me: two counselors, Dr. Baruch and Dr. Jennifer Bowe; my case manager; Aziz, the chaplain; two or three cops; and the warden, an older Italian guy who liked me. He had tears in his eyes.

"We've got bad news for you, Tom," Chaplain Aziz said. Jennifer took my hand.

"What? Oh, no. My mother?"

"No," said Aziz, "it's your daughter. Tom, Lauren was killed last night."

My knees buckled and everything went dark.

"There was a car accident," he continued, as Jennifer and a few others tried to catch me as I fell. "She was in the car with her friend and they were driving home. Her car veered off the road and no one knows why. They both died."

No! No, no, no, no! Not Lauren! Of all people, not her!

"Tom, your ex-wife Debbie is on the phone," someone said, as they put the receiver to my ear.

By now I was lying on the filthy prison floor, catatonic.

"Tom? Oh, Tom!" said Debbie's voice from far away. "We lost our baby!"

———

They let me go to the funeral for a few hours, which was against usual protocol.

It was the same church in which Debbie and I got married. The place was loaded with kids, all of Lauren's friends. My only friends to show up were Fat Pauly and Ray Esposito. Everyone else was too afraid to come. Lauren's face was so destroyed in the accident, the casket stayed closed. Nicky, Tommy Jr., and I held hands and followed the casket out of the church. Everybody has something that will break their spirit, and for my family, this was it.

After the funeral my mother doubled down on her drinking, as if she wanted to kill herself that way, and I sunk into depression. *I'm being punished*, I thought. *I was too greedy. I wanted too much, I had too much, and then I lost the only truly precious thing I had.* I was so distraught that the old Italian warden who liked me decided to let me out early to finish the last few months of my sentence in a halfway house.

When that day arrived, my mother was waiting for me outside the prison gates with a car and driver. But apparently my situational awareness had gone to shit because I didn't notice the cops and FBI agents hovering nearby. I walked toward the car and when I was fifty feet away, they surrounded me in golf carts. One of them was the US postal inspector and another was FBI agent Dennis Richards.

"You're not going nowhere," said Richards. "Your halfway house is canceled."

Richards had been with the FBI for thirty-five years, he told me as they handcuffed me and took me back into the prison.

"And you're gonna be my last case. You know why? Because there's nothing more prestigious than the FBI, and yet you went out and gave us a bad name and disgraced us."

Richards was in charge of the new investigation on me and he had news for me:

"You're in a lot of trouble," he said. "You're going to be under indictment again and face new federal charges. So, you better think about how to help yourself and start talking. We'll be back in a few weeks to see you again."

In December 1992 I'd served two-thirds of my sentence and they took me out of sissy-la-la camp and sent me across the street "behind the wire" to the low-security prison. Here, I was in a confined area and locked down. Every hour we had "the five-minute move" when you were allowed to go from one location to the next—the laundry room, medical, the commissary, or the chapel—they were all separate buildings or units. It was like playing musical chairs but when the music stopped, if you didn't have a chair, the doors locked and you either got shot or put in the hole.

Instead of "out of bounds" signs, the prison was surrounded by a double fence with quadruple barbed wire and trucks that drove around the perimeter day and night, carrying guys with shotguns and machine guns.

Everybody had to have a job so I got one at the chapel—Chaplain Aziz felt bad for me after Lauren's death so he gave me an easy job as his clerk, looking after the books and accounting. Wonder what my father would have thought about that. He did the books for the mob and I did the books for god. At least I was able to steal paper towel from Aziz's bathroom to hide in my locker back at the barracks. I needed it to scrub my filthy locker and dry my hands after their hourly washings.

At night, I lay in my bed and agonized over three thoughts while everyone else slept.

They plan to keep me in here for the rest of my life.

Someone killed my daughter and I am to blame.

My fucking father was right. I amounted to nothing—less than nothing.

———

I told the guards I was so upset about my daughter that I wanted to kill myself. I didn't really, but I was hoping they'd be easier on me or send me back to the camp if I said that. It had the opposite effect.

I was immediately taken to the medical unit and put on suicide watch.

They took my clothes away and put me naked into a freezing, padded cell and assigned an inmate to watch me with my balls hanging out 24/7 through a little windowed slot. The inmate wrote down every move I made: *"Inmate just took water." "Inmate just pissed." "Inmate just took a shit." "Inmate's lying down."*

The room had a cement slab to sleep on with four posts on it, in case they needed to chain you down. For five days, I lay on the slab as an air-conditioner blew cold air on me. It was a method of torture, like waterboarding, to snap you out of any suicidal thoughts. If I moved too much, the medical staff—who were also watching on camera—took it as a need to straitjacket or "four-poster" you, so I stayed as still as I could.

I tried to keep sane, to keep from breaking, but I was stripped bare—literally and figuratively—and afraid for the first time in a long, long time. I had no idea what was going to happen to me with this next indictment. I had no idea how strong I could be to handle prison life. I had no idea how to worm myself out of this jam.

So for the first time ever, since her death, I talked to Lauren out loud:

Honey, help me get through this. Help me stay calm and keep it together. Give me strength.

After five days of this, the medical team decided I wasn't suicidal after all and let me out on the provision that I went on antidepressants and saw the staff shrink, something I hadn't done since I was ten. I agreed. But I stuck the pills under my tongue and threw them out later.

Dr. Jennifer Bowe, the one who held my hand the day Chaplain Aziz told me about Lauren, was a pretty blonde. Even though I didn't believe in therapy bullshit, seeing a pretty blonde for an hour twice a week at least gave me something to look forward to.

"You're not eating, Tom."

"My life is over," I said, as I picked my fingernails with a toothpick until the cuticles bled. I'd lost fifty pounds in the six months since Lauren died. Sadness had a lot to do with it, yes. But so did their shitty food.

I had no intention of pouring out my soul to Dr. Bowe, but something about the softness of her voice and her eyes disarmed me.

"Why did I do this to myself and everyone else?" I asked her, and myself.

"*Why?* Why did I need a hundred Rolex watches? What was I trying to prove? I was so sure I could pay back all that money. All the Bentleys and the suits and the houses and the 45,000 tulips, what for? All gone. And yet, the one thing that was real, that was true . . ."

Dr. Bowe didn't tell me then, but the doctors at Fort Dix had written down some answers to my questions in their reports: words and phrases like "bipolar" and "history of mania" and "acute anxiety" and "dysthymia" and "personality disorder with narcissistic and antisocial features" and "major depression disorders."

"We're going to work on it, Tom," she said.

The next month I was shackled and taken into the US Attorney's Office in Newark to discuss a potential plea deal for all the *new* criminal activity I'd done since my *last* plea deal—which was a lot, needless to say. The group in the conference room included US attorneys, FBI agents, state police, and state detectives from the fraud division. One of them was Agent Richards.

They showed me a three-ringed binder of FBI 302 forms containing all the interviews with my friends and coworkers, at least two hundred of them. The names were blackened out but I could still read them. They even interrogated our maids at Saddle River.

"There's not one person here that hasn't pinned everything on you," they told me.

They *wanted* me to know who'd ratted me out, I knew that trick. Because now they would ask me to be a rat, too.

"Tell us about Nicky Ola, Nicky Calo, and Pauly Russo and all the money that disappeared. You wired hundreds of millions of dollars out of the country. We want to know where the money is, and we want to know everything about everybody."

In exchange, they'd give me a five-year sentence, buy me a house, and put me in witness protection when I was out, somewhere nice with a good dry heat, like Arizona, or Colorado. Or Oklahoma.

"You'll be just like Henry Hill in *Goodfellas*," one of them said, laughing.

"Go fuck yourself," I said, rattling my chains. "I'm not cooperating. I'm not giving you nothing."

That shocked them. But they didn't know I had my own ace up my sleeve to use as leverage.

"Okay tough guy, then we're gonna hit you hard."

"Oh, yeah?" I said. "How about we go to trial, huh? And the first thing I'll do is talk about Harry Mount and then put him on the stand. I'll say he knew about everything I was doing and that I thought I was acting as an informant on behalf of the government. And I'll say he told all of youse guys everything. So fuck all of youse.

Unless you have a better deal for me, I'm going to trial. If you think you look bad now, wait until I *really* smear you."

I knew Harry could be indicted for conspiracy and corruption if I went to trial, and that's the last thing the FBI wanted. Agent Richards was especially horrified at this thought, but he was still playing hardball.

"Giacomaro, you had power and you had money," he said, fuming. "And now we're going to take it all away from you."

That night, in search of a friend I wrote to Fat Pauly, even if he couldn't write me back.

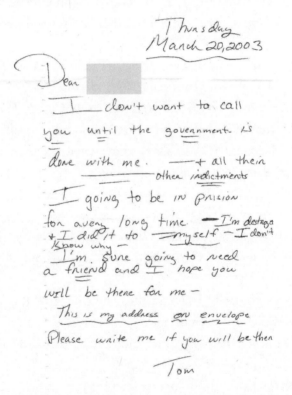

Another desperate, lonely letter to Fat Pauly—my last friend

Thursday, March 20, 2003

Dear Pauly,

I don't want to call you until this government is done with me and all their other indictments.

I'm going to be in prison for a very long time—I'm destroyed & I did it to myself—I don't know why.

I'm sure going to need a <u>friend</u> and I hope you will be there for me—

This is my address on the envelope.

Please write me if you will be there.

Tom

The Feds and I met each other halfway. We struck a deal in which I didn't have to rat, I'd get a fourteen-year sentence, and they wouldn't indict a long list of my friends and colleagues (who had ratted on me). Also, my cousin Anthony would receive a very, very short sentence.

In exchange, I wouldn't go to trial, and Harry and the FBI would keep their reputations and Harry would keep his pension.

Fourteen years was more time than some murderers and child molesters got. It was payback, punishment, for making the FBI look like fools. And extra time was tacked on because I was protecting my crew. I was going to do time for all of us.

("Who does all the time, Rob?" "You do, Boss!")

But even with our meeting of the minds, the fuckers *still* put me on Diesel Therapy that May, a month before I was to sign the plea agreement, just to make sure I didn't get any ideas about changing my mind and, I'm sure, to stick it to me.

I was taken to the US penitentiary in Canaan, Pennsylvania—a maximum-security prison with electric fences and giant towers all around it. Now my neighbors were murderers, rapists, and pedophiles. It was the kind of place you had to wear boots when you went into the gated shower so that if someone comes in and tries to rape you, you can stomp and kick your way out. Maybe. Here, the biggest, meanest guys would dress up the child molesters, put ChapStick on their lips, and fuck them up the ass.

From there, they chained and bused me with thirty other inmates to a hangar at Philly International Airport and let us out in front of a row of armed guards and US marshals standing in front of a jet. It was the real-life *Con Air*.

They flew to Oklahoma City and kept me in a high-maximum transfer station there for two days; it was the kind of place they put psychos like the Unabomber. From there, they sent me to Michigan for a few days, then back to Philly, then back to Canaan, then back to Fort Dix in Jersey to officially get sentenced. It was all done to torment me and keep me sticking to the plan.

On June 6, 2003, FBI agents picked me up in the morning and took me to state court, where I pled guilty to money laundering. Then they took me to federal court in the afternoon to plead guilty to eighty-eight counts of mail fraud, de facto ownership, tax evasion, and much, much more. I pled in a way that would make it possible for all the Wellesley investors to get back the $69 million I took using tax credits.

"All your sentences stack up to four hundred and forty years of jail time," one agent goaded me, "but don't worry, you won't get that much."

The new US attorney for New Jersey, Chris Christie, gave an official press statement after my plea: "Unfortunately, [he] was very good at his con-artist craft," said Christie. "The giant pyramid scheme collapsed on investors."

Once again, I was all over the local daily newspapers. On June 7, 2003, the *New York Post* had these headlines:

SCAMMER MADE FBI SUCKERS

SUPER CON: FBI SNITCH ADMITS $75M SWINDLE

I wouldn't be sentenced for another eight months so the US marshals handcuffed, chained, and transported me all over the country again. They were still trying to break me. The first prison was the barbaric Passaic County Jail, one of the worst prisons in the US.

Inside, I was waiting on a bench in the transporting area staring at the dirty floor. I was exhausted, hungry, and feeling hopeless when I felt someone standing in front of me and heard a kind, comforting voice.

"Tommy," she said, softly.

I looked up: *Tina*. She was wearing a blue uniform. In the years since I'd seen my upside-down-cake girlfriend, she'd become a cop working for the Passaic County Sheriff's Department.

"Tina," I said. I could barely talk.

"It's going to be okay, Tommy."

Passaic County was a twenty-four-hour-lockdown prison that made the others I'd been to look like the Hilton. I was put in a cell the size of a tiny bathroom and slept on a metal bed bolted to the wall. Food was a piece of meat with maggots on it slipped to you on a tray through the door. When you stepped into the showers, you stepped into people's shit, piss, and sperm. The COs patrolled the tiers with German shepherds and if you hung your arm outside the bars, the dogs bit it off.

For the three months I was there, Tina came to my cell door every day and talked to me through a little screen.

"Are you okay, Tommy? You're gonna be okay."

She called my mother every day, too, to report on our meetings.

"He's okay, Mrs. G. He's doing okay."

Tina told me later that she never, ever, thought I'd make it out of there sane or alive.

My sentencing in February 2004, just after my fifty-first birthday, was a spectacle.

The date, unlucky Friday the 13th, was chosen on purpose I was told, to specifically ram it up my ass. First I was taken to state court in Bergen County. The courtroom was packed with my angry victims—David Clark, Eric Reichenbaum, and others—looking like they wanted to kill me. I pled guilty to two counts of conspiracy to defraud the United States and one count of frauds and swindles. The judge sentenced me to ten years with a five-year stipulation.

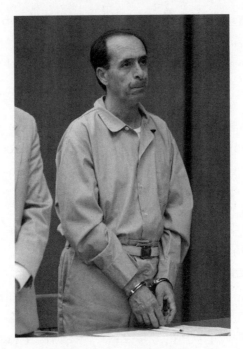

"I didn't have a Maserati!"

Photo by Christopher Barth/*The Star-Ledger*

"Mr. Giacomaro," the judge asked, as she went through the documents and heard the testimony, "is there a car you *didn't* have?"

My lawyer gave me a look: *Don't do it, don't do it.* But I couldn't help myself.

"Well, your honor," I said with a smirk, "I didn't have a Maserati!"

The courtroom went wild and my victims flipped out.

"Strike that from the record!" the judge yelled to the court reporter. "And get him out of my courtroom! You're despicable, Mr. Giacomaro. You're disgusting. Get him out of here!"

A team of federal marshals escorted me out of that courtroom and took me to Newark for the next sentencing. The angry mob followed, as if they were going to witness a modern-day public hanging. Now I stood in front of Judge Wolin in my handcuffs and orange jumpsuit.

"Mr. Giacomaro, you're back again after duping us for so many years," he said, and turned to the group of FBI agents and US attorneys in the room, pointing at them. "And it was all of *you* who wanted him!"

For crimes that would normally get two to three years, Judge Wolin sentenced me to the 168 months—fourteen years—agreed upon, and said in an official press statement, "[He] is an arrogant and resistant felon."

Four months later, Judge Wolin retired. As I said once, I was either a career maker or a career breaker. Before I went off to do my sentence, the new US Attorney Chris Christie had a final jab, as it was Friday the 13th.

"He's an extraordinary con man," said Christie, "but today, his luck ran out."

I took the pinch for everyone. They led me out of the courtroom and I caught sight of David Clark as I left. His mother was the only one who came out of the whole shitstorm shining. She got her investment money back from the government, and, as I suspected, she couldn't resist using me as fodder for her next novel.

That Christmas, Mary Higgins Clark published yet another best-selling novel: *The Christmas Thief*. And in a case of art imitating life, one of her lead characters was "a world-class scam artist whose offense had been to cheat trusting investors out of nearly $100 million in the seemingly legitimate company he had founded."

The guy even looked like me: "Fifty years old, narrow-faced, with a hawk-like nose, close-set eyes, thinning brown hair, and a smile that inspired trust."

You never can trust a writer; they're always looking for new material. At least she was more lenient on me than Judge Wolin. Mary sentenced her fictional scam artist to four months less of a prison term than what I got.

Maybe her con man gets out early for good behavior, I sniffed. But I had no intention of behaving—or breaking.

CHAPTER 20

FOOD, FAMILY, AND FRIENDS OF OURS

For a few minutes, we coulda been just a bunch of guys
eating linguine on Mulberry Street.

My mother died of a broken heart on Easter Sunday in 2006, waiting for me to get out of prison. Not that we ever had such a great mother-son relationship, but we were all each other had. After a lifetime of getting beat on by her husband, then watching her only child go to prison, then seeing her first grandchild dying young in such a horrific way, she'd had enough. She drank more and more to ease the pain and fell on Good Friday, went to the hospital, then died that Sunday. I think she gave up.

With her death I lost all connection with my blood family. Uncle Anthony had died years before. My cousin Anthony Bianco, who did the books for me at Wellesley, wasn't allowed to talk to me.

I'd been writing letters and cards to my children for years without getting a reply. When I telephoned Dorian's or Debbie's, my calls were either not accepted or blocked. So after my mother died, I gave up, too. I shut off what small part of my heart I had kept alive for them and started creating friends and family on the inside. You have to, to survive.

And in my case, I also met up with old friends—a lot of them.

At the beginning of 2008 I was sent to Allenwood low-security prison in Pennsylvania. It was one of the nicer ones and even got the "Best Prison in the Country" award one year. The living quarters were an open area with private cubicles with two bunk beds and lockers where you kept your stuff.

One day I was in my cubicle obsessively organizing my stuff when I heard a familiar voice behind me.

"You don't remember me, do you?"

I turned around and nearly shit myself. It had been about seventeen years. Fucking *Enzo Camino.*

"Don't worry, don't worry," he said, waving his hand and giving me a hug. "I know you talked to the Feds about me. But now we're together again, and you're gonna make up for that and help get me out. We're family, after all."

We were in the same unit; he was only five bunks down. There was no way the Feds and the US Attorney's Office knew about this; it must have been a total fuckup in the system. To put me five beds down from the guy I stole with and then gave information about? Enzo had been in prison ever since Harry's triumph in court a dozen years earlier, but he still looked great, the son of a bitch—still had that slick Tony Bennett look about him.

And now that I was living twenty feet away from him—a captive audience, so to speak—he was going to make the most of it.

He wanted out and was in the middle of yet another appeal and he had a scheme.

"I want you to concoct a story for me to use in my appeal," he said one day, as we ate egg sandwiches on my bunk. He was bribing me with food to cooperate, and it was working. Food was the most important thing in prison because it was so hard to get, and everyone was desperate for it. After my mother died, I didn't have anyone giving me commissary money anymore so Enzo gave me some of his, and he set up a few kitchen helpers to smuggle us a dozen egg sandwiches every few days, hidden in their clothing. Once a week, they'd bring us hamburgers. Other days, they'd bring us raw chicken pieces.

"You can say that the FBI set me up. Say the government lied and they made you lie and they trumped up the charges against me. I want you to reverse everything you said about me; I want you to recant."

I would have admitted to anything at that point just to get those egg sandwiches and raw meat, and I did for a while. I went along with it. I signed his documents that said I lied. When I didn't want to be pressured anymore, I knew how to get out of it quick. I wrote a letter to Chris Christie's second in command, Assistant US Attorney Ralph Marra (who took over for Joe Sierra), and mentioned that my old buddy Enzo Camino was my new jail mate. The next day four cops showed up, handcuffed me, and got me out of that unit. No matter how bad I'd been, the government always protected their people, and as a trained informant, I was their people.

But they didn't know what to do with me or where to put me so they stuck me in the hole. I was paired up in the same cell as a young member of the Aryan Brotherhood with a shaved head and a Nazi swastika tattooed on his forehead.

This guy was a killer. He slashed someone's throat in chow hall and did it again to someone in the hole. Fortunately, he thought I was a character. So much so that he gave me a nickname: "Old-School."

"Hey, Old School!" he'd say, with a punch on my shoulder. "Since you're an old man from the olden times with an old-man hip replacement, I'm gonna have mercy on you and give you the bottom bunk."

Everyone else was afraid of him but I wasn't. I was used to crazy guys; I was one myself.

Stabbing someone in the neck was apparently the murder method of choice in the prison. I saw a lot of neck stabbings when I passed through the maximum-security prison in Canaan. One time when I was waiting in the holding area, an inmate stabbed another—a child molester—in the neck and threw him off the second-floor tier onto the table where I was eating dinner with a bunch of mobsters. We were eating spaghetti and meatballs when his body splatted right on the table. The sirens went off and the unit went on lockdown, but we kept eating. It ain't so easy to make spaghetti and meatballs in a high-security prison, so we weren't gonna waste a good meal.

Another time I was playing cards in a cell with four guys; one was scheduled to testify against John Gotti Jr. three days later. Another guy started an argument with the Gotti witness and accused him of cheating.

"I don't think he was cheatin'," I said. Didn't matter.

The guy accusing him of cheating got up and stabbed the Gotti witness in the throat, over and over. The coroner later said it was ninety-two times. Then he wrapped a towel around the guy and sat him up in the bunk to let him bleed out into the towel. Me and the other guy didn't say nothing. We gathered the cards and carefully and quickly left the jail cell.

For three days, that guy stayed there dead like that, honest to god. Every day at the counts, the cops went by to check that we were in our cells, and the stabber would stand the dead body up next to him and turn him sideways a little so they saw two bodies in there, but they didn't notice one of them wasn't breathing. It wasn't until the smell of the dead body got so bad and other inmates complained that the COs realized there was a rotting body somewhere.

After Allenwood, they put me behind the wire at Loretto prison in Pennsylvania. Being at Loretto was just like being at a big mob sit-down.

My roommate for my first six months was Anthony "Fat Tony" Rabito, the consigliere of the Bonanno crime family—in for racketeering and extortion. Fat Tony and I used to walk around the track together outside to pass the time, him with his cane and me with my bad hip. He was in his mid-seventies and was a smart, funny, happy guy—even in prison. I was still fucked up about what I'd done to myself, and resistant to prison life. Fat Tony tried to give me fatherly advice.

"Look at the mess I got myself into, Anthony," I'd say.

"Tommy, this is the life we chose," he'd say, thumping his fist against his chest with his free hand, the way mob guys do in the movies. "We chose this mob life, you and I. You could have been a legitimate businessman, but you chose this. We can't have regrets."

We ate every meal together and he bought me commissary stuff. Whenever he had bags to carry, I carried them. I carried his tray in chow hall, too. I showed the proper respect for a man like him, you know? Every month I cut his hair with prison scissors, the kind little kids used in kindergarten with rounded edges and rubber tips on the ends. And I'd shave the little hairs from his ears—my grandfathers, both barbers, would have been proud.

Under Tony's wing I had the full protection of the Bonanno crime family while I was in prison, even though I was Genovese. We talked about our families, both personally and professionally. Fat Tony didn't have any kids and looked on me as a son. Still, I was shocked when he suggested I do the unthinkable and impossible—ditch my association with the Genovese family once I got out and become a made man in the Bonanno crime family, by his side.

"Nah, Anthony. I don't want to get involved like that."

"Think about it, Tommy. You're gonna be huge again when you get out."

Jesus. A quarter century later and they were *still* trying to make me. I'd stayed unmade this long, why would I change that now?

One by one, Fat Tony and I gathered more family members together at Loretto. We were in our cell one afternoon when someone knocked on our door and opened it.

"Tom! How ya doin'?"

In walked the towering Nicky Glasses to give me a bear hug and two kisses on the cheeks. The good news was that he wasn't in the pen 'cause of me, he said. But he had to be careful about being seen with me because the association could get him in more trouble than he already was.

"Listen, Tommy. Don't talk to me in front of everybody on the compound. I don't want nobody to know we know each other. But you're wit us here. We'll make sure you're taken care of."

Seems I was wit all of them, once again.

My prison ID . . . I was just a number

For breakfast, lunch, and dinner we had a mob table in the chow hall where a dozen of us sat together, guys from the Bonanno, Genovese, Lucchese, Gambino, and Colombo families—we were just one family in here. We'd meet at the entrance and walk in together like a high school gang and then sit down at our table together. All the other inmates knew not to sit at *our* table. It was a multigenerational, multifamily sit-down for the country's top organized criminals—many whose names I can't mention here, or I'll have myself a big problem.

We only had fifteen minutes to shove the shitty food in our faces. When we were done, we got up in unison and left together.

Because the food was crap, we often made pasta in our cells. This was an essential, jerry-rigged art form every Italian in prison had to learn if they were going to get their required spaghetti. There were a few ways you could do it. I got a guy working in the plumbing department to smuggle me two electrical cords with the ends cut off. Then I got a guy in the shop department to smuggle me a metal coil. I wrapped the exposed ends of the wires around the ends of the coil and now I've got a homemade "stinger." When you plugged it in and put it in a garbage can filled with water, you got boiling water.

From the commissary, we bought pasta, cheese, and sauce. From the kitchen, we stole garlic and hamburger meat. You put each item in plastic garbage bags and dunk them in the boiling water. I used to line up three garbage cans with three stingers in a row in my cell, like simmering pots on a kitchen stove—one had the pasta, one had the sauce and garlic, one had the meatballs.

Fat Tony, Nicky Glasses, and one or two other key Italians would be invited to my cell for dinner that night and we'd eat on stolen plates and cutlery from the kitchen. It felt good. For a few minutes, we coulda been just a bunch of guys eating linguine on Mulberry Street.

One night over dinner, I told the guys about how I duped Mary Higgins Clark. A few days later, one of the older, wiseguy Genovese guys showed up at my cell with a present from the commissary.

"It's for you to send to your friend . . . that writer, Mary," he said. He held up a little card with powder-blue raised lettering on it: "Thinking of You."

"Why don't you send it to her! Ha-ha!" laughed one of the other guys. "It can be your way to make it up to her!"

Why not? Inside I scrawled, "Sorry for what I did. I didn't really mean it," and put it in the mail. I wasn't trying to stick it to her, really, I wasn't.

Three days later the prison alarms went off and the warden locked the entire prison down. I was summoned to go to SIS office (Secret Intelligence Service)—never, ever a good sign. When I arrived, a bunch of FBI guys from Pittsburgh were there with the lieutenant of SIS. *Fuck, fuck, fuck.*

"How you doin'?" I asked.

"Giacomaro, sit down," the warden said. "We got an email from the FBI in West Paterson and attached here to the email is a scan of a card: 'Thinking of You.' It was sent to Mary Higgins Clark. And we have faxes here from the FBI in Paterson, 'cease and desist' letters."

"Yeah," I smiled. "I sent her a little note. To be nice."

"But . . . why the . . ." The warden started to laugh hysterically.

"Mr. Giacomaro," said one of the FBI agents, "we think it's really nice and all that you're thinking of her, but she's a victim of yours—a VICTIM. Do you understand that? Do you realize who this woman is?"

"Yeah."

"This is one of the top writers *in the country,*" says the other agent, sternly. "She's personal friends with the president!"

"Yeah. Well she's my friend, too."

"Giacomaro," the warden interrupted, still laughing, "just don't do it again, okay? We have to punish you if you do."

"I promise. Scout's honor."

They made me write it down on a piece of paper, too, like a little kid writing on the chalkboard after he'd done something bad in class.

I promise not to contact Mary ever, ever again.

I promise not to contact Mary ever, ever again.

I promise not to contact Mary ever, ever again.

The day Fat Tony left Loretto in the summer of 2009, I got his black jogging suit and brand-new Nike sneakers ready for him. I had the jogging suit washed and I ironed it personally and perfectly, and I laced and laid out his sneakers. The night before, I gave him a haircut. When it was time, I walked him to R&D (Receiving and Departure) and sat with him on the bench while they processed his departure paperwork.

"Don't forget what I told you, Tommy," he said, as we hugged goodbye. "No regrets. I know you'll do what's right."

Fat Tony was one of the few good friends I'd made in my seven years in prison so far, and when you don't have family, friends keep you sane and alive. A few months later when they sent me across the street to the Loretto sissy-la-la camp, I met another friend like that.

The Loretto camp was one of the nicest camps in the country. The barracks were immaculate, the grounds were lush, and the food in chow hall was edible. Compared to all the other prisons I'd been to before, this was paradise.

When you sat on the lawn chairs on the grounds, you could see roads of regular traffic just beyond the little "Out of Bounds" signs—freedom was close enough to touch. In fact, you *could* touch it. Inmates would get their girlfriends or wives to park across the street, and they'd run across for an evening quickie in between counts.

Manuto Nunez had already been at the Loretto sissy-la-la camp for a year before I arrived. He was a tall, young, good-looking jujitsu champ and Cuban drug dealer sentenced to more than a dozen years. Everybody, all the guards and inmates, loved him—he was the opposite of me in personality: nice, sunny, sensitive, like a big, handsome teddy bear. The kinds of qualities you look for in a cocaine dealer. But still.

We met while sitting in a pair of lawn chairs next to each other one afternoon, trying to get a tan. He being Cuban and me being Sicilian, that took about five minutes. But we got to talking and it didn't take long to discover that it was Manny and his crew who used to supply me with large quantities of coke when I was at the height of my own dealing days. Small world!

We began meeting for regular afternoon talks in the sun, after Manny worked out with the rusty weights in "the shack"—the out-door gym at the prison. I gave him advice about business and money, and he acted as my loyal bodyguard, getting me out of fights by tackling me to the ground or talking the other, bigger guy down. One day my temper was so crazy and out of control and I needed to fight, so I went after a bunch of big guys with a baseball bat that I got from the shack. Manny jumped me before I hit one of them, a guy who'd been annoying me, and took me down, taking the bat from me.

"You're gonna kill this guy and they'll keep you in here forever!" he said.

And yet, he was so loyal that if I told him, "Manny, go kill that piece of shit for me," he would have.

"When we get out of here," I promised him, "you're gonna work for me."

Manny had connections in the commissary and with the drivers who came into the compound so he arranged to smuggle in some designer jogging suits and half a dozen pairs of Nike sneakers for me. I kept my stash in plastic bins under my lower bunk. Manny did my laundry, and everything was meticulous and perfectly folded—he even wiped my shoes for me every day. He was my protégé.

Walking around the camp together like an oddly match buddy movie—Manny with his easy smile, Latin strut, and biceps like tree trunks, and me with my arrogance and bad-hip limp—we looked like Tony Montana and his sidekick, Manny Ribera, in *Scarface*. Or Joe Buck and Ratso Rizzo in *Midnight Cowboy*.

But it was more than that. During our talks, I told him about Lauren and how my family had cut me off. He told me about losing his father, who died a few months before he came to Loretto. Somewhere in the gap of pain and emptiness where I'd lost a child and Manny had lost a parent, we forged a father-son relationship we both needed.

The thing about Manny is he knew how to do jail. He knew how to make friends with the COs and play jail politics while I was confrontational. He waved at the guards when we sunned ourselves and I scowled. He always got extra food in the chow line—*two* hamburgers, *two* pieces of chicken—because he knew how to make them like him. It's what I knew to do and had done on the outside as a salesman, too, but not on the inside.

My first problem was that I could barely admit I was even there. In the nearly eight years I'd been in prison, I still hadn't given in to the reality that I was a prison inmate with nothing, just like everyone else here—nothing and no one special. I'd survived the worst of it and hadn't broken so far, and that was good; but I still hadn't *bent*. It's not that I didn't know *how* to; it's that I refused. Judge Wolin nailed it when he sentenced me: I was a "resistant, arrogant felon," and that was still true. For the first time in my life, I was floundering.

My job at Loretto was to wipe down five fire extinguishers with a wet cloth, that's it, and I'd be done for the day. It was a total of fifteen minutes of easy work. But I was such a pompous ass that I wouldn't even do that. When the guards confronted me, I'd say, "I ain't workin' today! I'm going to go lie in the sun!"

My first few years incarcerated, I got away with not working much because I was grieving over Lauren's death. Then, I lucked out with a warden or two who were easy on me. But at Loretto, I was expected to pull my weight and I wasn't. Manny tried to teach me, to talk to me, because he knew it would lead to trouble.

"Tommy, you gotta give in to these people or they'll send you away," he'd say. His job was to mop the kitchen floor for half an hour every day.

"They come to me to ask me why I can't talk sense into you, Tommy! Why do you keep resisting them? It's easy. We could have it good here for the next few years!"

"I don't want to do it," I'd say. "Fuck them."

He was right—we were sitting pretty, Manny and I. And I should have been more grateful, seeing that Bernie Madoff was arrested the year before and sentenced to 150 years for his Ponzi scheming. The laws changed for sentencing fraud crimes after I'd gone in and now they were massive. I don't care how many billions he took; he didn't take a life, yet they took his.

I was doing great in comparison. But like every other pretty deal I ever had in my life, I had to sabotage it.

A new warden came to the camp in early 2010 and when he heard I refused to work, he pulled the bins out from under my bunk during inspection and tossed my stuff into garbage bags and rusty old lockers. I was outside sunning myself at the time, like a billionaire back in my little fishing village in the South of France. When I returned and saw what he'd done, I blew a fuse. Manny wasn't there to diffuse it. I raced downstairs where the warden was inspecting the lower barracks.

"Hey, warden, why the fuck did you destroy my clothes?"

"What did you say to me?"

"You heard what the fuck I said."

Everybody around us was silent, staring at us. The warden didn't reply, or even hesitate. He turned to the lieutenant next to him: "Handcuff him and put him in the fucking hole. I don't want to ever see him again."

Four guys came and dragged me away. Just before I was out of the building, I saw Manny running down the stairs—someone had raced to get him and tell him what was going on. We had only a fraction of a second of eye contact. In that moment, I tried to wordlessly say: *We'll find each other when this is over.* But all I could think was *I'm sorry, I'm sorry . . .*

I was in the hole for one month. Then two months. I went two or three days at a time without food, and then maybe they'd give me half a hot dog or a few beans. Every morning, the warden would come by and bang on the glass window:

"Did they feed you last night, Giacomaro? You're never going to get out of this hellhole!"

Then three months.

Every night, I sent a letter to the US attorney for help. The COs would hand my letters to the warden, who threw them out. I went from 185 to 150 pounds. *He's trying to kill me.* They turned the cold air up and wouldn't give me a blanket. I got sick and feverish. I laid my head against the cold cement floor and closed my eyes. I was losing my mind.

Dad, you're going to be okay. You'll get out.

Lauren honey? How?

One of your letters will get through. The US marshals will come and get you.

But how will I survive the rest of my time in here, baby? I can't do it.

You've got to bend to them, Dad. Talk your way out. Use your smarts and charm. Play their game and beat them at it, like always.

You've got to con them in the way that only you can, Daddy . . .

CHAPTER 21

KING OF
THE CONS

My room was the village trading post, and my commissary
account averaged a float of $1,000 per month. It felt
good being a successful businessman again.

A concerned guard did smuggle out one of my letters and
mailed it.

A few days later, four US marshals showed up at my
cell at 6 AM with chains and belts. They bound me up, threw me
into a white van, and drove me six hours to Milan, Michigan. Along
the way they played Johnny Cash and gorged on Big Macs while I
alternately gagged and salivated at the pungent scent of that shitty
special sauce. Even with "Folsom Prison Blues" on high volume, I
couldn't get that old McDonald's ditty out of my head: *"You deserve*
a break today . . ."

By the time we reached the prison, I'd made a decision: I was
going to change.

I once asked Dr. Bowe at Fort Dix if people could change, and
I remember she said it was possible, but very difficult and very rare.
Then she told me a fable about a scorpion and a frog. The scor-
pion asks the frog to carry it across the river but the frog hesitates,

certain the scorpion will sting him. The scorpion assures him he won't because then they'd both surely drown. So the frog agrees to take him, but halfway across, the scorpion stings him and dooms them both.

"'But why did you sting me?' the frog asked the scorpion," Dr. Bowe continued. "'Now we will both die!' And the scorpion answered, '*Because it's my nature.*' Some people believe that certain natures cannot be altered," she said, "that what is fundamental about a person will not change."

"Is that what you believe, Dr. Bowe?"

She looked at me thoughtfully for a moment.

"Let's say I live and work in hope."

There was only one part of myself that I intended to alter and it was only temporary. I had to push my arrogance and narcissism aside (does a true narcissist actually *know* he's a narcissist?) enough that I could use my skills to help myself. After eight years in prison, I had to stop resisting the reality and laser focus on being the best inmate ever. Judge Wolin called me resistant and arrogant, but I was done being that guy.

Lauren was right: I was The Worm, I was Golden Tongue, I had—what did Mary call it?—*a smile that inspired trust.* I was going to take over this new prison and get out early; this was the plan.

———————

It was now spring of 2010 and the prison at Milan, one of the oldest in the country, was almost eighty years old. After I arrived the COs stuck me in a crappy, old unit built in 1933—a giant, open room that housed three hundred inmates, with half the bunks lined up on one side of the room and half on the other. It was a hot, sticky, loud, and leaky room of caged-up animals. The entire prison was built to hold one thousand inmates, but it now housed double that amount.

I paid no attention and got busy with my plan. I'd seen a gorgeous, new building on the compound when I arrived and asked around. It was for inmates in the residential drug abuse program (RDAP)—an expensive, six-month rehab course sponsored by the federal government, which cost the feds $250,000 per patient.

Inmates in the program not only got to live in the comfortable, modern, dorm-like setup, they also got a year taken off their sentences if they completed the entire thing. The course took up to three hundred inmates/patients each year, and they came in from all over the country.

You had to qualify to get in: diagnosed as an alcoholic or drug addict or have certain behavioral problems. The program's goal was to educate inmates about the biological and emotional reasons why they were addicts and teach them how to live a balanced lifestyle— something I knew nothing about—when they got out.

With the recommendation of my doctors at Fort Dix, plus my personal history—alcoholic parents, coke and drinking addictions, my OCD, ADD, and other psychological challenges listed on my intake paperwork—I was very qualified (some might say *over*qualified). The eight years I'd been in prison was the longest I'd been sober since my years leading up to puberty. Since then, except for blocks of time when I was focusing on work, I hadn't gone a day without being drunk, stoned, or high. You could easily get blow, hooch, and white lightning in prison, but I never did. Even though I was in denial about being there, and there were times when I was desperate to escape mentally, part of me wanted to keep my wits about me at all times.

"Tom, do you have any special talents?" Dr. Talbert, the lead doctor in the program asked, as he read through my files. "The kid who helped me run the program the past two years is leaving and the job is vacant. I see you're in for business fraud. Do you by chance have any talent organizing and motivating people?"

I could feel Golden Tongue rally to the surface.

"Dr. T," I said, with a warm familiarity and a smile that inspired trust, "I could run this entire unit for you better than it's ever been run before. If you give me this job, I'll do the morning openings,

I'll qualify the inmates for you, I'll keep the guys in line for you, I'll do your paperwork. You don't gotta lift a finger. Let me take care of everything for you."

Dr. T. looked pleasantly shocked. It was hard enough to get an inmate to work at all, never mind find a go-getter like me. After he spoke again to my doctors at Fort Dix I got the job, and the next day I lugged my stuff over to my new digs.

———————

The first thing I saw when I opened the door of my new "cell" was a window.

It was across the room and it looked out at an expanse of lush farmland behind the prison, dotted with trees, haystacks, and rows of crops. I went to the window and pulled at it and it opened. I breathed in the farm air and sighed. Such a simple, ordinary act was gratefully extraordinary to me.

It was a two-man room with air-conditioning, a work desk, a bunk bed, and the best part—a private bathroom with a porcelain toilet. Down the hall were four new microwaves and private showers that I could use any time, and they had doors on them. I didn't have to see everyone else's dick anymore! I felt like I'd scored a suite at the Plaza. (Ah, *the Plaza*. Limos, Bergdorf's, eggs Benedict, and a hooker named Berkeley . . .)

A few minutes later came the catch; he walked into the room. The gorgeous digs came with a big, fat monster of a roommate who pissed on the bathroom floor and was so heavy that when he slept on the top bunk, his mattress coils sagged and hit me in the face. He was *not* part of my plan. The next day I informed Dr. T that I was recruiting a new roommate and he said fine. I searched the drug unit for a nice, clean kid who had no money and was hungry. Food would be my bait. I had a plan for that, too—wait for it.

"Golden Boy" was a twenty-five-year-old blond, WASPy, all-American kid from Sioux Falls, South Dakota. He had little coke-bottle eyeglasses and giant arms—a weightlifter, in the clink for possession of methamphetamine. I nicknamed him "Golden Boy" because he was blond, and he was soon to become the next protégé of Golden Tongue.

"Hey, kid," I asked, "how would you like to eat good every day—extra hamburgers, extra chicken, fresh eggs every day, and all you gotta do in return is be my roommate and keep the place spotless to my exact specifications."

Within three days, the Monster was out and Golden Boy was in. Every day the kid mopped the floor, cleaned the toilet bowl, made my bed, washed my laundry (and folded it the way my mother taught me), chopped my garlic and onions for the pasta sauce, and washed the window that looked out to the hayfield.

In exchange, he got to eat like a horse. That's because in the time it took to exchange roommates, I'd also scored a second coveted job, in the kitchen—phase two of my takeover plan. If I hadn't had my head stuck up my ass for the last eight years, I would have zeroed in on the kitchens all along. Food was power in prison; everything revolved around getting better food and getting more of it, and the kitchen was the seat of that power.

I went to see Mr. Klemme, the supervisor of the chow hall. Klemme hailed from Toledo, Ohio, and was a former sergeant in the Marines. I knew he'd appreciate that I was a son of a Marine with Marine-style skills.

"Mr. Klemme, I organized two hundred employees as president of my last company," I told him, "and I can organize your kitchen and the inmates in your kitchen no problem."

Dr. T. had already put in the good word about me, and Klemme had looked me up on the internet.

"So, you're a trained FBI informant, is that right, Giacomaro?"

"Yes, sir, I am at that."

"That is exactly what I need in my kitchen. Some of the guys in here are child molesters, and I need someone who can make sure no one kills them during breakfast. I need someone who knows how to sense trouble before it happens and stop it."

I never thought my Quantico training would be used for prison, but there you had it.

"I'll take care of it," I told him.

"I'm making you my clerk, and you're going to run the kitchen, the COs chow hall, and the dining room. You're going to manage the one hundred fifty inmates that work here. I'm giving you everything to do."

As I told ya, a good salesman gives buyers what they need most. Dr. T. and Mr. Klemme needed someone to make them look good, make their lives easier, and make sure no one's neck got stabbed. I was their guy.

By my second week at Milan, I was juggling the two full-time jobs and working twelve hours a day, seven days a week. I didn't want a day off. Keeping busy gave me a purpose, something to focus on, and made doing the time go faster.

My day began at 3 AM when I opened the kitchen and started prepping and setting up. With each meal of breakfast, lunch, and dinner I had a staff of fifty working under me—busboys, servers, cleaners, and cooks. I reorganized the kitchen as soon as I arrived and designated "captains" who managed each area. This was my new crew.

Each meal had four different seatings during which three hundred inmates were fed within a fifteen-minute time segment. I had to get those hungry animals in, fed, and out the door fast. Then clean everything up and wipe everything down and get the next unit in and out.

It was ordered chaos. I patrolled the aisles and barked orders to my staff: "Pick up that tray! Take out that garbage!" Mr. Klemme would supervise for a while, then go to his room in the back to take a nap once he was confident I'd get everyone fed and keep them alive.

When I wasn't patrolling, I was sitting at my special table reserved for just me—my throne, you might say—because I was now the King of the Kitchen. I had the power to hire or fire these guys. I wasn't sitting there to eat; I sat there to oversee my workers and make sure my captains were on top of everything.

At 6:45 AM I'd leave the kitchen to get to the meeting room for a 7 AM start time of the drug program. I'd been instructed on what to do in front of the three hundred patients; I was to say good morning and lead them in the RDAP prayer:

We pledge to be honest with ourselves and with others; to be open to new ideas and criticism; to take responsibility for our actions; and to show humility both in success and failure.

Only I had my own idea of how I was going to do things—more like a master of ceremonies warming everyone up for a big rock concert.

"We gotta get these guys energized!" I told Dr. T, when I was explaining my grand vision to him in his office. "I was in class yesterday and nobody was paying attention. I'm going to engage them, like a comedy show. I'm going to wake everybody up!"

The night before my third day on that job, I went into the meeting room, moved all the chairs closer together, then put tape on the floor as markers for their new positions. When I got there the next morning, they were all talking to each other—which was a good sign. Dr. Talbert and six other shrinks sat at the side of the room waiting to see what I was going to do. I went to the podium and took the microphone. I was like Robin Williams in *Good Morning, Vietnam*.

"Good mornnnnnnnning, RDAP! My name is Thomas Giacomaro. You can call me Tom. How's everybody this morning?"

Grumble, grumble, grumble.

They wanted to go back to bed; they were sitting like lumps of shit. The inmates in the other units could do that—they could lie around in their bunks all day if they wanted to. But the RDAP guys had to earn their upscale rooms and year off their sentence.

"What? I can't hear you!" I yelled into the mike. "I want to hear noise, let's get going! Let's get the blood flowing! Everybody on their feet! Let's do arms, ready? Arms up, down, up, down! I want participation!"

Hundreds of inmates shuffled to their feet.

"If you like that Richard Simmons guy, you'll love me! Up, down, up, down. Now everybody clap their hands!"

Out of the corner of my eye, I could see Dr. T. and the six psychiatrists laughing their asses off because by now the inmates were hysterically laughing themselves.

"All right, all right. Everybody sit down. Now we're going to do the news," I told them. "I'm going to do the news today and I'll pick somebody else to do it tomorrow. We'll cover current events, US news, and international news. I'm also going to pick someone to be our weatherman. Sometimes, I'll pick someone to be our weather *girl*."

They roared at that, and the next day they understood what I meant when I trotted out an inmate—one of the child molesters—dressed up like a girl with bows in his hair, to deliver the weather. After the news and weather, we had a Q&A period and after that, I assigned groups to classes that went until noon. Some classes were drug related, some were about alcohol, and others focused on psychotherapy and psychology.

I sat in on the classes or used that time to book interesting speakers for the group or help the psychology team find other inmates who qualified for the program. In an empty classroom, I interviewed potential candidates while one of the psychiatrists monitored the interaction. It was a big responsibility, helping them make a decision like that. But what people on the outside don't know is that inmates are the ones who run their prisons. And in the psych department at Milan, I had become the go-between for prisoners and doctors. Milan was filled with rough Detroit characters, and they'd tell me details about the crimes they committed they wouldn't tell a doctor or a cop.

To get to the interview stage, an inmate ideally had to be in the last two years of his sentence (I was given special consideration because I was running the program) so that when he completed it, he could get back to regular society as soon as possible. Once they got to me, I had to figure out if the inmate would be compatible with the others and not interfere with the very serious treatment going on.

We didn't want guys who'd cause trouble. We didn't want guys who were gonna shit in the showers and ruin it for everyone else. It was my job to help weed out the potential shower shitters.

"This guy and this guy, you can't bring in here, Doc," I would say to Dr. T, when we went over my lists post-interview. He told me later that the caliber of inmates in the program rose dramatically after I got involved, and that affected their success rate once out of the prison as well.

As I saw it, we were in an inhumane place but we were all human beings. And it was my job to remind them of that when they weren't acting like human beings.

"Good morning, residential drug-abuse program! The first current event I have to report today is that one of you pooped in the shower last night," I'd say once in a while. "I'm not going to ask who did it, but if and when I find out, you're gonna be mopping floors for the next six months. Right, Dr. Talbert? Gentlemen, we do not poop in the showers. Please refrain from this!"

At noon every day, I took an afternoon siesta. I put one of my captains in charge of cleaning up the last lunch seating, and I set up a plastic lawn chair facing the hayfield to sun myself until 3 PM. Golden Boy sometimes joined me, like Manny used to. I'd wave to the guys above us in the gun towers and at the guards circling the perimeter in trucks. Manny taught me good.

———

After my siesta, there was more work to do. I had to review and sign off on the workbooks filled out by the inmates about the classes they took, like a teacher marking student homework. This was usually the job of the psychiatrist who taught the class, but I offered to do it—jumping at the chance to make myself even more indispensable.

After the workbooks, I went over the weekly pay sheets for the entire kitchen staff. Once Mr. Klemme learned I was good with numbers, he put me in charge of the money—a move that would have had the FBI, the US Attorney's Office, and my previous investors hooting and hollering. But there was no million-dollar pension fund to steal from these guys, that's for sure. The inmates made twelve cents an hour in the kitchen. If I was feeling generous, I could give them bonuses of a dime. That kept them in line and working hard; they needed every penny they could get for the commissary. Once again, I had the power of the pen.

When I was done with the pay sheets, I had the four dinner shifts to handle—that's usually when I stole food to take back to my room for Golden Boy and me. Mr. Klemme knew I was taking food, but I left the kitchen so immaculate he let it slide.

The warden even commented on it. He came into the chow hall once and was impressed.

"Giacomaro, this place is unbelievable! Hey, Klemme! What are you doing for Giacomaro in exchange for all this?!"

"What *don't* I do for Giacomaro?" Mr. Klemme answered, with a laugh. "I leave the refrigerator door open for him, that's what I do."

I fed Golden Boy well, as promised. Not only did I whip up pasta and sauce using the microwave (no more stingers!), I devised a method for pizza using my stolen kitchen groceries. I'd wet, layer, and spread out four flour wraps on a circle of cardboard as my pizza tin and press them together until they made a layer of dough, crimping the edges like a piecrust. Then I'd let it dry for ten to fifteen minutes before topping it with sauce, mozzarella, garlic, then two minutes in the microwave.

After dinner, I'd walk around the unit to make sure there was no trouble. Some nights I'd check the bathroom and see four feet under the stall.

"*Ahem!* We have a problem here. We're not supposed to have four feet in the toilet, gentlemen! You're a cunt hair away from getting expelled. Get to bed!"

But mostly, my unit was well behaved. For a lot of them, this was the first time they felt like themselves again since being in prison; the same was true for me. They also felt like they were learning something important and improving themselves; the same was true for me.

At twilight, my more lucrative moonlighting shift began.

Within the first few weeks working in the kitchen, I was selling food to the inmates who lined up with their trays at the chow hall. If you had an "account" with me, you stood in a certain line and I made sure you were slipped an extra burger or extra fruit or whatever you wanted. In exchange, you made sure to give me stamps later or get your family to send money to the central office in Missouri to be deposited in my commissary account.

Stamps, tuna, and mackerel in pouches were good commodities to have for trading because everyone needed stamps to send letters home, and the canned goods never went bad so you could stow them in your lockers. Some of the COs in chow hall saw what I was doing and looked the other way. I was so well liked now, and even *respected* because of the way I ran the drug program and kitchen, they let it go.

I really was a different person in Michigan. *I* knew that I was sucking the asses of the cops, shrinks, doctors, supervisors, and COs so I could get what I wanted. But on the outside, to everyone else, I was Tom Giacomaro, the cooperative, helpful, hard worker whom everyone wanted to know and be around.

Within a few months I expanded my business. I recruited a group of thirty "runners" who worked in the kitchen and smuggled food out to me, just like my cocaine runners in the old days.

"Whatever you bring, I'll give you your price for it," I told them. "If you bring me volume, I'll give you a lower price and make you my partner and you don't have to deal with fifty other people to collect from, just me."

They brought me pieces of chicken wrapped up in their pants, hamburgers on buns in their shirts, and egg sandwiches in their pockets. If ten runners brought me three hamburgers each, that was thirty burgers. I'd pay each runner with two stamps per burger, then mark up the price and sell the burgers for five stamps each. They inmates would rather pay the higher price than smuggle it out themselves.

The food came nonstop and I began to diversify. My runners brought me onions, tomatoes, potatoes, garlic, olive oil, pasta, fresh eggs, and tomato paste. I got plastic bins to store everything under my bed—one bin for produce, another for perishables, another for food in pouches. Without refrigeration, I kept the eggs in a cooler filled with ice from an ice machine down the hall.

My room was the village trading post, and my commissary account averaged a float of $1,000 per month. It felt good being a successful businessman again. Golden Boy and I sunned ourselves in the yard like billionaires on a beach somewhere as my runners were busy making me money.

In my prison world, I was stinking rich.

I had four new pairs of sneakers, Hanes underwear and T-shirts, ten pairs of Champion jogging pants—I had the best wardrobe commissary money could buy. My first Christmas at Milan, the shrinks pitched in and got me the most expensive watch you could get at the commissary—a $500 Timex. It was worth more than a hundred Rolexes to me.

Back at my room I now slept on *two* mattresses piled on top of each other and had *two* pillows. The staff doctor wrote a note ordering the extras for me on account of my hip replacement.

"You're going to live like a king!" the doctor said.

It was a miracle, but in Milan, Michigan, I was actually happy.

"Giacomaro, you walk in here every morning so upbeat and positive," Mr. Klemme said to me once. "How do you do it?"

Maybe it was because I felt like myself again. I'd found my crew, started my businesses, and was living large and looking good. I was more successful than anybody else there *ever*. (Okay, so maybe I didn't put *all* my arrogance aside.)

Some people find god in prison; I found myself.

CHAPTER 22

FREEDOM

I walked outside, past the barbed wire fence,
and didn't look back.

I intended to con them all, but in the end, it was me who was the unsuspecting mark.

The goal of RDAP was to help inmates become better adjusted people, help them explore the reasons why they drank or drugged themselves into oblivion, why they needed to escape themselves or the world. Often, that exploration led to an unraveling of the reasons why they committed the crime they were in prison for, too.

By the spring of 2012, I'd sat in on two years' worth of classes on psychology, addiction, brain chemistry, behavioral patterns, chemical imbalances, cognitive therapy, and more—taking the same ones over and over again. Essentially, I did the program four times. At some point, the stuff started to sink in.

I had taken a few required psych courses in college but didn't pay much attention during them. I thought it was crap. It didn't help me as a kid when I went to therapy, and when I got older, well, mob guys don't sit around and talk about their feelings.

Unless they were at the opera, Italian men didn't *cry*. My dominant emotion was anger. Any pain, sadness, frustration, or vulnerability I ever felt during my life I chose to ignore, erase, or turn into rage.

It was a survival mechanism, one of the psychiatrists told us in class. Except for my few hungover moments of self-introspection at Bear Mountain in the early eighties, I'd never been interested in analyzing my behavior.

But now I'd lost everything, including a daughter. And I wanted to know why.

It was one of the first questions I asked Dr. Bowe at Fort Dix soon after Lauren was killed. *Why* had I done this to myself and everyone else? Why did I need the Bentleys, the cash, and the mansions I'd never even live in? Why did I hurt so many people, including myself and the ones I loved, and not feel a thing in the process? Why did I spend decades drunk and coked up?

Sitting in class one day, my first major realization was when the doctor talked about addictions being genetic. I thought of my mother pouring her first of many drinks at the bewitching hour and popping Xanax at night to sleep. I thought of my father going into rages when he drank his vodka. I was so used to it growing up, I didn't realize until that moment in class that both my parents were classic addicts, and I'd inherited the gene from both sides. By ten I was swigging church wine from the chalice and drinking cocktails of gin, vodka, and scotch with Eddy and Danny in the woods.

But that was only part of it. There were also the emotional reasons why someone wants to drink too much or take drugs or over-eat—because doing so blocks out specific feelings you can't or don't want to deal with.

"Unless you understand that," said one speaker in class, "you won't be able to stop. And you'll find yourself back here."

As good as I had it at Milan, I had no intention of ever coming back if and when I ever got out. So I started paying close attention to what the doctors were saying about one's environment growing up and family dynamics.

Figuring out my mother was easy. She had a husband who abused her verbally and physically every day of their marriage—that was something for her to want to escape from with booze, and something I'd want to erase from my mind as well.

But there was also the hazy memory of her going away for six months to a mysterious place with gray walls and white coats, when I was little. She begged and cried to come home. I tried hard to remember what I felt during those Sunday visits I had with her there, and it took a while to dig it up: fear, horror, and abandonment. No wonder I let her wipe my ass for me.

When I dug further, as the therapists gently suggested I do, I found wells of anger at her—anger that she didn't protect me from my father and that she didn't protect herself.

"She didn't know how," said one of the Milan therapists. "She was frightened herself and did the best she could. Can you live with that?"

"I don't know," I said.

"Were you the perfect father?"

"God, no."

"Did you cause your children pain?"

"Yes."

———

My father wasn't a mystery to me at all; I knew why he drank and hit us: because I was bad, I was nothing, and he hated me. That was a truth I'd been certain of ever since I was three years old.

Then I remembered something. My mother and I weren't the only ones abused by my father. When I was a kid and my grand-mother Josephine, his mother, used to come to our home in North Haledon for Sunday night dinners, he'd insult and yell at her so bad she sobbed right there at the table. He was always so angry at her, but I could never figure out why. And then it dawned on me.

I called up a cousin of mine and asked her to visit my father's sister, Aunt Millie, who was now elderly and living in Virginia. I needed her to answer something. A few weeks later she called me.

"I asked her what you wanted," my cousin said on the phone, "and you were right. Aunt Millie said, 'My brother Joe used to get beaten badly all the time by our father—*and* by our mother, too. I was the favorite one. I was spoiled and could do no wrong. But he was the "bad" one. If Joe didn't come home at a certain time, they'd lock the door and make him sit outside all night. This is when he was a still a kid. They wouldn't give him dinner and made him sleep outside all night.'"

I slowly hung up the pay phone. *Son of a bitch*, so that's your story. He hit you so you hit me, is that it? Am I supposed to feel sorry for you, now?

I did, a little. I felt sorry for both of us . . . for what we lost as father and son and more. I realized that along with my many other failings as a husband and father, I'd stayed away from my own children for fear that my temper was like my father's, and I'd beat them the way he did me. Staying away from them, I reasoned, kept them safe. I suppose it was my way, unknowingly, of breaking the cycle of violence in the family.

Knowing my father got hit didn't take away the sting of my hundreds of beatings, but at least it made me understand some of the *why* of it. All those hours sitting on the rock behind our house as a kid, crying and wondering what I'd done wrong. And all along, I'd done nothing.

I wasn't born bad.

In my own class workbook, I wrote:

My father was hit by his father, and then beaten up even worse in the Marines. He drank to self-medicate, then took out his rage on my mother, so she drank. He beat me and beat me down, so I drank and took drugs. My desperate need for expensive cars, watches, homes, clothes, and women was another way to escape or numb the pain and lift myself up to a "grandiose" level. And it was a way to get him to love me. And it was a way to get my revenge on him without hitting him back. I fell into a self-sabotaging pattern where I built up my world, then fucked

it up because I didn't feel worthy. Everything I touched turned to plat-
inum, and then to shit.
    And all this led me here.

I understood what had happened and that was good. I wasn't
about to get all emotional over it, though. What's done is done. I had
no need to think or talk about it anymore.

The rest of my unit, though, wanted to talk about their shit.

My unit was mostly made up of guys aged twenty-five to
thirty-five. Because I was older and in charge of the kitchen and the
meetings, they began to look up to me and trust me. They gave me
my new nickname, "Old Gangster," or "OG" for short. They wanted
to talk to *me* about their shit instead of the therapists. Most of them
came from bad, fatherless families living in the Detroit ghettos and
they looked up to me. This was a first for me.

I'd been presenting myself as a completely different version of
Tom Giacomaro in front of them—reliable, helpful, of service, car-
ing—they didn't know the other Tom, the *real* one, the asshole Tom.
He wasn't the kind of guy you told your problems to.

They didn't know that. So as I rushed around on my twelve-hour-
plus work schedule, they began coming up to me to talk.

It started with Golden Boy, who was having problems with his
girlfriend. Then other guys in our unit began approaching me after
the morning meetings to talk. Soon my kitchen crew started spilling
their guts as they pulled hamburgers from their pants, and guys in
the chow hall started plopping down next to me at my special table,
my throne, where I was not to be disturbed.

"Hey, Mr. Tom," they said, or, "Hey, OG, can I sit with you a
minute?"

"Yeah, sit down."

"You won't believe what happened."

"What happened?"

"Betty-Sue didn't take my call last night. She said she was sending me a letter. I didn't get no letter. I think she's cheating on me. I'm depressed. What should I do?"

Every inmate lost his girlfriend or baby-mama while in prison; there wasn't one who didn't. These bad, rough guys from the ghetto broke down crying telling me about it. I was embarrassed for them that they cried, never mind that they did it in front of me. I wasn't a fucking therapist; I didn't know what to tell these kids. I barely knew how to be a good friend.

They were desperate for letters from the people they loved, and I didn't care about that anymore—I'd given up on that six years earlier. No visitors at holidays and no mail from family hurt me in the beginning, but by the time I got to Milan, I was so disconnected from them I didn't feel it no more. I'd hardened up.

"Oh, shut the fuck up, you crybaby!" I'd tell them. "Get rid of the broad. You'll get a new one when you get out! You were cheating on her with three other broads anyway!"

After they stopped their whimpering, I'd attempt some practical advice.

"You gotta stop going to mail call," I'd say. "It's bad for you."

Somehow, my unique brand of tough love made them feel better and helped them.

Word got around outside our unit that I was "a good listener," and soon I had at least three inmates a day approaching me. I began booking "sessions" and keeping a notebook for appointments. I even had a waiting list.

Because of my phenomenal memory, I remembered every detail about everyone's life. ("You got that photogenic memory," Frankie used to say.) I knew whose dad walked out, whose moms were addicts, who was married and the names of their kids. I knew who killed a guy, who was suicidal, who was innocent, who didn't finish high school.

The doctors encouraged me to keep going because a lot of the guys didn't want to reveal themselves to a cop, and the psychiatrists were federal officers. Soon, I was doing my "therapy" sessions for three to four hours a day, and it even cut into my sacred suntan time. Dr. T unlocked a conference room for me after hours so I could hold sessions after midnight.

Why did I keep listening? Some of these guys were my crew, and I had to make sure they weren't too fucked up to work. Plus, I wanted to keep scoring brownie points with the staff, which went toward my plan to get out of there early.

But . . . it was something else, too.

When the twentieth tough guy broke down sobbing in front of me, I started listening for real. I actually *wanted* to help them. It also felt good being useful, using my mind in a way I never had before, in a way I never knew I could. I could hear Lauren's voice: *Just like the Tin Man and the Scarecrow, Daddy. They followed the yellow brick road to get a heart and a brain and realized they had it all along.*

I was also curious about the raw feelings they expressed so freely. It was foreign to me, like I was Spock in *Star Trek* observing these primitively unrestrained humans.

With Dr. T's guidance, I started giving better advice.

"Listen, you've got to move on with your life," I'd say. "You've got to start planning for when you get out."

A lot of them had never held a real job before, so I counseled them about where to start: "Go to a supermarket; they're less stringent on requirements. Take a job at night stocking shelves when the store's closed so you don't have to deal with customers, and it keeps you out of trouble. We have job placements in this unit to help you."

Dr. T was amazed at how much I helped them.

"They look up to you like a father, Tom," he said. Which amazed me. My own kids didn't look up to me like a father.

These kids were the same age as my eldest two with Debbie: Tom Jr. was now thirty-one and Nick was twenty-nine. I'd never talked with them about girlfriend problems or jobs, like a real father would. Maybe that's why I was doing it now with these fatherless kids. I was a childless father and maybe it was a way to make it up to my own children.

I'd started out telling my fellow inmates to ignore mail call as I'd done for years myself, and forget about friends and family who deserted them. But the truth was, the RDAP program promoted and encouraged family connectedness. They even gave out free greeting cards so you could write to your family and develop or mend your relationships with them.

In the fall of 2012 I took one of the free cards the unit offered and wrote a letter.

My daughter Stephanie was three years old when I went away, and probably had little memory of our fairy-tale home in Saddle River, or of me. Even at such a young age, Dorian used to call her "Tom with hair" because she was most like me in looks and personality.

Stephanie was thirteen now and living outside Detroit with Dorian's mother, a thirty-minute drive from the prison. Her world was vastly different from how I'd left it. A few months after I went to prison, the government took the $25 million I'd hidden for Dorian, and they'd been struggling ever since. I wasn't sure what Dorian told Stephanie about me or if she'd ever given her and her brother and sisters the cards and letters I'd written from various prison cells all over the country. I was a stranger to her.

Still, in the spirit of family connectedness I wrote, asking if her grandmother would bring her for a visit.

One day that November, Stephanie and her grandmother were waiting in the visitor's room. As soon as I saw her from across the room I choked up. She had my features but she reminded me of Lauren—the same soft hair, something in the eyes. Or maybe, seeing her simply reminded me that I was a father.

We weren't allowed to hug so we sat down across from each other at a table. For a minute, I couldn't speak. I felt sick inside—it was the sickness of regret. I was about to say something when her grand-mother cut in.

"You really made a disaster of everything," Dorian's mother began. "You ruined my daughter's life, you ruined the kids' lives, you . . ."

The list went on and on as Stephanie sat silent, slumping lower and lower in her chair. When Dorian's mother was done, I asked Stephanie questions about school, her siblings, but she barely answered. After fifteen minutes, they left.

It was a start, I thought.

A few days later I called Stephanie to see if we could try again—this time without her grandmother?

"Lose my number," she said. "I never want to see you again." *Click.*

That Christmas I worked double shifts in the kitchen. Most everyone else had family or friends visiting so I gave them the time off. It was the best time to work in the kitchen anyway, because I could steal the steak and make a big profit.

At Thanksgiving, we had turkey; on Memorial Day, we barbecued thousands of hamburgers, hot dogs, and sausages outside; on Christmas and New Year's, we got Applebee's steaks. They were delivered frozen the day before, so right after 3 AM count on Christmas Day, I raced to the chow hall in anticipation. I checked in, did breakfast, and organized my captains to do the cleanup. Mr. Klemme was ready for his morning nap about then.

"Mr. Klemme, I need to get salad from the freezer to prep it for lunch. Can you unlock the freezer for me?"

"Giacomaro, you know we don't freeze the lettuce."

"Right. I'm craving an ice cream, then."

"At 7 AM?"

I shrugged.

"Okay, okay. I'll unlock the freezer for you."

After he unlocked it, he went to his office for a little sleep. That gave me time to get out cases of steaks hidden at the back of the walk-in freezer and load up my crew, who smuggled them out of the chow hall in their pants. At my price of three dollars per steak I made at least $1,000 that day, which cheered me after the Stephanie fiasco. *Merry Christmas to me*, I thought, as I microwaved my steak alone that night, slathering it with stolen butter.

The New Year's present I gave myself was even better; it was my freedom.

After learning about psychology and medical stuff in class, I was hungry to learn more and started borrowing books from Dr. T's medical library. Every month he lent me a new one. I read about anatomy, the nervous system, and the circulatory system. Then I read all his psych books—Freud, Fromm, Jung, Kinsey, Pavlov, and Skinner.

"Giacomaro, you already know way too much about how people's minds work and how to sway them," Dr. T said, as he handed me a book on abnormal psychology. "With what you're learning now you could be a very dangerous character on the outside."

It was similar to what Harry said after I got out of the FBI Academy. Dr. T was only half serious, but he needn't worry. My goal in learning this time wasn't about that. I was always a smart kid but for so many reasons, never applied myself in school. Now, I really did want to learn.

After I read all the medical books, I devoured the law books. Every prison in the country has a complete law library so an inmate can read up and file appeals—it's our civil right. One at a time, I took out each law encyclopedia from A to Z and read all night in the conference room. I speed read—I could look at a page and see it in its entirety. I read about criminal law, civil law, and more. Had I not told Princeton to go fuck itself forty years earlier, I might have done this reading on campus at their goddamn law school.

In January 2013 something in one of the updated law books caught my eye. I was reading a section about the Federal Bureau of Prisons and I came across something called the Second Chance Act, which allowed inmates to serve their entire final year of a sentence in a halfway house. President Bush signed the order in 2008, the year

I arrived at Allenwood, but it wasn't exactly advertised at the prison—I'd never heard about it, but it was something I was qualified for.

I immediately wrote a letter. The US Attorney's Office hadn't heard from me in a long time—*too long*, I smiled. One more request and they'd be rid of me for good, I wrote. I urged them to grant me early release under the Second Chance Act. I wrote that letter, and then I wrote another, and a dozen more after that. They already knew what a persistent son of a bitch I could be.

A few months after I sent that first letter, I was playing cards with the guys as my tomato sauce bubbled in the microwave when a counselor came over with the news: I was being given the Second Chance.

Packy Noonan carefully placed an x on the calendar he had pinned to the wall of his cell in the federal prison located near Philadelphia, the City of Brotherly Love. Packy was overflowing with love for his fellow man. He had been a guest of the United States Government for twelve years, four months, and two days. But because he had served over 86 percent of his sentence and been a model prisoner, the parole board had reluctantly granted Packy his freedom . . .

Mary Higgins Clark
—The Christmas Thief, *November 2004*

On August 28, 2013, I put on my new sweatpants and Champion sneakers and packed three laundry bags with my stuff—commissary clothes, spaghetti, olive oil, cheese—to take on the nineteen-hour Greyhound bus ride to New York and the halfway house that would be my new home for the next year.

Like I did with Fat Tony, Golden Boy walked me to the admissions and orientation area with a handful of my young crew. They waited on the bench with me until my name was called.

"How are you guys gonna eat without me?" I asked, and they laughed. But I wasn't kidding—these poor kids were gonna starve unless one of them got industrious and snagged my kitchen spot.

"Who ya gonna tell all your sob stories to, huh?" I worried about them a bit.

"Giacomaro, let's go!" a corrections officer called out.

We all got up and one by one, the kids gave me a hug.

"Thanks for being there for me, Mr. Tom," said one.

"You always made time to talk to me and I really appreciate it," said another.

"Yo, Old Gangsta . . . thanks, man."

What those guys didn't know was that it was me who should have been thanking them. Over three years I became their counselor, big brother, mentor, and father figure. But in helping them, this Old Gangster ended up helping myself.

"You bunch of crybabies!" I said, laughing at their sniffling. "Toughen up!"

I didn't know what else to say, so I left them with the same send-off Fat Tony, Hoffa, and The Chin had given me. By now it was tradition: "Always remember," I told them, as I walked toward the metal exit door, "do the right thing."

I walked outside, past the barbed wire fence, and didn't look back. A white van was waiting to take me to the nearest bus station.

What did you expect, a big dramatic exit or something? A getaway car? A shoot-out? This ain't no bullshit Hollywood movie, and at sixty years old I'd had enough melodramatic endings to last ten lifetimes.

On the bus many hours later, I looked out the window at the road ahead as we passed little towns between Cleveland, Pittsburgh, and Philly.

I didn't want to close my eyes; I didn't want to miss a thing. I felt something I hadn't in a very, very long time, and I couldn't place it at first, but it was strong.

It was freedom, yes, but not only the physical kind. I felt happy, sad, excited, exhausted, relieved, regretful, grateful, hopeful, and scared—all those feelings welled up inside me. I leaned my forehead against the cool glass as another transport truck barreled by in the night.

After nearly sixty years of damming them, a river of emotions began pouring out of me and I couldn't stop it.

For once, I didn't even try.

And ya know what? It felt fucking fantastic.

EPILOGUE: EVERY DAY IS CHRISTMAS

July 3, 2017

It's a warm summer morning and before Marty arrives for my 6 AM haircut, I put on the Sinatra Christmas tunes.

I'll be home for Christmas . . .

Except for my stint in prison, Marty's been cutting my hair for forty-five years now. We got history together. He knows all the different crews and still has the Cabbage Patch doll I gave him for his kid that time I got arrested thirty years ago. Marty's a witness and one of the few still alive, like me, to attest to it all. These days, our conversations go like this:

"Marty, whatever happened to Freddy Minatola?"

"Dead," says Marty, as he trims the nape.

"And Streaky and his son? Joe Albino?"

"Dead. Dead."

"Tommy Barnetas?"

"Dead."

It's a little game we play, and the list goes on and on. Most of the guys in my crooked tale are dead and buried, but somehow I survived.

When I got out of prison, I returned to a bizarro world I didn't recognize.

Harry Mount was teaching a course on organized crime at a local university; Kim DePaola was now "Kim D" and starring on a reality show called *The Housewives of New Jersey*; Tina went from being a cop to being a dog whisperer; and my attorney, Cathy Waldor, is a New Jersey district court judge. One of the guys I bought a garbage company from, Jimmy Rotundo, was now Mayor of Palisades Park, and Nicky Ola's son is now a street boss. My kids grew up, got married, and made me a grandfather. I felt like Rip Van Winkle. Tom Jr. and Nick are good fathers, Debbie tells me. And with that, they put a final end to the cycle of violence between father and son in our family.

I came back to a country where guys marrying guys was the law of the land and we had our first black president. Then last year, America went and elected a con man into the White House.

"He's like a dumb mob boss!" I tell Marty, as he snips away and we listen to CNN over top of Sinatra. "I'm the king of con, but this guy? Son of a bitch conned more than half the country. And he's such a disaster."

Oh yeah, there was hope for me yet to take over the world.

———

After I got out of the halfway house in the summer of 2014, I moved into a hotel in Jersey near my old neighborhoods. That's where I've been for three years now, until I figure out my next move. In my room, everything I have is in plastic boxes and I still wear my prison-issued T-shirts. When Tina came by to see my room, she shrieked: "You're so institutionalized! Oh my God!"

I hoard canned goods in my closet with the labels forward, my clothes and socks are folded and lined up like my mother taught me, and at least twice a week I raid the maid's cart in the hallway. I load up on paper towels, toilet paper, shampoo, towels, anything I can get my hands on. Yeah, I'm a still a thief—only now my crew is the hotel staff.

At least once a week I get the unstoppable urge to steal something bigger, more dangerous, more challenging.

It usually hits me at 4 AM, the time I used to steal from my father's wallet. With my hands slathered in Vaseline under white gloves, I take a bunch of plastic grocery bags downstairs to the hotel kitchen, just off the lobby. From the freezer and fridge, I steal pints of Häagen-Dazs, breakfast sausages, cut-up fruit, whatever catches my eye that's easy to clip. If the night manager on duty catches me, I slip him a twenty and tell him to keep his mouth shut. If he still complains, I slip him another twenty and he goes away. They gotta have tons of surveillance video of me by now, roaming the hallways like a looney tune. But they all know me. I'm the Old Gangster on the outside, too, and my hotel is my new home and safe house.

For a while, I was spending my days watching Netflix, devouring the news, eating my favorite deli, and loving every minute of it. I don't give a shit about going out to clubs or buying five Cadillacs or dating broads. I really don't. I'll smoke a Maduro cigar once in a while and buy a nice suit, and I bought one nice car—I had to do that. But that's it. I don't fucking need or want what I had before.

Greed nearly killed me. It may have been good for Gordon Gekko, but not me. I'm happy with my stolen paper towels and ice cream. Especially because I've had plenty of time to lie awake at night and look back at my life with regret, over and over.

What the fuck did I do to myself? I still ask out loud, while the rest of the hotel and world sleep. I had everything, and now I'm a sixty-four-year-old man getting a pension, living on the money my mother left me.

Yeah, I know what you're wondering. Where's the rest of the money I took? The millions in banks all over the world? Everybody asks me that. All I can tell you is: I have no fucking idea. That's my answer and I'm sticking to it.

I'll tell you this, though: I got plans, big ones. My mother used to say: "Give my son a pencil and a dollar and he'll make a million." I plan to get back on top again, and this time it's not for the glory and not to prove anything to my father. This time it's to prove something to myself—that I *can*, because I'm good at it. I'm the kid with a business mind who's talented with numbers and can convince anybody of anything. The kid who coulda been somebody, a contender, without going bad.

"Just don't go into trucking," warns Mr. G, my parole officer, who visits once a month to make sure I'm on track. "And don't go into the garbage business," he says, "or the courier business. Or funeral homes, or investment companies, or . . ."

Okay, okay, I get the picture. I'm in trouble even if I fart wrong.

"Hey, Mr. G. Maybe you can work for me after you retire?"

He didn't hesitate for a second before responding.

"Never going to happen," he says, and we laugh. But I'm serious, of course.

I'm putting my new crew together, and it will include some of the old guys and some new ones.

After I got out, some of the old crew slowly reappeared—the best and most loyal ones: Fat Pauly, Wayne, and a few others. We get together at the old Tick Tock Diner in Clifton to make plans, the place where Tony Pro recruited me at nineteen.

You might be interested to know that Fat Pauly ain't so fat no more, so we'll have to come up with a new nickname for him. Wayne recently kicked cancer's ass. And my Fort Dix buddy whom I didn't say goodbye to, Manny, found me after I got out, and he's gonna be my right-hand guy in my next big business venture.

Some of the other guys are calling, too, the ones I should stay away from. Because once you're known as a Big Earner, they never leave you alone. I made a lot of money for a lot of guys, and they're lining up to get a piece of what I do next. They want me to part the Red Sea for them again; they want me to be their golden goose one more time.

But I made two promises to Lauren in prison, and I'm trying to keep them.

The first was to find out who killed her, and you better believe I'm on the trail of that motherfucker. The second was to stay straight once I got out.

After Marty finishes my hair, I get into my car—a black Mercedes with black interior—and drive to the cemetery. Today is the fifteenth anniversary of Lauren's death so I'm going there to talk to her. I still don't believe in god, but I believe in Lauren.

"Baby, I'm getting it all together again," I say, putting flowers on her grave. She's buried in the same plot as my parents. "I'm going to be bigger than ever. And this time I'll do it right, you'll see."

I can hear her voice in my head: *Don't get tangled up again like last time, Daddy. Be careful. Be good.*

"I'll be good."

I look at my parents' names on the stone and all I can think to say is: "I'm sorry." They'd never said those words to me and part of me is saying it for them, to me. I'm still working on how to say those words to Tom Jr., Nick, Alison, Joey, Stephanie, and Kristina.

When I get back to the car I have a voice mail waiting. It's a high-ranking made guy I'd done business with before I went away.

"Hey, Tom. We hear you're working on a big idea. You're wit us, don't forget. We wanna see youse."

I drive away from the cemetery and pass the mansions in my old neighborhood, each one grander than the next. It would be easy, so easy, to call that guy back and duplicate the life I had before. I can smell it, I can taste it; all it would take is one phone call. My hands are itchy.

I lean over and hit play on the CD player; on comes Frank singing "Hark! The Herald Angels Sing."

I'm not going to get tangled up. I'll climb back on top of the mountain without those no-goodniks. I never needed them, anyway.

I was the one who made it happen and took the Smurfs to the Super Bowl. *I* was the genius mastermind behind the deals that proved miraculous. I still *am*.

Glory to the newborn King!

Peace on earth, and mercy mild . . .

At the next stoplight I listen to the voice mail again, then hit delete. I know where to find that *stunard* if I want him. I take the turn for my hotel, singing along with Frank, a fellow Jersey boy, as I drive:

God and sinners reconciled . . .

In this world of saints and sinners, heroes and bad guys, real and fake news, I'm an old gangster returned home, trying to learn new tricks. And that's the truth as I see it.

Because after all, a guy can change.

Can't he?

END

ACKNOWLEDGMENTS

To my brave, talented, and patient coauthor, Natasha Stoynoff . . . thank you for tolerating my lunacy and years trapped in a New Jersey hotel room with me force-feeding you pasta at 4 AM.

Many thanks to my true friend and loyal supporter, Vincent Brana, who has been there for me from the beginning.

To my agent, Frank Weimann, at Folio Literary Management and to Glenn Yeffeth and the team at BenBella Books—I'm grateful for your belief in us and your hard work on this project.

Thank you to all my crews—past, present, and future.

And finally, thank you to my daughter Lauren. You are my best girl and the reason I get out of bed every morning.

Structure, organization, discipline, and control: You must fight every day for success. This is how I live my life.

—THOMAS GIACOMARO
King of Con
January 30, 2018

ABOUT THE
AUTHORS

THOMAS GIACOMARO was the owner and president of dozens of million-dollar companies and M&A consulting firms that acquired, consolidated, and sold privately held companies in the fuel, energy, trucking, transportation, commercial and residential, recycling, and waste industries. He graduated from William Paterson University with a degree in business administration.

NATASHA STOYNOFF is a two-time *New York Times* bestselling author with thirteen books to her credit. She graduated with a BA in English and psychology from York University in Toronto and studied journalism at Ryerson University. Natasha began her career as a news reporter/photographer for the *Toronto Star* and columnist/ feature writer for the *Toronto Sun*. A two-time winner of the Henry R. Luce Award for excellence in journalism, she was a longtime staff writer in *People* magazine's New York bureau and a news reporter for *TIME*. She currently writes an ongoing series about sexual harassment and assault in *People* called "Women Speak Out." Natasha lives in Manhattan and is finishing her second screenplay.